SUPPORTING STRUGGLING READERS AND WRITERS

SUPPORTING STRUGGLING READERS AND WRITERS

Strategies for Classroom Intervention 3–6

Dorothy S. Strickland

Kathy Ganske

Joanne K. Monroe

Stenhouse Publishers
Portland, Maine

INTERNATIONAL
Reading
Association
Newark, Delaware

Stenhouse Publishers
477 Congress Street
Portland, Maine 04101-3451
www.stenhouse.com

International Reading Association
800 Barksdale Road, PO Box 8139
Newark, Delaware 19714-8139
www.reading.org
ISBN 0-87207-176-6

Library of Congress Cataloging-in-Publication Data
Strickland, Dorothy S.
 Supporting struggling readers and writers : strategies for classroom inter-
vention 3–6 / Dorothy S. Strickland, Kathy Ganske, and Joanne K. Monroe.
 p. cm.
 Includes bibliographical references (p.) and index.
 ISBN 1-57110-055-5 (alk. paper)
 1. Language arts—Remedial teaching—United States. 2. English lan-
guage—Composition and exercises—Study and teaching (Elementary)—United
States. I. Ganske, Kathy. II. Monroe, Joanne K. III. Title.
LB1576.S83 2002
372.6'044—dc21   2001049274

Cover design by Judith Arisman
Cover photographs by the authors

Manufactured in the United States of America on acid-free paper
07 06 05 04   9 8 7 6

Tell me, I forget.

Show me, I remember.

Involve me, I understand.

CONTENTS

FOREWORD

This book is intended to offer the best research-based practice on the literacy learning and teaching of low-achieving students. It grows out of our observations and discussions with teachers who are frustrated by youngsters who lag far behind the expectations for intermediate-grade work and by their feelings of inadequacy as they attempt to address students' needs.

All three of us work with teachers and administrators on a regular basis and understand teachers' concerns, having been classroom teachers ourselves for more than forty years. Dorothy and Kathy are teacher educators and researchers at universities. Joanne is a curriculum director and teacher educator.

Because each of us works regularly with teachers, administrators, and students in a variety of school settings, we are aware that literacy problems of intermediate-grade youngsters are a common and growing issue. Several factors may account for this: (1) recent emphasis on early intervention and beginning reading may have caused some to assume that all children would automatically be ready to do the more content-focused work of the middle grades; (2) overreliance on remedial programs such as Title I and Basic Skills may have resulted in their misuse as a replacement for regular classroom instruction rather than as a supplement to it; and (3) even the most successful supplementary programs require strong classroom support and intervention, which some teachers may not be trained to provide. We further believe that for most students the intermediate years provide the last opportunity to address the prevention of continued failure in reading and writing. These years are a critical bridge to middle school, where the tendency is to be less personalized and focused on individual needs. We start by centering on grade 3 in the belief that this is a turning point in the content standards, expectations, and instruction that link to grades 4 through 6. We would add that the instructional approaches and strategies we offer are suited to many students in middle school as well.

This book is intended for preservice and inservice teachers and administrators. Our goal is to provide a guide to a systematic and ongoing approach to classroom intervention to prevent continued failure in reading and writing. Key to the entire premise of the book is the emphasis on differentiated and tailored instruction, which we believe leads ultimately to better instruction for all children. We urge you to begin by turning to the last section of the Strategy Bank, which provides some suggestions for how this book may fit into a professional development program.

D.S.S.
K.A.G.
J.K.M.

ACKNOWLEDGMENTS

We are grateful for the genuine interest our editor at Stenhouse, Philippa Stratton, has shown in our topic as well as for the patience and support she and Tom Seavey have demonstrated. We also want to thank Martha Drury for her careful attention and guidance through the editorial process. Jeanie Eye and Cindy Mershon have enlivened the work with their photos of many of the strategies in action. We greatly appreciate the reading, reviewing, and commenting of Rebecca Brittain; the editorial assistance of Christina Longo; and the secretarial support of Veena Shastri. Finally, the stories of many teachers are woven into the fabric of this book. We heartily thank them for sharing their classrooms and informing our work.

PART ONE

LEARNERS
AND CONTEXTS

In this chapter we describe the settings in which children are likely to be at risk for failure. These children can be anywhere, from the poorest communities where teachers are overwhelmed by the chronic low achievement of large numbers of students, to the most affluent districts where teachers are baffled by a few low-achieving students for whom nothing seems to work. We explore highly prevalent concerns about factors such as linguistic and cultural differences, learning disabilities, and students' lack of motivation.

"But what do I do with the child who can't read?" Teachers in the middle and upper elementary grades are quick to pose this question. In some cases, they are talking about only one or two youngsters, who seem to defy everything they try. At other times, the queries come from teachers overwhelmed by virtually whole classes of children functioning well below expectations. In either case, these teachers are aware that for many children, adjusting to the more challenging and diverse demands of the upper elementary curriculum is extremely difficult. Middle and upper elementary grade teachers are faced with the task of making sure students gain knowledge in the content-area subjects. They must also improve students' skills and strategies in the English language arts. The fact that access to and use of content-area knowledge is largely dependent on one's abilities in the English language arts is lost on neither teachers nor students. Following is an overview of the key contextual issues causing the middle and upper elementary school years to emerge as a focus of great concern.

Changing Contexts for Teaching and Learning

The Changing Nature of What It Means to Be Literate

The notion of what it means to be literate has changed in our society. Although it is still true that becoming literate requires developing some basic skills and strategies, low-level basic skills that merely involve surface-level decoding and recalling information are hardly enough. Critical thinking and the ability to personalize meanings to individual experience and apply what is read or written in the real world, under many different circumstances, and with many different types of texts, may now be termed the "new basics." As Kibby (1993) reports,

> At the turn of the century, high school completion rates were less than 5% and illiteracy was the norm even for second generation Americans; today, high school completion rates range between 75 and 80%, and less than 4% of young adults cannot read. But the era of taking pride in graduating a mass of literate students accompanied by

only a sprinkling of critical readers and critical thinkers may have passed; such standards may no longer be sufficient. (p. 39)

It is not only what we are required to do with texts that has changed, but also the texts themselves. Texts are presented to us and generated by us in endless variety: books, magazines, and pamphlets of every conceivable design; letters and memoranda arriving via fax, e-mail, and snail mail; television screens, computer screens, and numerous other electronic screens and displays in our kitchens as well as our offices; and the indecipherable array of documentation for every thing we buy that must be assembled, cared for, or operated. The list goes on and on. Today's learners need skills that help them adapt to constant change. It serves as a reminder that the definition of what it means to be literate has evolved with the increasing demands of all aspects of our lives—personal, social, and economic. It is also a reminder of the critical role schooling plays in making literacy accessible to every child. For most children, it is during the middle and upper elementary years of schooling that the complexity of literacy learning receives full attention for the very first time.

Increased Expectations at the Elementary Level

Public awareness of the critical need for proficient readers and writers has never been greater. Nor has public criticism of the job that schools are doing. An unprecedented amount of open dissension and debate about the content of literacy instruction has led to state directives and legislative mandates that dictate specific curriculum content. National, state, and local school reform efforts have raised expectations for what readers and writers should know and be able to do. Increased accountability for student achievement is often determined by high-stakes assessments administered during the upper elementary grades. This has led to a growing concern about struggling readers and writers at these levels. It is no secret that achievement in literacy, most specifically reading, remains the key barometer by which success or failure is measured in elementary school. There is good reason for this. Children who experience difficulty learning to read are also less likely to be capable writers and spellers. In fact, they are less likely to achieve well in every area of the curriculum. The cycle of failure often starts early in the child's school career.

Longitudinal studies (Juel 1988) reveal that there is a near 90 percent chance that a child who is a poor reader at the end of grade 1 will remain a poor reader at the end of grade 4. As they move through the grades, these youngsters experience continued failure and defeat, which is directly related to the tendency of many of them to drop out of school. These facts are well known to educators. The educational reforms and effective practices set forth in this book have been initiated in many schools and classrooms to address these problems. Many are based on what has been learned from early intervention programs, designed to prevent failure before it becomes ingrained. Some were initiated in an effort to help classroom teachers think beyond "remedial-type" pullout programs as the main source of extra help for struggling students. All are based on what has been learned from helping struggling learners in balanced literacy programs. Today's balanced instructional programs are characterized by differentiated instruction and include a variety of intervention activities for struggling learners.

Learning from Early Intervention Programs

In an effort to address issues associated with the prevention of reading failure, recent research and programmatic efforts have focused heavily on the early years of schooling. Most often, these efforts have centered on intervention programs at the first-grade level. Some intervention programs have been highly effective for children at risk for failure in reading (Pikulski 1994). Research on these programs has helped provide insight into effective practices for helping struggling readers and writers. Some of these approaches are suitable for adaptation at the upper elementary levels. Teachers of older elementary children recognize that many of the children who have benefited from early intervention programs need continued support and special attention beyond the formative years. In addition, many children enter the middle grades with inadequate literacy skills and strategies and without the benefit of any previous special help, either in the regular classroom or in an intervention program. These children may need assistance with the most basic understandings and strategies generally taught at the beginning stages of formal instruction. Teachers at the middle elementary levels often need help in tailoring instruction to the needs of these students and incorporating the best prevention and intervention procedures into daily classroom instruction. The following list outlines some of the key ideas learned from early intervention programs that may be applied to differentiate instruction in the regular classroom.

Intervention Strategies for the Classroom: Some Key Considerations

Time: Children experiencing difficulty need more time. Large blocks of uninterrupted time work best. Schedule for continuity.

Organization/Management: Flexible grouping is required.
- Whole group
- Small group—revisit, review, teach, reteach

- One-to-one reinforcement
- Peer dyads

Materials: A variety of materials are needed for use in an integrated and balanced manner.
- Integrate core literacy program, trade books, technology, and content materials.
- Layer texts for various purposes.

Nature of Instruction: The types of instruction offered should allow for diversity of response.
- Direct and indirect instruction
- Individual and small-group application
- Multilevel assignments/tasks

Documenting and Monitoring Learning: Progress should be monitored in a systematic, ongoing manner.
- Establish goals; benchmarks.
- Employ rubrics, checklists, conferences, and observations.
- Assess learners in terms of their own individual growth first, then compare with the group.

Home/School Connections: Establish a systematic program of home support.

Students experiencing difficulty need more time on task than others do. Even in the upper elementary grades, a schedule that allows for large blocks of time for language arts is advantageous for these children. This allows teachers to follow up instruction to the whole class with more focused small-group and individualized instruction for those who need extra support. Instruction that is delivered in brief intervals of forty or fifty minutes may be too fragmented to promote the continuity and follow-through these children need. Organization and management involving a variety of types of groupings is essential and also easier to schedule in larger blocks of time. Teachers can monitor to see that struggling readers have opportunities to practice skills and strategies, using materials they can handle. Opportunities to work in heterogeneous groupings, using a variety of materials, can also be provided.

Early intervention programs have also taught us about the nature of the instruction that best serves children who are struggling. For example, these children may need more direct instruction, but they also need an abundance of opportunities for independent application. These activities are planned by the teacher, but are considered indirect. Without them, these children will not build the confidence they need to become independent learners. Keeping track of student progress and establishing home/school connections are also important parts of an effective instructional plan for children experiencing difficulty. Each of these components, essential to most early intervention programs, will be dealt with in Chapter 4 as frameworks for planning instruction. Specific examples of lessons and activities follow in subsequent chapters.

Moving Beyond "Remedial" and Supplementary Programs

Supplementary remedial programs, such as Title I and "replacement" programs that substitute for in-class instruction, have had mixed results over the years. It has been argued that such programs cause many classroom teachers to over-rely on special help and thus neglect their responsibility for less able students. Others complain that the type of instruction offered in these programs, whether or not it is pedagogically sound, is often at odds with that offered in the regular classroom, resulting in confusion for the very students most in need of consistency and continuity. Even the most successful early intervention programs appear to work best where there is a compatible instructional "home base" in the student's regular classroom. Some have suggested that the resources expended on these programs would be better used to provide smaller classes and improved instruction in regular classrooms. No doubt there will always be room for improvement in literacy instruction, whether in the regular classroom or through special intervention programs. It is safe to say, however, that for most students the regular classroom will continue to be the mainstay of instructional performance, and that regardless of the supplemental help offered, more attention needs to be given to incorporating the best prevention and intervention procedures into daily classroom instruction. For some schools and in many classrooms, this requires a major overhaul of how the curriculum is conceived in terms of classroom organization, the use of materials, and the very nature of the literacy activities in which students engage. Practical suggestions for addressing these areas of concern will be covered in later chapters as well as in the Strategy Bank at the end of this book. But first, let us go beyond the context that makes this topic both timely and critical to consider the learners themselves.

Knowing the Learner

What Is Known About Successful Readers and Writers

For most children, learning to read and write follows a typical pattern and evolves in relatively predictable and satisfactory ways. Such children generally have normal or above average language skills and a fair amount of motivating and pleasurable early childhood experiences with books and literacy. They are cared for by adults who involve them in purposeful literacy experiences during the early childhood years and provide them with opportunities to identify letters and environmental print, including their own names. Through rhyming, singing, and language play, these children are given opportunities to develop an awareness of the internal structure of spoken words. They also have the advantage of explanations about language from responsive adults who listen to them, talk with them, and help them become aware of the contrasting nature of spoken and written language.

The schools these children attend offer experiences that help them understand and use reading to make meaning with print; give them frequent and intensive opportunities to read and write; and help them learn about the nature of our alphabetic writing system, the structure of spoken and written words, and the joys of literature. Although some of these children may have periodic difficulties with specific aspects of literacy learning, their overall progress is steady and sure. They build successfully on the informal experiences with literacy from their earliest years as they encounter the more formal and complex tasks involved in conventional reading and writing.

What Is Known About Young Learners at Risk for Failure

Just as we know a great deal about the characteristics of children who learn to read adequately through "typical" home and school experiences, we also know a great deal about those for whom learning to read is a highly challenging and difficult task. The brief outline below lists factors often found to place children at risk for failure in learning to read and write. They are not offered here to place blame on the child or the child's circumstances. Rather, they are offered as a way to alert teachers to certain variables that may have an effect on the learning situation. Knowing learners as individuals, who come to the classroom with well-defined influences on their lives, is equally (if not more) important than paper and pencil screening devices designed to yield information about children's knowledge of letters, sounds, and words. It should be noted that some of the risk factors refer to the child's personal development. Others refer to the group or situation in which the child resides. Learning to read and write may be extremely challenging and difficult for

1. *Children with a history of preschool language impairment.* Although children vary widely in their early language development, there are indicators outside the normal range, such as severe delay in pronunciation accuracy and use of complex sentences, that signal language delay to parents, pediatricians, and caregivers (Scarborough 1998). Language delay is often part of a broader condition such as general developmental disability, hearing impairment or deafness (Conrad 1979), or a neurological condition. Reading problems are most likely when the language impairment is severe, broad in scope, and persistent.

2. *Children with limited proficiency in English.* When a child's home language is other than English, the likelihood of reading difficulty increases. This is particularly true if reading instruction in English begins before the child has acquired oral proficiency in English (August and Hakuta 1997).

3. *Children from homes in which a nonstandard dialect of English is spoken.* When a child's home language or dialect is other than standard English, the likelihood of reading difficulty increases, particularly when the differences between the child's dialect and the dialect of instruction are not taken into consideration or when the child's language is viewed in a stereotypical way to make judgments about his or her learning capacity (Labov 1995; Smitherman 1977).

4. *Children whose parents had difficulty learning to read.* If a child receives a diagnosis of a reading disability, there is a higher than normal chance that other family members have also had difficulties with reading (Volger, DeFries, and Decker 1985; Gilger, Pennington, and DeFries 1991).

5. *Children with attention deficit hyperactivity disorder (ADHD).* Long-term studies show that from the beginning of formal schooling, reading disability is relatively common in children with inattention problems—31 percent in first grade, becoming even more frequent as the child matures; more than 50 percent in ninth grade (Shaywitz, Fletcher, and Shaywitz 1995).

6. *Children who lack motivation to learn to read.* Children who have never experienced purposeful and pleasurable experiences with books and literacy are apt to be unenthusiastic about learning to read and write. Those who experience continued failure tend to avoid reading and thus deny themselves the most important means to improve their reading abilities (Snow et al. 1991).

7. *Children from poor neighborhoods.* Children who attend schools and live in communities where low socioeconomic status is widespread are more likely to be at risk for failure in reading.

8. *Children who attend schools in which the classroom practices are deemed ineffective.* Classroom practices in ineffective schools (regardless of community socioeconomic status) are characterized by significantly lower rates of student time-on-task, less teacher presentation of new material, lower rates of teacher communication of high academic expectations, fewer instances of positive reinforcement, more classroom interruptions, more discipline problems, and classroom ambiance that is generally rated as less friendly (Teddlie, Kirby, and Stringfield 1989).

Today's teachers are likely to work in situations where many of the factors listed above are characteristic of the children they teach, the circumstances in which they find themselves, or a combination of both. It should be noted, however, that none of these factors is an automatic barrier

to literacy development. Nor do any of the characteristics usually function alone as a single causal factor or predictor of an individual child's reading problems. For example, low reading achievement is a widespread problem among Latino students, but linguistic differences are not solely responsible for the high degree of risk these children face. Many children who have limited English proficiency come from homes where their parents are poorly educated and the family income is low. Similarly, African American students who speak a nonstandard dialect are apt to live in poor neighborhoods and attend schools in which achievement is chronically low. In such cases, co-occurring group risk factors, such as the socioeconomic circumstances of the child's family, the child's home literacy background, the neighborhood where the child lives, and the quality of the instruction in the school the child attends, must be taken into account to fully comprehend the problem. A child of low socioeconomic status in a generally moderate- to upper-status school or community is far less at risk than that same child in a whole school or community of low-socioeconomic-status children (Committee on the Prevention of Reading Difficulties in Young Children 1998). Simply put, the factors listed here are among those often associated with reading difficulties and thus are among those that must be considered in decisions regarding policy and practice for children experiencing difficulty with reading and writing.

The Challenge of Student Diversity

Ironically, as children progress through the grades, their strengths and abilities are likely to become more divergent than similar. They become increasingly complex human beings with interests and attitudes that vary across subjects and tasks. Moreover, the demographics of today's society make it much more likely that the children in any given classroom will vary widely in their linguistic and cultural backgrounds, their special needs requirements, and their dispositions toward reading and writing. These factors have emerged as significant challenges for teachers in the upper elementary grades. Fortunately, the knowledge base for improving literacy has never been richer. Researchers and practitioners have filled the literature with both a research base and practical suggestions for educators, policy makers, and others as they consider how to help all children meet today's higher literacy standards. Following is a discussion of three critical issues that teachers often find perplexing and challenging: linguistic and cultural differences, learning disabilities, and motivation. If not understood and addressed, these issues have the potential to adversely affect children's literacy development.

Linguistic and Cultural Differences

An increasing number of children enter school speaking either a language or a dialect that is other than standard English. Like many others before them, these children and their families immigrated from other countries or other parts of the United States to seek a better life. For a variety of economic and social reasons, these families usually remain within their new communities, thus helping to maintain existing similarities in culture and language. This tendency is most pronounced in rural areas and inner cities.

Over the years, educators have expressed growing concern about the differences between home and school language and culture in some communities. As mentioned earlier, this topic has received considerable attention as a possible cause of school failure. The low achievement of poor African American and Hispanic children, in particular, has often been associated with their dialect or language. During the 1960s, linguists looked closely at language diversity as a cause of school failure. Focusing primarily on black dialects, these studies revealed important principles about language diversity that have remained helpful to teachers and curriculum developers today. The principles were summarized by Cullinan (1974) and confirmed more recently by Gopaul-McNicol, Reid, and Wisdom (1998):

- All language varieties are equally valid;
- All language varieties can accommodate all levels of thought; and
- Any variety of standard English is not intrinsically better than any nonstandard dialect. (p. 7)

Similarly, research in the language development of children for whom English is a second language supports the belief that the learner's home language should be valued and accepted as part of second language acquisition and learning (Cummins 1984). *Preventing Reading Difficulties in Young Children* (1998), a recent report that received widespread attention, supports the notion of bilingualism and biliteracy. Research has shown that being able to read and write in two languages has cognitive, social, and economic benefits and should be supported whenever possible. The report also suggests that to the extent possible, non-English-speaking children should have opportunities to develop literacy skills in their native language as well as in English. Moreover, evidence is mounting that much of the low achievement of language-minority students may be pedagogically induced or exacerbated and therefore amenable to change (Rueda 1991). There is growing recognition that teachers involved in teaching English Language Learners to read need special training in their students' curricular and cultural needs.

None of this denies the fact that the form language takes has economic, social, and political importance. As teachers, however, we must resist the tendency to equate the use of language other than standard English with incompetence or a lack of intelligence. Keep in mind that all children learn the language to which they have been exposed. Within any language community, speakers vary in their communicative competencies and their dispositions toward learning. To be sure, all children growing up in the United States need access to standard English. The important issues center on helping this to happen without denigrating the child's home language and culture. Following are some principles for teachers working with students whose first language or dialect is other than standard English. Chapter 3 addresses instructional strategies for English Language Learners.

Language Diversity in the Classroom

Teachers of children who speak a dialect or language other than standard English need to keep in mind that:

1. Language diversity is present in all classrooms.
2. Every speaker has an individual dialect, or "idiolect." Some speak in a more "standard" form than others.
3. Some speakers may differ in their style of language use (e.g., in some cultures, children may be considered impolite if they look directly at adults as they speak).
4. Correcting all nonstandard utterances should be avoided. Repetition in a standard form followed by a question related to the meaning of the utterance is a more helpful response.
5. Learning as much as possible about students' culture as well as their dialect or language is helpful in forming judgments about the quality of their language use and in assessing its development.

6. For English Language Learners (ELL), language instruction in the native language should accompany language instruction in English when possible.
7. Opportunities to talk about what they read, write, and study is essential for language development and for helping students make sense of what they are learning.
8. It is important to create a safe, supportive, and meaningful environment in which students can practice their evolving language skills.

Learning Disabilities

About 10 percent of the school-age population has learning disabilities and qualifies for special education services (National Research Council 1997). Students may be learning disabled for a variety of reasons, including medical and environmental causes. They also vary widely in their characteristics and educational experiences. However, the vast majority have some difficulty with reading. Some learning-disabled students receive specialized curricula and instruction. An increasing number, however, are served in the regular classroom setting with some time spent in resource rooms (Beattie 1994). These students are said to be mildly disabled and participate extensively in the less restrictive environment of the general education classroom and curriculum.

Johnston (1999) lists several characteristics of students termed mildly disabled. Such students

- do not read or write strategically, or actively theorize about language;
- do not take control of their learning;
- do not view themselves as readers and writers;
- are slow and inaccurate at figuring out words;
- have poor spelling;
- do not apply their personal experience to their reading;
- do not enjoy reading and writing.

Because most classrooms at the upper elementary grade levels include one or more mildly disabled youngsters, these characteristics are well known to teachers. Following are some general suggestions for working with mildly disabled learners:

1. *Mildly disabled learners need to experience success as readers and writers.* Many of the materials used in the curriculum will be difficult for these learners. Nevertheless, they must have daily opportunities to practice decoding and comprehension skills on materials that they can handle successfully. Multilevel literacy tasks, such as writing a story or a report, work

best. These include all students while allowing them to perform to their own abilities.

2. Mildly disabled learners need to be viewed as learners who can achieve. Teachers communicate their expectations of students, both through what they say and what they do. Positive reinforcement, when warranted, encourages students to make the extra effort required of many of them. Focusing on what students can do as well as what they are working toward helps them gain a sense of accomplishment.

3. Mildly disabled learners need instruction that emphasizes self-monitoring and control over their own learning. Rather than focusing on the accumulation of isolated skills, these students need to acquire and learn to be strategic in their use of skills. Teacher and peer demonstrations and modeling of how to solve problems help make reading and writing strategies transparent to them. Then, they need many opportunities to practice what they have learned.

4. Mildly disabled learners need special efforts at motivation. Helping these students find materials that are interesting to read and topics that are interesting to write about is extremely challenging and difficult. Yet it may be the key to what makes them continue to try. Needless to say, these students must be academically and socially engaged as participants in class activities.

Motivation

Struggling readers and writers often find themselves caught in a cycle of failure. They have difficulty learning to read and write, so they avoid literacy activities. Avoidance means they don't get the practice they need to apply and strengthen their skills.

The absence of abundant reading practice with materials that are interesting and important to them may be the most harmful aspect of these students' reading development. Cunningham and Stanovich (1998) make a compelling argument for the positive consequences of children's reading volume. Their analyses of the research suggests that the amount children read contributes significantly to the development of other aspects of their verbal intelligence, such as vocabulary knowledge, spelling, and verbal fluency. Reading volume also builds students' background knowledge, an important contributor to reading comprehension that is discussed in Chapter 8.

During the 1980s, interest in motivational issues surged among researchers and teachers in the fields of reading and writing (Guthrie and Anderson 1999). The National Reading Research Center was formed to conduct research on reading instruction with a special focus on developing motivated and strategic readers, who use literacy for pleasure and learning.

Key ideas from the National Reading Research Center (Baumann and Duffy 1997) that inform instruction at the upper elementary levels are

- Instruction should be systematic and integrated with quality children's literature.
- Motivation to read and reading ability are synergistic, mutually reinforcing phenomena.
- Connections between home and school enhance children's learning in both environments. Parents are receptive and supportive of programs that help them promote their children's reading.
- Thinking and talking about books promote children's critical understanding of what they read.
- The use of multiple documents, as opposed to a single textbook, fosters students' interest and learning of social studies content.
- Using analogies between familiar ideas and unfamiliar science concepts aids students' learning and appreciation of science content. (Adapted from pp. 5–6)

Researchers in the area of motivation place heavy emphasis on promoting students' intrinsic motivation to read and write (Deci and Ryan 1985; Guthrie and Anderson 1999) but recognize that outside sources may be needed to initiate student interest (Gambrell 1996). They stress the need for students to feel both competent and in control. Focus is put on language arts instruction that considers the appropriateness of the task, offers instructional support, and encourages students to internalize what they have learned. Instructional frameworks such as scaffolding student learning, which is explained in Chapter 4, allow students to move from easy to more challenging tasks in ways that help them gain control and increasing independence. Many of the strategies offered throughout this book use scaffolding as the basic instructional device. Collaborative activities in which students work with others provide an engaging and risk-free environment. Finally, teacher sensitivity to task appropriateness is an important aspect of motivation. Tasks should be neither too easy nor too hard if they are to contribute to students' sense of competence. Monitoring student learning so that moderately increasing degrees of challenge are offered helps keep them engaged and willing to try. Further strategies for motivating students to read and write are discussed in the next chapter.

MOTIVATING RELUCTANT READERS AND WRITERS

In this chapter, we examine a number of approaches that teachers can take to encourage students' motivation for reading and writing. Recent research suggests that motivation is multidimensional. Taking a broader view of the multiple factors that contribute to motivation can be particularly helpful to teachers who work with struggling readers and writers. Although no single "quick fix" will motivate all students, certain classroom practices can influence every child's motivation to read and write. The issue of motivation is a particular concern to us as we consider the needs of literacy learners who struggle, because we know that without diligent, frequent, and extensive practice, these students will not improve.

Background and Issues

Motivation is recognized as a crucial element in all learning (Csikszentmihalyi 1990). According to the National Reading Research Center (Baumann and Duffy 1997), children need to be motivated to read and use literacy to develop into fluent readers. Becoming competent users and producers of text requires a great deal of practice, and students who have difficulty with these activities often lack the motivation to invest in the practice required.

Many factors contribute to children's motivation in learning to read and write—their interest, attitude, and engagement. Findings from recent research suggest that not only does motivation to read have many dimensions but also different students are motivated in different ways. Researchers assert that students cannot be characterized as either motivated or not motivated, but simply as differently motivated (Baker and Wigfield 1999; Ivey 1999).

Some children may be impelled to read or write because of the challenge of a particular text/genre or because of a sense of obligation; others may be encouraged by the possibility of recognition or other factors. For struggling readers and writers the bases for motivation may be their interest and familiarity with a topic, the ease with which they can understand what they are reading, and the classroom circumstances in which they are reading (for instance, in a small group rather than a large group).

Once we recognize that all intermediate-grade students, regardless of their gender, ethnicity, or reading achievement, are motivated to read in certain circumstances, we can accept the challenge posed by students who seem to be unengaged and apathetic. Hidi and Harackiewicz (2000) suggest that teachers "hook" these students into reading by manipulating situations and goals. Most of our classroom strategies are designed to build self-driven intrinsic motivation, typified by personal interest and mastery goals so that students learn for the sake of learning, but struggling readers and writers may initially need purposes beyond their own self-satisfaction to motivate them.

Although extrinsic motivation has been avoided in recent years out of concern that it might hinder the development of intrinsic motivation, findings from current research suggest that outside sources of motivation can play a role in bringing students to read and write (Baker and Wigfield 1999; Gambrell 1996; Hidi and Harackiewicz 2000). The judicious use of rewards for completing reading or writing tasks, and *situational interest* may serve as a "jump start" for students who are otherwise unmotivated. Situational interest is created when a teacher gets students eager to read and write by setting up a situation that appeals to them, despite their personal lack of interest in reading and writing. Situational interest does not have the staying power that personal interest does, but for some reluctant readers and writers it may be a necessary first step that will spur their engagement in other literacy activities. Indeed, there is evidence that situational interest can lead to personal interest (Reinking and Watkins 2000; Hidi and Harackiewicz 2000).

As teachers plan lessons for students who struggle with reading and writing, they need to think about motivation as well as instructional objectives. Students who are otherwise indifferent to literacy tasks may become absorbed when reading and writing topics are geared toward their personal interests, when small-group cooperative learning strategies are used, or when fun and game-like situations or technology are incorporated into the instruction. It is important to keep in mind that the specific rewards and situations that interest and encourage individual students will vary. Instruction can and should be adapted to inspire students who might otherwise avoid reading and writing, or who do it in such a cursory way that it has little effect on their learning.

Classroom Implications

When we are motivated by an activity it is easy to devote our full attention to it. This type of total engagement has been described as *flow* (Csikszentmihalyi 1990). The writer who is so involved with what he is doing that he is oblivious to the distractions of the classroom around him is an example of a student who is experiencing flow. For this to occur, the challenge level at which the learner is working must be demanding enough to keep attention engaged, but not so demanding that she feels unable to succeed. Ivey (1999) found that a reader who struggled with grade-level and whole-class work enjoyed reading when the text was at her own level and when she worked in smaller groups. Small-group instruction that features instructional-level text, such as guided silent reading described in Chapter 5, can be highly motivating to many struggling readers. This approach allows students to engage with text at an appropriate challenge level, one that requires their effort and thought but does not overly exceed their skill levels.

Creating Classrooms That Inspire Reading and Writing

Gambrell (1996) identified six characteristics of classroom cultures that foster reading motivation for most students: the teacher as an explicit reading model, a book-rich classroom environment, opportunities for choice, opportunities to interact socially with others, opportunities to become familiar with lots of books, and appropriate reading-related incentives. Some of these characteristics have their matches in behaviors that have been found to motivate writing. All of these characteristics are worthy of consideration for teachers who want to build motivation in their classrooms.

The Teacher as an Explicit Reading Model

Although the importance of the teacher as a model of literate behavior has been implied in numerous descriptions of effective literacy classrooms, Gambrell (1996) points out that teachers are not effective models if they are not explicit models. Merely reading and writing along with the students in the first ten minutes of an independent reading or writing lesson is not sufficient. Teachers who serve as inspiring models of reading and writing are passionate about their own literacy. They read aloud to students from their own writing and reading; they talk with their students about the importance of literacy in their own lives. Their love of books and of words is something about which their students know a great deal. Not all teachers are passionate enough about reading and writing to serve as explicit models. However, through their interest in motivating their students, they may be inspired to become more enthusiastic and involved in their own literacy.

Joanne has found this to be true through personal experience. Though she has always loved to read, writing was something she did only when she was assigned to do so, such as for schoolwork, for the record-keeping needed in her work as a teacher, or for necessary correspondence. When she studied the writing process as part of her involvement in the New Jersey Writing Project, she learned the importance of becoming a writer and serving as a writing model for her students. She began to keep a journal and to share bits of her writing with them. She found herself becoming more willing to write and more interested in developing her writing ability but openly admits that she was motivated by her desire to serve as an explicit model for her students. As she recalls, "My purpose for becoming a writer was more to improve my ability to teach writing than it was a need or desire to express myself." She notes that what she learned about writing through writing helped her to better coach her students in their writing and led to a genuine enthusiasm for writing.

The interest in reading and writing that is developed in the explicit model classroom is situational. The classroom environment provides a situation in which students become interested in reading and writing. However, teachers who explicitly model and encourage literate behaviors help many of their students develop a personal interest in reading and writing that stays with them long after they have left the teachers who first inspired them.

A Book-Rich Classroom Environment

Situational interest that might become personal interest is also developed in a book-rich classroom environment. Although access to books is an important factor in developing motivation, the types of books and the ways they are made available to the students also make a difference. When teachers build a classroom library to motivate independent reading, they may need to provide books that are different from those selected for instruction or even for the school library. For example, regardless of their gender, reading achievement, reading attitude, or family income, sixth-grade students specify scary books as their first choice of reading material, and comic books or magazines as their second (Worthy, Moorman, and Turner 1999). Because choices may vary among other populations and age levels, we recommend using a reading survey, such as the one in the Strategy Bank, to determine both individual and group reading preferences. To encourage students to browse for books, classroom libraries should be conveniently located, not tucked behind the teacher's desk or other furniture. Teachers can increase the effectiveness of the classroom library by giving students time to look for, select, and read their books. Also, letting individual students know about the "perfect book" for them, and being able to immediately provide it, encourages many students to read.

The classroom library is also an area where teachers need to take into account the wide differences in students' reading ability. Including books that range from the weakest readers' independent level to the strongest readers' instructional level (see Chapter 7 for further information on reading levels) will take time and effort, but it will result in an effective collection. In many school districts, teachers are not provided with funding to support the development of rich classroom libraries. Most teachers build their collections using bonus points from student book clubs, such as Troll, Trumpet, and Scholastic. In some districts, the PTA holds an annual or semiannual book fair, and teachers receive book donations for their classroom libraries as part of the arrangement. Schools have also had success with making a birthday book club part of the school culture. Instead of, or in addition to, a birthday snack, parents send a book for the classroom library on the child's birthday, inscribed with their child's name and birth date. Many teachers who make the classroom library an important focus in their teaching and in their dialogue with parents receive gift certificates to bookstores and copies of children's books as holiday and end-of-the-school-year presents. On occasion, families contribute books from their own home collections. Yard sales, too, are sometimes a source of affordable books for the classroom library, with teachers purchasing some books and students and their families purchasing and donating others. When particular topics or genres are being studied or have widespread interest teachers can augment their classroom collections by borrowing books from the school and public libraries.

To effectively motivate students, the classroom library must be incorporated into classroom procedures. Simply providing lots of appropriate and potentially appealing books is not sufficiently motivating: students must be enticed to read them. Using materials from the classroom library for read-alouds and think-alouds and giving book talks about them (see Chapter 5 for an example) builds student interest. Changing book displays near the library and showing the covers rather than spines of as many books as possible is also effective. Ending independent reading time with a share session in which two or three students tell a bit about their books is yet another way to arouse interest.

The classroom library can motivate and assist student writers if books are readily available that can serve as models or provide background information (see Chapter 9). Teachers who know their students and their collections can easily suggest ways for students to use books to improve their writing. For example, during a conference with a student who was writing haltingly about visiting his relatives in Jamaica, Elaine Delany, a fifth-grade teacher, offered the following suggestions:

> To help the reader better understand the things you did with your family, you may want to make this a picture book. I notice that you have single sentences about many different things you did with your family. Like here where you say, "This is my grandmother's house deep in the forest," a drawing might help the reader to picture what it's like. Also, creating the pictures might give you more ideas for what to write about and how to revise what you have. Take a look in the poetry section of our classroom library for a book called *Not a Copper Penny in Me House* by Monica Gunning. It has great illustrations of places that are very similar to Jamaica. I think you'll find it helpful. Check back with me after you've had a look.

Even the mechanics of writing can be supported by selections from the classroom library. For example, struggling writers who need help with paragraphing, punctuating, and capitalizing dialogue can be encouraged to use fiction books as models for the correct format. Several resources are available to help teachers forge connections between children's literature and writing (see for example, Gillet and Beverly 2001; and Ray 1999).

Classroom libraries that include several titles by an author and several titles within a genre make it possible for teachers to capitalize on students' enthusiasm after a successful independent reading experience by helping them select the next book on the spot. Series books can also be helpful in promoting continued reading, and among fourth- and fifth-grade low-achieving readers, they rank within the top reading preferences (Worthy, Moorman, and Turner 1999). When Michele, a fourth-grade teacher, noticed that one of her less able readers had finished and enjoyed Lensey Namioka's *Yang the Eldest and His Odd Jobs*, she was able to provide him with earlier books by the same author that featured the same family.

Opportunities for Choice

Choice is another motivating factor for readers (Gambrell 1996) and writers (Graves 1994). Literature circles, silent sustained reading, writing workshop, and fluency-building activities (topics discussed in later chapters) all present students with opportunities to make choices in their literacy learning. Students who make and prefer their own choices are intrinsically motivated to read and write. Unfortunately, students who haven't had many positive literacy experiences often cannot select a book they want to read or choose a topic for writing. Teachers commonly express concern about this, but all too frequently they respond by supplying these children with a book or a topic. In some situations this may be appropriate; however, in most cases the better answer is to teach these students to make choices. Turning to students' personal interests and areas of strong background knowledge is a great first step.

When teachers know the interests of struggling readers they can introduce them to books that are potentially appealing and assist them in the selection process. One way to do this is by helping students stay focused on making a choice: talking with them and guiding them through a review of the books using the *five-finger test* is effective. The five-finger test is a simple technique that helps ensure that only relatively easy books, those within the students' independent reading level, are chosen. Students quickly read any passage in the text that has at least 100 words, holding up one finger each time they come to a word they cannot read. If by the end of the reading students have all five fingers raised, the book is probably too difficult for them to read independently. Carefully guided decision-making sessions like these allow students to understand how to go about choosing a book they will enjoy.

Teachers can also help struggling writers learn to select topics. Discovering students' interests is an important part of this. Teachers who have their students complete a writing survey at the beginning of the school year, such as the one in the Strategy Bank, become aware of ideas the students may want to write about through the lists of possible topics they create. These lists provide a backup for students, a place they can turn to throughout the year when they need help deciding on a topic. As students develop new interests and have new experiences, they often want to add topics to the list. Talking with students about potential topics before they choose one (see Chapter 8) and modeling the decision-making process are other ways teachers can help.

Often, struggling writers have an interest in a topic but are unsure of what to share about it in writing or of how to get started. In his workshops, Donald Graves has modeled a technique that we have used with great success in classrooms at all grade levels and even with very reluctant writers. The topics that we use to model the technique are personal and everyday in nature; they are the sorts of experiences and ideas that we imagine our students writing about. The strategy works like this:

1. The teacher stands at the front of the room and draws a large + sign on an overhead transparency to divide the space into quarters.
2. Then the teacher begins to think aloud about a possible writing topic, making bulleted notes of important ideas about the topic in one of the four quarters.
3. Next, the teacher considers a second possible topic and goes through the same process of thinking aloud and making notes in one of the other quarters.

4. The procedure continues with two more topics. Filling in all four quarters generally takes about seven to ten minutes. (Figure 2.1 shows a grid that was completed for a fifth-grade class.)

5. The teacher then says, "Now take a blank sheet of paper, and fold it into quarters. You're going to do what I just did with a partner. What did I do?" Student responses should reveal an understanding that the teacher talked about possible writing topics and made notes of some of the ideas.

Figure 2.1 Teacher Demonstraton: Finding a Topic

Mr. Parris's visit
- paleontologist's background ②
- working at the NJ Museum ①
- the tools paleontologists use ④
- information about local fossils ⑤
- questions Mr. Parris answered ⑥
- descriptions of the samples Mr. Parris brought ③

Thank-You Note to Mr. Parris
- make sure all parts of the friendly letter are there! (use p.145 of Writers Express)
- appreciated the samples he brought
- enjoyed the video of his Kansas finds
- learned a great deal from his stories
- was amazed that so many fossils can be found locally

Poem for Mother's Day
- appreciate kindness and all of the care
- remember special things –
  - visits to other family members
  - time "alone" – mom & me
  - learning to read, reading books together
  - learning to print, writing letters
- try free verse first: look for rhythm – rhyme??

Garden Journal
- perennials that are coming up – especially spreading one
- bulbs that filled in this year
- ground covers that need to be divided, moved, and groomed
- annuals to be planted and where
- wish list
  - more lavender
  - more perennial geraniums
- draw "map"

6. The teacher next explains to the students that they will talk to a partner about possible writing topics and jot down some ideas while he or she listens. Then the roles will change.
7. The teacher allows partners to decide if they will trade roles after each writing topic or after all four topics have been discussed. Students are given about fifteen minutes to talk to each other and are notified of the halfway point.

At the end of the fifteen minutes, most students will have three or four ideas with some details, but every student will have at least one idea, and in reality, one idea is all anyone needs to begin writing. Most students find it far less threatening to identify several things they might write about than to identify the *one* thing they will write about. The comfort of the teacher's modeling and the encouragement of talking to a classmate about an idea further reduce their anxiety.

Sometimes Kathy slightly altered the strategy for her students. After the initial modeling she asked students to individually brainstorm topics and record them in three or four of the quarters *before* they met with a partner. Then she allowed the students ten to fifteen minutes to take turns talking with their partner about the topics and jotting down details. Students tended to show much greater enthusiasm for one of the subjects and spent more time telling their partner about it. This helped them identify which topic they really wanted to write about. They came away from the activity focused on an idea and with many details recalled to fuel their writing.

Students need many opportunities for choice, but some may require additional instruction and guidance to reap the motivational benefits. When we recognize this we can plan the time for small-group and individual interventions that will help them become more confident and capable in selecting books and topics.

Opportunities to Interact Socially with Others

Many teachers who use literature circles (see Chapter 5) recognize and praise their social component as a major motivating force for students. Given that student talking is the most frequently observed and corrected misbehavior in intermediate classrooms, it makes sense that an instructional format that promotes conversation would appeal to many students. Social interaction is incorporated into many simple teaching techniques, such as Think-Pair-Share (Kagan 1994). In the Think-Pair-Share strategy, students are given time to consider something (a quote, question, or concept, for example), then directed to tell the person sitting next to them about their thoughts and to listen carefully when it is the other person's turn. After every student has talked to a partner, the teacher calls on a few students to share their responses with the whole class. In many situations, such as that previously described for choosing and thinking about a writing topic, partner sharing alone is a sufficient motivator. In such cases, the strategy is simplified to "turn to your partner and tell; then listen while your partner tells you."

Social interactions occur when students have time to work with classmates in dyads, small groups, or as a whole class. They talk about their reading or writing with a classmate or collaborate with a partner on an activity. They discuss reading and writing ideas or explore how words work with a small group of classmates. They share a response with the entire class or pose a question for others to consider. In classrooms where opportunities are provided for these social interactions, students who struggle benefit from the motivation that comes from being part of a community of learners.

Opportunities to Become Familiar with Lots of Books

Students who have difficulty with reading and writing have a wealth of opportunities to become familiar with lots of books when all of the previously discussed characteristics of classrooms that motivate reading are provided. If their teacher is an explicit model of literacy, students are the recipients of read-alouds, think-alouds, and book talks that make them familiar with lots of books. They are exposed to books that are easy enough for them to read independently, books that they can read with instructional assistance, and books that they cannot yet read themselves but can enjoy as listeners, or perhaps remember as choices for later when their reading ability has grown. When struggling readers and writers are fortunate enough to be members of classrooms where a classroom library is available and used, they have ready access to books. If they are given time to read and provided with the assistance they need, they become intimately familiar with many books. When students are taught to choose their own books, they are exposed to a wide range of possibilities: new authors, genres, topics. When reading is enhanced with social interactions, students have opportunities to become familiar with the books their classmates read.

It is interesting to note that the more students know about books, the more they are motivated to read books. This is perhaps the best rationale for creating classrooms in which books, sharing, and time for browsing and reading are provided, particularly when our goal is to encourage more reading and writing from students who seem reluctant to pursue literacy activities.

Appropriate Reading-Related Incentives

Gambrell (1996) found that first-grade students who were rewarded a book for reading did not name the book as what they liked best about the program. They named reading activities instead. Although the book reward served as a strong initial motivator for the children, the reading itself (particularly reading with a friend) became the real motivator. When the reward is reading-related, students read so they can read more. Unfortunately, many of the reward programs provided by commercial establishments provide an incentive (e.g., a pizza party) that is not related to reading. This concerns educators who fear that students will read only for the purpose of attaining the reward.

Simply being noticed for having worked hard at a demanding task is often enough encouragement for students who are competitive or need the acknowledgment of others. Teachers have used incentives such as certificates and postcards mailed home to parents to document and celebrate the number of books or pages read by the student in a certain period of time. When these simple rewards are given along with their teachers' genuine praise, students are motivated to continue to work toward accomplishing reading goals.

Creating Situations That Inspire Reading and Writing

When regular classroom activities are not motivating enough for some readers, teachers may need to create new situations that encourage reading and writing. When they do so, they know that the interest they have effected is temporary and that it may not develop into a long-term interest for many of their students. However, engaging projects, such as those that follow, provide opportunities for students who lack a personal interest in reading or writing to invest more motivated time in literacy activities than they would have otherwise. These experiences improve their literacy abilities and may lead some of them to the life-changing discovery that they do, in fact, enjoy reading or writing.

Multimedia Book Reviews

Reinking and Watkins (2000) developed a program through which fourth- and fifth-grade students learned to use HyperCard to produce multimedia book reviews. Because of their interest in using the computer some low-achieving, low-interest students read and wrote more and paid greater attention to their writing skills. One low-achieving student's reluctance to write reviews because the books he read were easy was completely reversed when his teacher announced to the class that they should produce reviews of easier books for younger students in their school. For some of the student participants, interest in reading became a personal interest that endured even after they knew how to use the HyperCard program. Teacher involvement and interest were important factors in the results: there were significant variations in the level of students' engagement, depending on the teacher, indicating once again the critical effect of the teacher on generating enthusiasm for reading and writing.

Biography Parades

Kathy's students were motivated to read for a project that had become a tradition at her school—the Fourth-Grade Biography Parade. In preparation, every fourth grader chose and read a biography, wrote several clues that they thought the famous person might give as a way of introduction, and dressed up as the subject of their selected book. For Thomas Jefferson one student gave the following clues:

> I wrote the Declaration of Independence. I was the third president of the United States. I doubled the size of the United States when I made the Louisiana Purchase. My home, Monticello, is pictured on the back of the nickel. Who am I?

On the day of the parade, third graders, fifth graders, and parents of the fourth graders gathered in the multipurpose room with anticipation. They were handed a sheet that listed in alphabetical order all of the featured "celebrities" and a sheet with numbered blanks. The costumed fourth graders paraded in, sat down, and one at a time came before the audience to share their clues. After each speech, members of the audience scanned their list of people to try to guess the presenter's name, then recorded it on their numbered sheet. At the end of the Biography Parade the celebrities revealed their identities, and the audience checked their answers. It was an enjoyable time for everyone, and as a result, even struggling fourth graders entered school with great anticipation for their biography reading and the parade that would follow it.

Visiting Authors

Dorothy has a vivid memory of the reaction her fourth-grade students had to a local writer who visited their classroom:

> The children were thrilled to meet someone who had actually published a book. The notion of how someone's ideas eventually get to print came alive for my students, and they were inspired by it. They began to write quite a lot more than they had before, and the struggling writers were encouraged to write.

As Dorothy points out, it is hard for intermediate-grade students to imagine how books are made. A visit from a person who has actually written a book and can talk about the experience of researching, writing, and revising provides the students with details that make the process real for them. The writer who visited Dorothy's class was not a famous author of children's books, but rather a local person who had written a nature book for children. For Dorothy's class, the visit gave new meaning to the word *author*, motivating students to involve themselves in more reading and writing.

Publishing Possibilities

Being able to publish for an audience beyond the classroom is motivating for many student writers. In some communities, the local newspaper publishes student writing in a weekly supplement along with the authors' and schools' names. Frequently, students are given a specific topic for response. Students who resist revising and editing class assignments are often willing to polish a piece of writing in hopes of having it selected for publication. Teachers who do not have the local newspaper option may find that their hallway walls provide a publication opportunity. Selecting only students' best work and providing a colorful construction paper backing and a photo of the author for each student's display can elevate hallway postings. Since teachers who use this technique include writing on a wide variety of topics (it is highly unlikely that a single assignment will lead to each student's best work), passersby will find the students' pieces interesting enough to read. This is seldom true of the "cookie cutter" writing samples—all in response to a single prompt—that many teachers post outside their classrooms.

The district writing fair in the Flemington-Raritan School District in Flemington, New Jersey, provides a situation that motivates every student in the school district with a publication opportunity. This spring tradition has a history of more than ten years. On a given evening, every school in the district is open to parents and children who come to read the writing that is placed on tables and posted on walls in cafeterias, classrooms, and hallways. Every child in the district has at least one piece of writing on display. Entire families visit the writing fair together, many moving from elementary schools to the district's one middle school, reading the pieces submitted by their children and their children's friends. Because the children participate year after year in this event, they know that any piece of writing they do during the year may be the piece they select to revise, edit, and polish for the writing fair.

Creating classrooms and situations that inspire reading and writing requires that we consider students' feelings about literacy learning. Effort is required of teachers who decide to provide instruction that will not only inform students but also motivate them. It is important that teachers recognize the effect they can have on motivating students to engage in literacy activities. Knowing the difference they can make for students who are having difficulty acquiring literacy should encourage teachers to focus their attention on providing the "something special" that might engage and motivate such students.

MEETING THE NEEDS OF ENGLISH LANGUAGE LEARNERS

3

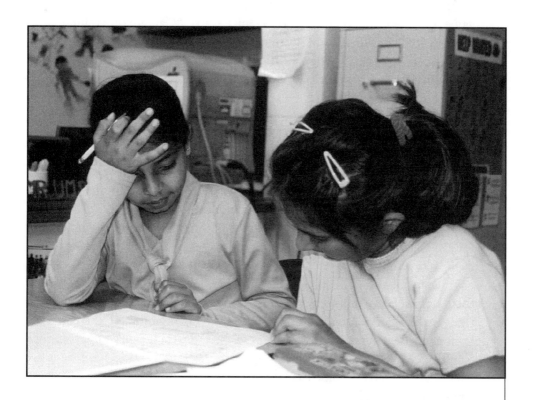

Our discussion in this chapter focuses on the special challenges faced by teachers who seek effective approaches to teaching the growing number of students whose first language is other than English. The diversity among these youngsters in terms of their linguistic and cultural backgrounds, the degree of competence in their first language, and their competence in English combine to make a complicated mix of variables for instructional decision-making.

Denise Ammon and her fourth-grade students sit on the floor surrounding a large street map of the school neighborhood. They are about to play the game Tell Me How to Get There. Denise starts. "Can anyone tell me how to get from Jake's Hardware Store to the gas station on 15th Street?"

Ramón begins, "Well, you have to go to the end by the park."

"To the end of what? Can you give me more information?" Denise asks.

Elisa attempts to help. She points to the map. "Well, you go here to the park and turn right."

"See if you can give me the directions without pointing to the map," Denise says. "Pretend that I can't see the map. I want you to use the words you know about directions. Should I go north to get to the gas station? What street should I walk down, and where do I turn?"

Denise continues to coax the children. She urges them to look carefully at the map and think about the words they need to help someone get to the gas station.

Many of the children in this class are learning to speak English as their second language. Though most come from Spanish-speaking homes, three other languages are represented as well. Some of the English Language Learners have a fair degree of competence in conversational English. Others are new to the country and know very little English. This particular activity is one that both native and non-native speakers of English enjoy and learn from. It involves concrete materials and ideas, and students realize that it will be useful in their everyday lives.

As their teacher, Denise has a dual purpose in mind in using the game. Map reading is a part of the social studies curriculum. This activity provides an excellent foundation for the more complicated map-reading skills they are required to learn. Also, the language and concepts that are needed to read maps and to give and follow directions are important aspects of the literacy curriculum.

In the Tell Me How to Get There game, students of varied abilities and competence in English can participate at their own levels. Some children are acquiring basic vocabulary, such as directional words and the words for thoroughfares, such as *street*, *avenue*, and *boulevard*. Other students are learning how to give the directions in complete sentences, using appropriate terminology. Still others are learning to be precise and accurate in their directions. Advanced students may be asked to write down some directions as well as to give them orally. Denise is aware of where each student is and coaches each accordingly.

Challenges for Teaching and Learning: An Overview

In the United States, the number of schoolchildren whose home language is other than English continues to grow rapidly. Yet there is still a great deal to be learned about successful strategies for working with these children (Garcia 2000). A recent survey on the quality of teachers in American classrooms revealed that 54 percent of the teachers surveyed taught students who either had limited English proficiency or were culturally diverse. Relatively few (about 20 percent) felt well prepared to meet the needs of these students (National Center for Education Statistics 1999).

Many English Language Learners find it difficult to participate successfully in school-based literacy activities. Many are newcomers to this country who find themselves in strange and emotionally disquieting surroundings at home and at school. Even those who are not newcomers often face daily adjustments between the language and culture of home and school. The school's most fundamental and challenging job is to make the educational environment nonthreatening and emotionally supportive for these children. At the same time, the school must make a comprehensive program of language, literacy, and content-area studies accessible to them. This is no small task. Yet researchers who have studied instructional practices that work with English Language Learners agree on some fundamental ideas. Gersten (1999) reviewed a range of research on teaching speakers of other languages when English is the primary language of instruction. The following principles were derived:

1. *Avoid oversimplified materials.* These may be insulting to students. Although the students are learning new vocabulary for familiar things, the materials should not suggest that students are immature or unintelligent. The use of concrete objects is extremely helpful.

2. *Make use of visuals.* These help both students and teachers come to a clearer understanding of what is being discussed. Misunderstandings are less likely when students are helped to visualize what is being discussed in what is a new language for them.

3. *Integrate oral and written modalities.*

4. *Focus on a few core vocabulary words in each lesson.* Words may be selected because they are key for understanding a text or the content under

study. Where possible, enlist the help of other students and teachers to link words or concepts to the student's first language.

5. *Avoid simultaneous translation.* However, at times it may be helpful to make limited use of a student's first language and English in a lesson. Again, the help of native speakers can be enlisted. Of course, when there are multiple languages in a classroom this could slow down the pace of instruction to the point where it might be counterproductive.

6. *Be sensitive when providing feedback to the new English learner.* Students need to be encouraged to try out their new language and to risk error. As students progress, specific feedback on errors should gradually be increased.

Keep in mind that it is not the purpose of the school to *replace* students' home language with English. However, where English is the language of instruction, it is the school's responsibility to provide opportunities for students to expand their language repertoires to include proficiency in English. The organization of Teachers of English to Speakers of Other Languages (TESOL) has produced a set of standards for second language learning (TESOL 1997). These standards set forth a vision of effective education for English as a Second Language students that includes the goal of native levels of proficiency in English; the maintenance and promotion of students' native languages in school and community contexts; a recognition that all educational personnel assume responsibility for their education; the comprehensive provision of first-rate services and full access to those services by all students; and the recognition that knowledge of more than one language and culture is advantageous for all students (p. 3).

Intervention Strategies for English Language Learners

Learning to Use English to Communicate in Socially and Culturally Appropriate Ways

Opportunities should be provided for English Language Learners to adjust the tone and variety of English they use so that it is appropriate for their audience, purpose, or setting. Creative dramatics in response to a story or poem is an excellent vehicle for this purpose. Students may act out a scene from a story, portraying the tone and sentiment of the characters and using language similar to that of the story. In writing, students may be encouraged to use words that convey the emotions of their characters.

Gasparro and Falletta (1994) describe their experiences using drama with poetry in the middle and upper grades. In this approach, the teacher provides students with the background to a poem and introduces difficult or unusual vocabulary. The teacher then reads the poem aloud to all the students. This is followed by discussion and another reading by the teacher. Next, students read the poem aloud chorally and then take turns reading it aloud individually. They are now ready to prepare for the dramatization. Scenery and props may be used. Students are given time to rehearse their dramatization, much of which is improvised. They perform for one another, experimenting with character interactions and dialogues.

The key to success in using drama with English Language Learners is placing the learners in situations that are real to them. As students use their new language to communicate their interpretations of the poems, they experiment with body language, gestures, and facial expressions, as well as intonation, rhythm, stress, slang, and idiomatic expressions. Effective use of all these is obviously an important goal for all students who participate, whether or not they are English Language Learners. Gasparro and Falletta recommend poems such as "Woodpecker in Disguise" by Grace Taber Hillock or "Read This with Gestures" by John Ciardi as good selections for advanced beginners and low intermediate level children. Further fine works for dramatization may be found in

Elephant Games and Other Playful Poems to Perform by Brod Bagert and Paul Fleischman's *Joyful Noise: Poems for Two Voices.*

Small-group activities that involve talk about the content under study in science and social studies is another way to help students get a sense of what is acceptable socially and culturally in their new linguistic environment. Working in a group involves an exchange of ideas, a willingness to listen to others, and an opportunity to make opinions heard. Group activities that include some concrete materials, such as painting a mural, conducting an experiment, or constructing a representation of something for display, work very well. Each of these should involve writing and reading as well as talk and activity.

Gina Goble uses interesting paintings, drawings, and photos to stimulate discussions in her classroom. Images that allow students to "put themselves into the picture" work best. Here again, the concrete stimulus serves to spark discussion. Students are encouraged to use appropriate English labels for items in the picture. They expand their knowledge of synonyms as they are reminded that in English, objects are often called by several different names. Students draw on their knowledge of English to offer descriptions for the scenes and actions. They attempt to use suitable sentence structures, often self-correcting as they go along.

Gina makes a deliberate attempt to create experiences that are low-risk so that students are willing to participate fully. Her goals are clear, however, as she builds in enough modeling and gentle correction to promote learning. Most important, students are compelled to concentrate on language and their need to think and express themselves in the new language they are attempting to learn.

Yvonne Cramer uses idioms to help both first and second language speakers of English engage in a study of the English language in a way that is both thoughtful and fun. She starts by presenting some idioms to the group for discussion, such as "out on a limb" or "off the wall." Over a period of weeks, the students search and gather idioms to note in their journals and discuss with the group. This activity has the added benefit of raising awareness among native English speakers of how difficult learning a foreign language can be, particularly English.

Idiom Search

An idiom search fosters familiarity with idioms and a greater understanding of them. It also helps students use contextual clues to identify the meaning of unknown words and clauses.

The process:

1. On a given day each week, have each student take a small notebook home and write down any idioms that they encounter. They can find

examples from the radio, television, books, or even from conversations they hear.

2. The next day, take about ten minutes to have students write some of the idioms on the board, explain the context in which they found them, and provide tentative definitions. The other students may also want to contribute their ideas regarding possible definitions.

3. Have the students record the new idioms in their notebooks.

4. Divide the students into groups and have them discuss an idiom that you have written on the board. Read the idiom in the context of a couple of different sentences. Have the groups talk about the way the idiom is used as well as give a possible definition. Discuss the definitions with the entire class and comment on any possible situations where its use would be inappropriate.

5. If desired, the students could write short dialogues that incorporate these idioms and then read them to the class.

Assessment considerations:

- Are the students using context to figure out the meaning of idioms?
- Are they developing a sense of when the use of given idioms is appropriate?
- Can the students create dialogues that reflect some of the nuances of the idiom?
(Based on *ESL Standards for Pre-K–12 Students* (1997). Teachers of English to Speakers of Other Languages, Inc., pp. 96–97)

Some Frequently Used Idioms

Below are frequently used idioms to start a discussion about our colorful language.

At the drop of a hat
At the end of your rope
Beat around the bush
Beating a dead horse
Bed of roses
Clean bill of health
Cost an arm and a leg
Drive you crazy
Eating out of house and home
Easy as pie
Hold your horses
Get out of my face
Go fly a kite
Gone bananas

Left out in the cold
Pull a fast one
Sweet tooth
That's the way the ball bounces
Your name is mud

Chapter 6 includes additional information on the use of idioms.

Learning to Use English to Read, Write, and Speak Effectively

Studies with younger children show that repeated readings are useful for helping students acquire a comfort level with a new language (Baker et al. 1999). In studies with young children, books were introduced and read to the children in school. They were recorded twice, once in a slower voice, making it easier for children to follow along, and the second time at a regular "conversational" pace. Books, tapes, and in some cases even tape recorders were sent home so that students could practice reading and rereading there.

Repeated readings can help older, intermediate-level students gradually become comfortable with more difficult texts. Providing repeated reading experiences with a few short, relatively easy, high-interest books on tape is a good way to begin the transition. A careful introduction to the book is important so that students have some basic understanding of the text. Listening to the English language speaker and reading aloud along with the tape combine the written and oral in a meaningful way. Other opportunities for repeated readings include group or independent readings of short rhymes, poetry, songs, or any texts meant to be read aloud. (For further information on repeated readings, see Chapter 7.)

Because comprehension of texts is so difficult for English Language Learners as they attempt to speak, read, and function effectively in a new language, they require special attention and support with self-monitoring for understanding. Klinger and Vaughn (1999) describe a technique called Collaborative Strategic Reading (CSR) that combines a number of familiar strategies to foster students' comprehension of text. In CSR students work together in small, heterogeneous, cooperative learning groups. First, the students collaborate to preview the passage to be read. Then, as they read, they *click* or *clunk* unknown words and definitions. "Clicking and clunking refer to the self-monitoring strategy that students are taught to apply while reading" (p. 741). When students are moving through a text with understanding, they are clicking. Running into a brick wall of misunderstanding is referred to as a clunk. Students record clicks and clunks as they read. Later they discuss them with each other and with their teacher to clarify their understanding and reinforce their repertoire of independent fix-up strategies. Thus, they talk not only about the content but also how they came to understand the content. This is an excellent strategy for English Language Learners because it allows them to use talk to further their understanding and to reflect on it in a metacognitive way.

Yvonne Cramer uses a similar strategy with her fifth graders. Her students use sticky notes to record the "roadblocks" (sometimes called *potholes* by the students) to their understanding. She finds that the talk surrounding the notes they make reveals a great deal about where the difficult concepts lie. According to Yvonne, she is sometimes surprised by the kinds of things that impede comprehension even though she attempted to anticipate the troublesome vocabulary and concepts with a good introduction to the text. The discussion also provides a window into how the students are thinking about the content and what might have contributed to their misunderstanding.

Another strategy used in the Collaborative Strategic Reading technique is called Get the Gist. Students read and then provide the gist or essence of a passage in as few words as possible, being careful to convey the most meaning while excluding unnecessary details. Stating the main idea is often problematic for students who are simultaneously learning English and dealing with new content material. The right words to express key ideas in a text may elude the reader. Therefore, this is a good task for cooperative learning groups. Here, students exchange ideas until they come up with just the right words to convey the meaning they wish. Jan Rivera encourages groups to brainstorm their ideas. One person acts as the recorder and writes down suggestions from the others. Then the group goes through the list discussing the pros and cons of each suggestion, making changes as they go along until they find the words that they think best describe the main idea of the passage. Each small group shares their suggestion with the others. These, too, are discussed, with the understanding that several responses may be equally suitable. Jan sees this activity as having three positive outcomes: students are required to think about the most important ideas in a passage, they are required to express their ideas in English, and they are required to discuss the content as well.

It is important to keep in mind that careful supporting by the teacher is the key to success with these strategies. For instance, before students are asked to note points at which their comprehension breaks down, they need to be shown through modeling and demonstration just how that works. Yvonne did several think-alouds with passages on an overhead projector to illustrate her own comprehension processes and what she might jot down as perplexing parts of a passage. She demonstrated for the students by simply reading the passage aloud and noting the problem points in the margin. (Photocopying a piece of text, then enlarging it and making a transparency is the ideal way to conduct this type of think-aloud. All of the students attend to the same stimulus, and the problem points can be noted right on the transparency.) Later, Yvonne and the students went back to discuss the points that were troubling and what she might do to help her understanding. The think-alouds were followed by similar small-group activities in which the students worked together to identify difficult words and ideas. Finally, the students were guided to use the same strategies on their own, with their content-area texts; they were encouraged to treat any difficult text in much the same way.

Learning to Acquire and Communicate About Content-Area Knowledge

The concept and vocabulary load of content-area books is especially difficult for English Language Learners. Strategies that involve cooperative learning and talk about a text are helpful to learners who need support in monitoring their comprehension. The use of learning logs, in which students reflect on their thinking, can be helpful as follow-up to cooperative group discussion. This is a particularly useful strategy for students who have at least some facility with literacy in their first language. The logs allow students to write down what they have learned about a particular topic at the end of a lesson. English Language Learners should be encouraged to use as much English as they can in their logs. However, a combination of first and second language can be allowed as long as students are obviously attempting to incorporate more and more English into their writing.

A typical content lesson that makes use of learning logs might start with a whole-group discussion of the content area under study. Reading from a textbook or other material might be included. After the whole-group activity, a prompt would be given for small-group discussion and problem-solving. The small-group discussion would be followed by a personal reflective entry in students' individual learning logs.

For example, ancient Greece is one of the social studies topics required of sixth grade in Pam Slepian's district. During one lesson, Pam introduced the topic of Greece as the birthplace of the public library. She showed the students reproductions of ancient Greek scrolls, which they handled and discussed. Then they read from their textbook about the topic. Pam took care to spend considerable time showing and talking about the scrolls, comparing them with modern books. She used short, simple sentences with plenty of repetition as she previewed the chapter before guiding the students in reading and discussion.

After the whole-group discussion, Pam placed students in heterogeneous groups, taking into consideration their general competence in literacy and their English language proficiency. This resulted in a varied mix of students working together. Each group was given a set of three questions to answer based on the text that was just read. The questions required factual recall as well as inferential responses, so students had to use information from several parts of the text to respond. The students were asked to choose a different member of the group to act as scribe for each question. Scribes recorded their group's answers on index cards. The small-group responses were then shared with the whole group, and Pam placed them on a large chart. Finally, without using the charts or texts, students were asked to record in their logs three key things that they personally had learned from the lesson.

Instruction of this type is powerful in its integration of the language arts and the content areas. Pam combined *visual representation* and *listening* as she introduced the lesson with artifacts and reading aloud; *reading* as the students were introduced to their text and guided through the textbook material; *speaking* as students engaged in discussion both as a whole group and in small groups; and *writing* as they reflected on what they had learned as individuals. All students had the benefit of visiting the same material in several different ways. When students are struggling with a variety of new concepts and vocabulary, planned redundancy of this type can be useful in solidifying subject matter in their minds. It also provides multiple opportunities for them to use language to discuss the ideas under study.

English Language Learners and Standardized Tests

High-stakes tests present a special challenge to English Language Learners. Increasingly, states are requiring that these students be included in the testing cohort, though many are limited in English proficiency. Strategies that require students to monitor their understanding as they go along have important implications for high-stakes test-taking. Today's standardized tests often contain long passages that require students to construct and sustain understanding of a considerable amount of text in order to address a series of tasks at the end. Struggling readers and writers frequently read through with just a surface understanding only to find that they must go back and read the entire text to complete the questions at the end. Offering students concrete suggestions for monitoring their comprehension as they go along helps them save time on standardized tests and makes it easier for them to remember what they have read when they get to the open-ended questions and other items at the end. Teachers need to

- discuss this as a problem that many students encounter;
- model techniques that students might use to help remember each section of the passage (note taking, underlining if allowed, and so on);

- model the use of techniques, such as note taking, to find the specific information needed to complete the tasks at the end of the passage; and
- call special attention to the importance of using notes to support answers to open-ended questions.

The Strategy Bank contains some tips for helping students approach reading passages on standardized tests more effectively. These are especially useful for English Language Learners.

INSTRUCTIONAL FRAMEWORKS FOR FOCUSED INTERVENTION

4

I n this chapter we expand on the background information we presented earlier about learners and contexts and translate it into concrete suggestions for instruction. We discuss strategies for organizing and managing the classroom, adjusting the nature of instruction, monitoring progress, and collaborating with the home and with special programs. These overarching instructional frameworks allow teachers to differentiate instruction and accommodate the needs of all learners.

Addressing the needs of struggling students is one of the most perplexing problems teachers face. Low achievers need extra time, materials with which they can feel successful, and strategies that work for them. Regardless of the supplemental help offered through special programs, attention must be given to incorporating the best prevention and intervention procedures into regular classroom instructional practice.

Organizing for Differentiated Instruction: Flexible Grouping

One of the misconceptions paralleling the advent of holistic approaches to literacy was the trend toward total whole-group instruction throughout the day. Indeed, teachers were continually warned of the dangers of long-term ability grouping—and rightly so. Considerable research evidence supports these cautions (Allington 1983b; Hiebert 1983; Pallas et al. 1994). However, resistance to any ability-based instruction in the regular classroom is misguided and often renders lower-achieving students with few opportunities for instruction that is tailored to their needs. Students who are progressing rapidly may also miss out on opportunities for more challenging special projects that extend ideas previously introduced to the entire class. Even where teachers attempt to provide frequent individual conferences in reading and writing, there are times when gathering together a small group of students who have similar needs is the most effective and efficient way to provide extra support. As Roller (1996) so aptly says, "We must remember that ability grouping and special pull-out programs arose as a solution to the real problem of variability in children's acquisition of literacy. To return to uniform instruction, uniform materials, and uniform expectations is unrealistic. Variability exists" (p. 9).

Organizing instruction to account for variability offers students opportunities to work within a variety of types of groupings. Students interact with those whose literacy development is most like theirs as well as with those whose skills and abilities differ from theirs. Groups based on instructional needs are continually reformed according to the results of ongoing evaluation, and all children are exposed to a wide variety of heterogeneous grouping for a variety of purposes (Fountas and Pinnell 1996; Worthy and Hoffman 1996). Students receive regular, planned opportunities to learn through varied formats, including whole-group, small-group (including pairs), and one-to-one formats; heterogeneous and homogeneous groupings; and direct and indirect instruction. Although variety is emphasized, flexible grouping structures are highly predictable so that students and teachers have a sense of order and continuity.

Considerations for Flexible Grouping

Flexible grouping allows teachers to differentiate instruction according to

1. *Teacher/child ratio.* Students work with the whole group, in small groups, and with the teacher one-to-one.
2. *Group constituency.* Students work in homogeneous and heterogeneous groupings.
3. *Abilities and needs.* Students work with students at similar levels of development and with similar needs.
4. *Teacher guidance.* Students work with teachers in situations that involve direct (teacher-led) instruction and indirect (teacher-planned, independent) instruction.
5. *Materials.* Students are provided with materials appropriate for their developmental levels and interests.
6. *Modalities.* Students are exposed to work with texts through a variety of media (books, computers, etc.) and given opportunities to respond to texts in a variety of ways (discussion, writing, graphic representation, drama, etc.).
7. *Intensity and duration.* Students work in long- and short-term groupings. (A homogeneous, special needs group may be short term; a heterogeneous research group may work together for several weeks.)

One framework used in planning for differentiated instruction starts with the assumption that a large block of time is designated for language arts each day. This block of time is devoted to planned, systematic instruction in reading, writing (including spelling and grammar), and oral language. However, it is important to note that language and literacy are addressed all day long in all areas of the curriculum. Conversely, topics under study in subject areas, such as science and social studies, may provide the content through which the language arts are taught during this block of time. We have worked with teachers in self-contained classrooms who have 90 to 120 minutes specified for their language arts block. Other teachers, responsible for the language arts in departmental settings, often have an

80-minute block of time that is actually two 40-minute periods scheduled back-to-back. Regardless of the grade level, a large, uninterrupted block of time is essential. Table 4.1 outlines the suggested format for planning. The format allows all of the flexible grouping considerations identified above to be included.

The language arts block begins with a whole-group segment for approximately 30–45 minutes, followed by a brief planning time of 5 to 10 minutes and a workshop period for an hour or more. Following are some tips for planning.

Start by Planning the Whole-Group Activity

Consider each weekly plan as part of a larger unit of work or thematic focus, extending over several weeks' time. Among the objectives targeted for a particular week might be fluency, getting meaning from figurative language, and using the structure of informational books to retrieve information. During the week under consideration, decisions must be made about the materials to be used. These might include a particular story or group of stories, selections of poetry, and some informational text linked to the science curriculum. The materials might consist of trade books, core literacy textbooks, or content-area materials. To balance skills and meaning, lessons should be planned using a *whole-part-whole* framework (Strickland 1998), shown in Figure 4.1. Start with *whole*, meaningful texts and encourage a variety of types of response. Focus on students' comprehension and construction of meaning. Follow this with explicit attention to specific textual features (the *parts* of written language) and conventions of print. Whole texts provide students with a purposeful basis for looking closely at parts of language. These may include specific word structure elements such as meaning-based prefixes useful for reading and spelling, the use of quotation marks in dialogue, or interesting leads that authors use to grab and hold readers. After highlighting the parts through explicit instruction, reinforce the attention given them by returning to the original text or extending into other *whole*-text activities.

Whole-group instruction usually ends with a follow-up assignment for the entire class. It is important that this task be *multilevel*, that is, all students should be able to approach it with a degree of success. Multilevel instruction acknowledges that children come to the classroom with varying backgrounds and abilities. It allows teachers to engage students in similar educational processes with the expectation that individual responses will be varied. Thus, each child truly has an equitable opportunity to move forward toward meeting the curriculum performance standards. A writing assignment such as creating alternative texts (spin-offs based on works students have read and discussed) is an example of a multilevel activity. This is

Table 4.1 Planning for Differentiated Instruction, Grades 3–6

I. Whole-Group/Direct Instruction: 30–45 minutes

Types of Activities	Instructional Notes
Reading/Writing Aloud Teacher models; students observe and respond. **Interactive (Shared) Reading/Writing** Teacher leads; students participate to the extent they can. **Strategic, Reading/Writing, and Word Study** Teacher engages students in systematic manner with support.	**Whole-Part-Whole Framework** Starts with whole text, focuses on skills and strategies within that text, and leads to application with the same or new whole texts in new situations. May involve core literacy program, trade books, or content-area materials. **Follow-up Activity** Whole-group instruction ends with assignment of follow-up activity. May consist of rereading, writing, art, library research, follow-up on specific strategy or skill, etc. Differentiate by offering multilevel tasks.

II. Planning Time: approximately 5 minutes

Discuss who, what, where, when of workshop activities.

III. Reading/Writing Workshop: 60–75 minutes

(Includes teacher-assisted and independent activities and individual and collaborative activities)

Types of Activities	Instructional Notes
Teacher-Assisted Reading/Writing: Small Group and One-to-One Guided reading. Direct instruction for special needs intervention group and other groups. Individual conferences. **Independent Reading/Writing Activities: Individuals, Pairs, and Small Groups** Voluntary reading/writing Center-based activities Projects Library research Computer activities Teacher-assigned tasks, etc.	**Time Allotment** Plan to meet with one or two small groups each day. Allot no more than one-third of the activity time for each small group. Use remaining time for individual conferences and for circulating among students as they work independently. Students experiencing difficulty should meet for small-group or personalized instruction at least three times per week. Others may meet less often. **What the Other Children Do When the Teacher Is Working with Small Groups and Individuals** Follow-up assignments to whole-group instruction as noted above. Other short-term tasks and long-term projects.

Figure 4.1 Blending Skills and Meaning Using a Whole-to-Part-to-Whole Framework

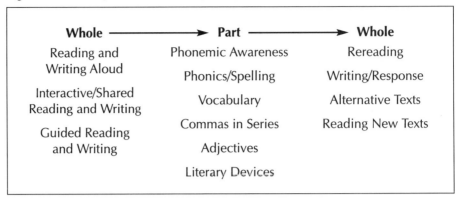

Whole ⟶	Part ⟶	Whole
Reading and Writing Aloud	Phonemic Awareness	Rereading
Interactive/Shared Reading and Writing	Phonics/Spelling	Writing/Response
Guided Reading and Writing	Vocabulary	Alternative Texts
	Commas in Series	Reading New Texts
	Adjectives	
	Literary Devices	

a major departure from traditional seatwork activities, which are usually of the clone variety. That is, all children fill in the blanks, copy from the board, or answer a set of factual questions in which the goal is to have every student produce precisely the same product. Clone assignments keep children busy while the teacher works with small groups. But, because they are geared to the average student, they tend to frustrate struggling learners and offer little or no challenge to those who are progressing rapidly.

Use the Planning Time to Make Sure Everyone Knows What Is Expected

Take a few minutes to discuss the who, what, where, and when of the workshop activities to follow whole-group instruction. Use name charts, lists, and other devices to help children ascertain who will work in small groups today, who has a one-to-one conference with the teacher, whose turn it is to work with a buddy at the computer or on a word study activity, which small group may go to the library, and so on. These procedures as well as classroom routines related to conduct during activity time need to be introduced gradually during the early part of the year and reinforced as the year proceeds. Each new routine or activity must be explained, demonstrated, and even rehearsed, where applicable, so that students may work as independently as possible.

Use the Workshop for Both Teacher-Assisted and Independent Activities

One useful way to think about the workshop time is to envision it in terms of three smaller segments. Each child spends at least one segment to do the follow-up (to whole-group) assignment already described. For some stu-

Supporting Struggling Readers and Writers

dents, one-third of the time is spent with the teacher in a small-group, direct instruction format in which the materials and instructional focus are tailored to meet group needs. These students will spend the remaining one-third of their time at centers, doing research, working on projects, involved in buddy reading, having a one-to-one conference with the teacher, working in a reader response group, or a variety of other options that may be available. Some students may spend two-thirds of the time involved in two or more of these activities. On occasion, three mixed-ability literature response groups, such as the literature circles described in Chapter 5, might be operating simultaneously with the teacher circulating among them. Establishing a clear pattern for these activities is extremely important and takes time. Response groups, in particular, need to be introduced in whole-group settings and then modeled by small groups with the remainder of the class observing. In this way, students will experience the process in advance and understand what is expected. Our experience shows that once the patterns are established, these classrooms run smoothly. And, in fact, teachers tell us that having a well-organized and varied instructional period results in fewer discipline problems, because students have opportunities to work in a number of ways rather than all whole-group, teacher-directed instruction.

Adjusting the Nature of Instruction

Educators often remark that in the primary grades children learn to read; beyond the primary grades they read to learn. In actuality, both occur throughout the grades. Kindergarten children share in the reading of enlarged texts from which they often gain knowledge about science and social studies as they acquire understandings about literacy. Sixth graders continue to refine their abilities to make sense of figurative language and to synthesize and analyze informational texts. To be sure, at the intermediate levels, the emphasis shifts toward using literacy to accomplish increasingly complex tasks. For this reason, much of the reading and writing instruction occurs in conjunction with the content-area subjects. This is highly appropriate, since learning to read and reading to learn are perfect partners when instruction is meaningful and purposeful. The teacher's task is to ensure that all students have a point of entry into the process. Struggling learners, in particular, need guided instruction that helps to make assigned tasks transparent to them. They don't function well in classrooms where there is a heavy emphasis on merely giving assignments and little emphasis on techniques such as modeling and coaching. Teachers who make assumptions about what all children *should* already know about literacy put these children at a great disadvantage.

Adjusting the nature of instruction to include strategies that make learning easier for children is appropriate for all learners. It is essential for those who are experiencing difficulty. In the previous section, we discussed two important ways to adjust the nature of instruction so that struggling readers and writers have an opportunity to perform to their abilities: multilevel instruction and using a whole-part-whole framework.

Multilevel instruction allows all learners to work up to their highest potential. Struggling students engage in the same intellectual processes as everyone else, with challenging but realistic expectations. Teachers not only expect but demand variability, seeking growth over time on the part of all learners. Another aspect of multilevel instruction has to do with materials. Struggling readers need materials they can handle successfully so that they can practice the skills and strategies they are taught. Whole-group activities will usually employ materials beyond their reading levels. Small-group, guided reading instruction (see Chapter 5) should make use of texts at students' ability levels. Independent reading activities that encourage children to select books that match their interests and their reading abilities also provide the kind of practice they need most. Whole-part-whole instruction allows learners to place skills within a contextual frame, so that they have a sense of how and when to use them. Too often, students may know the definitions for parts of speech or certain rules of grammar but lack a frame of reference for when and how to apply what they know.

Another key teaching strategy is *scaffolded instruction*. It may be the single most important approach to teaching that makes a difference in how well learners succeed. Cazden (1988) defines scaffolding as a process in which the learner participates in the full performance of a given activity to the degree to which he or she is capable. The adult provides the "helping hand." As the learner gains competence, the adult gradually increases expectations of how much of the full performance the child can be responsible for.

When teachers scaffold students' learning, they begin by exposing children to the task through modeling and providing examples. Gradually, students are invited to take part in the process although minimally at first. Students may work with partners or in small groups as they take more and more responsibility for the task. They are helped to solve problems and to focus on specific strategies related to what they are learning while gaining competence in the task. Gradually, they move toward independence, applying what they know to similar but new situations. With independence, students are guided to think and talk about what they are now able to do.

Below is a summary of the process of applying strategic scaffolding to writing in a particular form, such as a memoir or list poetry.

From Writing Together to Writing Alone

Immersion and Exploration (Showing Examples and Discussing)

    Expose children to the genre/form; help them generate and crystallize ideas

        How do professional writers do it?

        How do writers among us do it?

        What are the features?

        What key ideas should be kept in mind?

Experimentation (Moving Toward Independence)

    Model by generating and organizing ideas/language

    Guide students through collaborative writing

        Whole group

        Small group

        Writing dyads

    Encourage independent writing

        Share/Publish/Respond

Using this model, a teacher would begin with *Immersion* and *Exploration*. During immersion, students are exposed to the forms under study as they listen and respond to examples read aloud and share examples they discover on their own. Throughout the sharing, students are encouraged to notice patterns and similarities and to decide what makes this particular form unique. They observe, reflect, and discuss. This exploration of the form helps students crystallize their ideas. *Experimentation* begins with the teacher modeling the form as a "think-aloud" demonstration for the children. During a think-aloud, the teacher actually writes while saying aloud everything that is going on inside his or her head: "I think I'll choose rain as my topic. When I think of rain, I think of wet, soggy, shiny. It cleans the streets," and so on. The teacher generates ideas, organizes, and changes them out loud as if the children were not present. Think-alouds are useful because they provide a window into how a skilled writer thinks and what the teacher is eventually going to ask students to do on their own.

After the demonstration, teacher and students might collaborate as a whole group to create another example, thus offering another opportunity for a mental rehearsal for the students who need extensive support. Throughout, students are guided to notice certain patterns and similarities within the form. For example, if list poetry is the instructional focus, students would notice that poets simply select a topic that interests them and then brainstorm everything they can about it. The ideas generated are then organized in a poetic way. Experimentation moves students, in a gradual way, from observing and participating to working independently.

Another example of scaffolded instruction is a strategy designed to help students deal with difficult texts in the content areas. Less able readers need specific instruction in the use of strategies for comprehending texts (Dole et al. 1991). The kinds of activities that follow can help smooth the way for readers who need extra support as well as promote better access to key ideas for more capable readers:

1. Determine vocabulary or concepts that you anticipate may be troublesome. Lead students in a discussion of the words and have them predict what the selection might be about. Write their predictions on the board and periodically confirm or disconfirm them during the reading.
2. After introducing the selection, read aloud the first paragraph or two as the students follow along. Reflect aloud about what you read and note something you learned. Encourage the students to summarize what they learned or tell one new thing they learned from the passages that you read. Students may volunteer their contributions individually or collaborate in pairs or groups and then share with the class.
3. Ask students to read the next paragraph or two silently. Then continue by asking an individual to reread the passage aloud as the others follow along. After the oral reading, have students summarize or tell something new they learned, being sure to include some of the struggling readers. When appropriate, guide students to use some of the new vocabulary in their responses.
4. Record their statements on a chart to form a student-created summary of the selection. The chart then serves as a reduced version of the key ideas in the passage. It may be referred to and reread periodically as a review of the topic, both with the whole group and as a follow-up in small-group, teacher-directed activities with less able readers.
5. After the guided practice and sharing, provide opportunities for the students to read and respond to other short passages on their own.

Monitoring Progress: Documentation Is Not Enough

Monitoring progress is at the heart of a successful program in which instruction is differentiated. Teachers who respect and respond to variability are constantly alert to individual needs and the implications for instruction. They use assessment to focus on students' strengths rather than just their weaknesses (National Center for Fair and Open Testing 1998). New forms of instruction in the language arts, such as literature response circles and cooperative learning groups, have created a need for new forms of assessment. "Conventional standardized tests, in which students can respond only in a multiple-choice format, cannot adequately assess students' learning of complex forms of reading and writing" (Au, Carroll, and Scheu 1997, p. 281). Students' progress must be documented on an ongoing basis, but merely documenting progress is not enough. The instructional decisions that are based on that documentation are what really count. Increasingly, teachers are integrating a system of ongoing, informal classroom assessment into their instructional programs. They have discovered that this type of documentation more truly reveals student needs as opposed to norm-referenced standardized tests or even teacher-developed paper and pencil tests alone (Calfee and Hiebert 1991). Viewed in this way, assessment is used to support better teaching and transform schooling, rather than reify existing problems and inequalities (Darling-Hammond 1994).

A distinct advantage of informal classroom assessment is that behaviors can be observed over time to determine when they are characteristic of a student's reading behavior and need attention or when an apparent problem is more likely related to a specific text or situation. For example, students who lack fluency when reading orally may be helped through practice reading aloud with easier texts. This might be accomplished through a buddy reading arrangement, in which students take turns reading aloud to each other (see Chapter 7). Students who over-rely on the first letter of a word when employing decoding strategies might benefit from activities that help them attend to the entire word (see Chapter 6). Students who "read" through a text and have difficulty recalling anything about it might benefit from reading small sections at a time and telling what they remember. Teachers who emphasize targeted reading instruction to address individual and small-group needs are apt to see greater student progress.

Students need to know that everything they do in the language arts class is important and that in one way or another it counts. Self-selected, independent reading and reader response groups are sometimes viewed by students as less important than a test or other types of written work: "After all, we chose the books ourselves," or "We're just talking about what we read." Teachers complain that these activities are difficult to monitor. They want simple but useful management systems for documenting student progress in a variety of areas.

By keeping district curriculum objectives in mind and offering students many opportunities to participate in activities of the type described under "covering skills," teachers can engage students in holistic, literature-based activities and still chart progress on targeted strategies over time. The information gathered can be analyzed in at least three ways: (1) progress of the individual learner in relationship to him- or herself; (2) progress of the individual learner in terms of the group; and (3) progress of the group as a whole. Each of these offers teachers insight into what skills need extra emphasis. Most important, teachers have a sense of where that emphasis should be placed: at the whole-group level; through small, needs-based groups; or through more personalized attention. Following are two examples of systems for monitoring literacy activities that many teachers find difficult to assess. (See also Anecdotal Records, in the Strategy Bank.)

Monitoring Reader Response Groups

Literature circles offer teachers an opportunity to use oral response to literature as a window into how children are thinking and responding to text (Roser and Martinez 1995). Very often students experiencing difficulty are not given opportunities to read and discuss materials that they can handle. They are often at the periphery of discussions centered on materials that are far too difficult for them, or they are excluded from response groups in favor of skills-focused groups. All students need a balance of both. We agree that response groups work best when children of various levels read and discuss what is read together. It is possible, however, to organize groups so that students are not so disparate in their ability to handle the material for their group. Teachers who like working with a class text, at least to some degree, may choose to carefully guide and extensively support that reading. Smaller, somewhat heterogeneous groups focused on the same topic, genre, or author (whatever is under study) are then formed for literature circles. Strickland (1998) worked with several teachers to construct a method for evaluating the reading skills and strategies during such discussions. Peterson and Eeds also (1990) offered a system for monitoring students' preparation for and participation in literature study groups. A scheme for documenting discussion in these groups, which is based on both efforts, uses a response group assessment form that includes the date, the prompt or focus for the discussion, and the name of the students in the response group. During the discussion, the teacher makes comments next to each child's name regarding

- preparation for the discussion;
- quality of participation;
- application of knowledge about literary concepts (e.g., plot, theme, genre, characterization, etc.);
- application of knowledge about aspects of reading comprehension (making predictions, getting the main idea, using supporting details, comparing and contrasting, etc.).

Teachers may participate in the discussion or merely observe. The strategy has undergone several mutations as teachers have attempted to keep the form as simple as possible without sacrificing the content they are after. It works extremely well as a means for maintaining quality and accountability in small-group settings. (See Assessing Reader Response Groups, in the Strategy Bank.)

Keeping Track of Independent Reading

Reader response journals are a major resource for helping students and teachers keep track of independent reading. Brief one-to-one conferences with children about their self-selected reading go a long way toward giving this kind of activity the stature it deserves as the most important practice for reading development (Greaney 1980; Anderson, Wilson, and Fielding 1988). Too often in the past, only those children who finished their work early had time for independent reading. Enlightened about its importance, today's teachers are more apt to make independent reading, in and out of school, an integral part of their reading programs. Teachers are also aware that this is an effective way to adjust materials to students' reading levels and interests. Children can, of course, keep their own records. However, personalized conferences transform the record-keeping into a time for documenting and monitoring progress. A three-ring binder with pages for each child provides a quick and easy method for recording information. Pages should be arranged alphabetically, according to each child's last name, for easy reference. Conferences are scheduled for each child every one or two weeks and include

1. *Questions and discussion.* Questions that can be asked about any book are useful to get the conversation started: "How are you enjoying this book so far? How does this book compare with other books of this type? by this author?" At times, the reader response journal may become the focus of the discussion.

2. *Oral reading.* After a brief discussion the child is asked to read a portion of the book aloud. This may be selected by the teacher or prepared in advance by the student. Some teachers keep a cassette tape on hand for each child and record the oral reading or the entire conference. Over a year's time, each child will have several such conferences recorded to be placed into a portfolio or sent home to parents as a gift.

3. *Documentation.* The teacher engages in a type of diagnostic record-keeping in which information about the child's reading strategies, reading preferences, and his or her ability to talk confidently about books is noted.

This simple method of conducting individualized conferences fits easily into the framework for organization already outlined. When several pages are accumulated, they may be stapled together and placed in students' portfolios as evidence of the amount, breadth, and overall proficiency of their independent reading. At times, of course, teachers will want

to use personalized conferences to conduct Running Records (Clay 1985) or Modified Miscue Analysis (Goodman and Marek 1996) to assess children's reading development (see Chapter 7).

Connecting the Classroom, Homes, and Special Programs

By the time children reach the upper elementary grades, a variety of support programs may be available to them. Many teachers involve parents in some type of systematic home support program. Special pull-out programs staffed by reading specialists are also available in school. Community partnerships and school-based programs in which adults tutor students or older students read with younger students may also be available. Although all of these may indeed be helpful, they may also contribute to discontinuity and fragmentation for the very children who need consistency and continuity in their lives. Without question, the classroom teacher is best equipped to coordinate all of these activities so that they complement, rather than compete with, one another.

Reaching out to the home is an absolute must for a number of reasons. Parents and caregivers want and need to be involved with the literacy development of the children in their care. Involvement need not take the form of formal lessons in reading and writing. Fostering encouragement for learning, limiting the amount of television viewing, providing a quiet place to read or study, and establishing a consistent routine for homework may be the best gifts that parents can give to any child. These are of major importance to children who are not succeeding as well as hoped. We encourage teachers to send home class newsletters on a weekly, biweekly, or monthly basis. Newsletters are an excellent vehicle for reminding families about the routines they can establish at home to help their children become more successful learners. They are also a great way to keep parents and guardians informed about classroom activities that have been completed or are upcoming. Parents seem to especially appreciate a monthly calendar with project due dates and special events highlighted; these can be conveniently posted on a refrigerator or kitchen bulletin board.

Finding time to confer with those responsible for special services to students is a major challenge for classroom teachers. Too often, conferences are limited to brief conversations conducted on the run when children are collected or returned to the classroom, in the teachers' room, or in the parking lot. These meetings tend to be brief and almost accidental. Obviously when immediate attention is needed for a problem, a quick conference between classroom teacher and specialist is appropriate. However, there should be a more systematic method for sharing progress and information about areas of need. In some school districts, at least one or two days per marking period are set aside for scheduled conferences between teachers working in supplementary programs and classroom teachers. A "floating" substitute is hired to move from one classroom to another as the teachers meet for thirty-minute periods. A simple form of record-keeping is used to note student progress, record recommendations for instructional emphasis, and jot down comments by both teachers. A copy of the form is kept by anyone participating in the conference and used as a reference in future conferences. This is important because it provides the documentation for decision-making used to inform parents and administrators.

Focusing instruction to meet the needs of students who have difficulties with reading and writing requires orchestration of many elements. Teachers need a wide range of instructional techniques, a varied set of classroom management skills, a broad view of assessment, and an understanding of how to differentiate instruction by effectively picking and choosing from all of these tools. Because these students' needs are greater than those of the average student, teachers often need to include other teachers, their administrators, the students' families, and the students themselves in the process. Although these considerations can seem overwhelming, a "big picture" plan that includes all of them allows each to be addressed in turn, in manageable and effective ways.

5

MAKING THE MOST OF SMALL-GROUP INSTRUCTION

Guided silent reading and literature circles are at the heart of our discussion in this chapter. These two types of small-group instruction enable classroom teachers to make interventions for struggling readers during their regular reading instruction. When both techniques are used, teachers are able to work with struggling readers in homogeneous groups for focused instruction (guided silent reading) as well as foster independence in reading through heterogeneous groups that include more able readers (literature circles). Benefits and management techniques for each approach are presented.

Background and Issues

Today's classrooms serve a diverse population of students who range from capable, independent readers to struggling readers. Most teachers of grades 3 through 6 are aware that all of their students require instruction to comprehend the increasingly complex and less familiar text that confronts them at these grade levels. In heterogeneous classrooms, whole-class reading instruction is frustrating for teachers and students. Most teachers who are worried about children who "just can't read" really mean that these students can't read the book that was selected for the whole class. Despite their frustrations, many of these teachers continue to use a single text. Some believe that it is required by their school administration; others think that small-group instruction is too difficult to manage, or that it is damaging to the self-esteem of struggling readers.

Whole-class instruction that involves reading is generally aimed at teaching subject matter rather than at teaching students how to read. When the objective is for all students to learn particular content or become familiar with a particular story, whole-class instruction can be successful. However, accommodations should be made to ensure that the material is accessible to all students, regardless of their varying abilities. This may mean pairing struggling readers with more capable readers or even making the text available on tape. When the goal is to teach specific reading strategies, small-group instruction is necessary.

In the small-group setting, teachers are better able to observe, monitor, and attend to the needs of individual readers. Students whose confusions might go unnoticed and unassisted in whole-class instruction are likely to receive the help they need in a small group. Similarly, students who are easily distracted or hesitant to participate in a whole-class lesson are likely to be more engaged in small-group learning, where their participation is more frequently required and the situation is less intimidating. A further advantage of small-group instruction is that it can target the specific needs of the group members. Although this is helpful for all learners, it is crucial for struggling readers, whose need for improvement is so great that they cannot afford to devote their instructional time to experiences that do not help them become more capable readers.

Organizing the Classroom for Small-Group Instruction

How to Manage the Independent Work Time

Teachers' concerns about managing the classroom during small-group instruction are legitimate. When teachers meet with one group at a time, the question of how to manage the learning and behavior of the other students is a critical one. Whether working with or without the teacher, the learning of *all* students is important. Small-group instruction suffers when the rest of the class is not engaged in meaningful work. The teacher's attention is drawn to monitoring those students, and this disrupts instruction and learning in the small group. Effective small-group work requires an attentive, responsive teacher.

Independent reading is one of the easiest activities to arrange for students who are not meeting in the group. The need for extended reading practice in grades 3 through 6 has been well documented (Anderson, Wilson, and Fielding 1988). Setting aside a quiet time for students to read self-selected material fosters their enjoyment of reading (Gambrell 1996) and is a valuable way to build their reading stamina and ability. In addition to the obvious reasons for providing independent reading time, there is another. One of the most overlooked test-taking skills for students in the intermediate grades is the ability to read silently in the classroom, surrounded by other readers, and for periods of up to forty minutes at a stretch. Yet children face such demands in standardized test situations and need to be given opportunities for regular practice under less stressful conditions.

Students who are already comfortable with SSR (Silent Sustained Reading) or DEAR (Drop Everything and Read) time will welcome the opportunity to read silently. Those who are not, or who have difficulty doing so for longer periods of time, need help learning this skill. Many struggling readers need explicit direction from their teacher before they can choose a book that appeals to them (see Chapter 2). Helping children to identify areas of interest, authors they have enjoyed, or types of books they have read successfully in the past is a good start. Taking children through the classroom or school library to find possible selections is a sensible next step. Teachers can help children determine whether they can independently read the books they have chosen by encouraging them to use the five-finger test described in Chapter 2. Once students have made their selections, teachers can begin providing short daily reading periods; ten minutes works well at first. The time can gradually be increased as students develop reading stamina and become better able to select engaging books.

During small-group instruction, many teachers use a chart or board area to list tasks that students can do independently. These are not busy-work activities. All of the assignments are familiar to the students, at their ability levels, and relevant to their learning. The tasks might include independent reading and writing, word study activities, handwriting practice, and even assignments they are completing for their content-area learning.

Students may be engaged in these tasks for as much as sixty minutes while their teacher meets with small groups. To work independently and complete all of the activities, they need to be taught the procedures for each task and how to monitor their time. An established routine makes the whole process run more efficiently. Figure 5.1 shows the technique that two fourth-grade teachers, Jean Anderson and Sheri Laman, use to guide

Figure 5.1 Jean Anderson's Literacy Laboratory (Lit Lab) Workboard

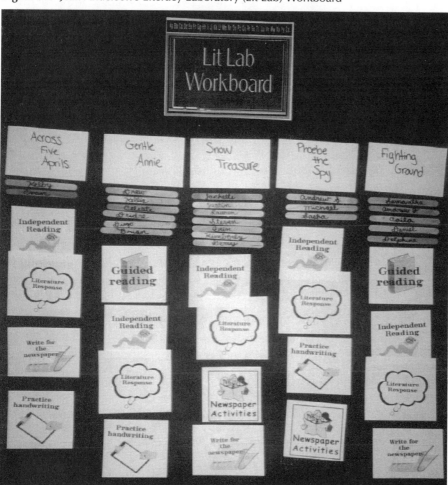

their students through independent work time. Jean and Sheri use a type of *work board* (Fountas and Pinnell 1996) to inform students in each small group of the tasks they need to complete and the order in which they should be carried out.

Which Type of Small-Group Instruction to Use

Various formats can be used for small-group instruction. Two that work well in the intermediate grades are guided silent reading (Whitehead 1994) and literature circles (Daniels 1994; Keegan and Shrake 1991). Both enable teachers to group children in ways that serve everyone's needs, including those who struggle as readers. Because each involves all students in the class, those who are experiencing difficulty with reading are not singled out. Both techniques also call for some level of teacher guidance and instruction, peer collaboration, and consideration for students' reading abilities and interests. Despite these similarities, there are also differences, and it is the differences that make these two techniques complementary partners in classrooms that provide special interventions for struggling readers.

The goal of literature circles is for small groups of students with varied reading abilities but a common interest to be able to discuss and analyze their reading with gradually decreasing support or intervention from the teacher. Peer collaboration and discussion are especially important aspects of this approach because the text is one the students have chosen to read and may therefore at times be more challenging for some group members than the texts used for guided silent reading. The interactions during literature circles enable children to explore their "rough draft" understandings (Short 1995, p. x) by sharing, reflecting, clarifying, and changing ideas in much the same way they revise their writing (see Chapter 9).

In many classrooms, teachers provide a half hour of silent reading time for all students and follow this with a half hour for everyone to meet and discuss in depth what they read, often a chapter. Teachers typically join one or two of the groups daily. Because there may be four or more literature circles in the classroom, students spend more time in discussion without their teachers than they do with them.

By contrast, when a guided silent reading format is used, students meet as groups only when their teacher is working with them. Because teachers find it difficult to meet with more than two or three groups a day, most groups generally meet every other day. Those who may come ~ether daily are students with the greatest needs, for many teachers make ~roup time a high priority and manage to work out the logistics. ~less of the meeting schedule, all students have large chunks of time ~eading silently and reflecting on their reading through note taking and response writing. As a result, discussion at group meetings usually covers more than a single chapter. Students who struggle with reading can be quite successful with this approach: they read books at their instructional level, and the teacher guides their reading through purpose setting, note taking, and a focused instructional session at least every other day.

Whether guided silent reading or literature circles is used depends on the teacher's purpose. The former is the better choice when the aim is to enable struggling readers to learn and practice comprehension strategies under teacher guidance while reading text that is not overly challenging with children of similar reading abilities. Literature circles are a better match when the teacher wants to provide students with opportunities to select their own reading material (even though it may be more challenging) and to work with children who can model more fluent reading. Each strategy supports a variety of teaching objectives, and when both are put to use in intermediate-grade classrooms, struggling readers are provided with a rich and challenging instructional program that is supportive and engaging.

A Comparison of Guided Silent Reading and Literature Circles

Guided Silent Reading	Literature Circles
Small-group reading instruction	Small-group reading instruction
Homogeneous grouping	Flexible (and most likely heterogeneous) grouping
Text at instructional level for all group members	Text at instructional level for some group members
Teacher-selected text	Student-selected text (from teacher-determined options)
Teacher guides group in *all* instruction	Teacher initially guides to teach roles, then facilitates and observes groups. Groups meet frequently without teacher
Teacher sets reading purposes and note-taking tasks to provide structure for students' reading and discussion	Teacher assigns student roles to provide purpose for students' reading and structure for discussion
Benefits struggling readers with text at their instructional level	Benefits struggling readers with with choice, flexible grouping, and a supported opportunity to learn to cope with more difficult text
Groups may work independently to complete culminating activity	Groups may work independently to to complete culminating activity

Instructional Strategies: Using Guided Silent Reading

Why Students in Grades 3 Through 6 Need Guided Silent Reading

Guided silent reading is an intermediate-grade variation (Monroe 1998) of *guided reading* (Fountas and Pinnell 1996), a strategy often used in the primary grades, which brings children with similar reading behaviors together for instruction that supports and extends their reading processes. During guided reading, young children typically "whisper-read" or read orally, so it is easy for teachers to determine when and how to intervene to help them become more strategic readers. By contrast, at grades 3 through 6, students generally read silently and often not in the presence of the teacher. This makes it more difficult to tell when and how to assist. Because intervention is still important, other means are needed to discover where readers are running into problems. Many teachers find it helpful to teach students to take notes on paper and to use sticky notes to mark important or confusing parts while they are reading. These notes provide the students and teacher with a record of the reading experience and serve as springboards for conversations and problem-solving when the small group meets. Through these discussions, teachers are able to learn about the students' reading behaviors and intervene accordingly.

The small-group lesson also gives teachers a chance to model effective strategies that the students will use in their reading, note taking, and discussion. Students must learn to notice when their comprehension is disrupted and to apply fix-up strategies. Because the process of recognizing confusion may be new and difficult for struggling readers, it is especially important for teachers to talk about self-monitoring strategies during the group lesson and to encourage students to use them during their silent reading and note taking. The following exchange from a guided silent reading lesson on Laurence Yep's *The Imp That Ate My Homework* demonstrates how fourth-grade teacher Judy Torres thinks aloud and uses praise and prompting to help a student monitor and clarify her understanding.

Teacher: Did anyone note a part that needs to be clarified?

Jena: I did [*turns to a page marked with a sticky note*]. On page 14, this part where the imp talks, I don't get it. It says: *"The imp held up the paper and nibbled at the corner. 'Hmm, rather bland,' he said. He went on taking small bites. 'No wit for spice. No insight for seasoning.'"* I don't get what he means.

Teacher: Nice work, Jena, you caught yourself not understanding something, and that's the first step to figuring it out. This part is confusing. What do you think the imp is talking about?

Jena: I'm not sure . . . the paper? The homework? You know . . . the essay Jim did about his grandfather?

Teacher: I think so, too, especially because the imp says it's *"rather bland."* Do you remember: Jim the narrator had similar thoughts about the essay.

Jena: Yeah, that's right; he didn't like it.

Teacher: Look back, and find that part for us in the book.

Jena: Here it is, on page 11. *"It was kind of boring"*; that's what he thinks. Jim thinks his teacher won't like it.

Teacher: And *bland* means the same thing as *boring*, so it makes me think that the imp and Jim both think the essay is dull. But how about *"No wit for spice. No insight for seasoning,"* back on page 14? The imp is talking about the essay like it's food!

Jena: And he's eating it!

Teacher: So what does the imp think the essay is missing?

Jena: Wit and insight.

Teacher: Does that make sense?

Jena: I think so, like the things Jim said—that he only said nice things about his grandfather—made it boring.

Intermediate-grade readers need this type of direct instruction in comprehension strategies (Baumann, Hooten, and White 1999; Duffy 1990; Tierney, Readence, and Dishner 1995). Although struggling readers are most obviously in need of it, even students who have been successful primary-grade readers may begin to have difficulty as they encounter texts with fewer and fewer pictures and more and more challenging vocabulary and concepts (see Chapter 6). For students who independently monitor their reading for meaning, and reread, infer, and problem-solve when they lose meaning, the need for direct instruction is less pronounced. Nonetheless, all students benefit from comprehension strategy instruction with text that is appropriately difficult.

Making the Groups

Teachers begin the process of homogeneously grouping students for guided silent reading by looking at the range of readers in their class. A comparative list can easily be created by alternately rank ordering the students as follows:

1. Number a sheet of paper to correspond to the number of students in the class.
2. Consider everything you know about your students as readers, and identify the strongest reader in the class. Write that student's name on the first line.

3. Identify the weakest reader in the class, and write that student's name on the last numbered line.
4. Decide which student in the class reads most like the first listed student and record that individual's name on the second line.
5. Identify the student who reads most like the final student on the list, and record that student's name as the next-to-the-last name.
6. Continue alternating from top to bottom of the list, matching students to most-similar classmates.
7. List the last two or three children, who are in the middle of the class, in any order. These students are so similar in ability that they will ultimately be grouped together.

When the ranking is complete, teachers determine groups of four to seven students (groups larger than seven are too big to function as a small group). They base their decisions on how similar the children are as readers and know that the groups will not be equal in number. The important issue here is that the group consists of students with similar reading abilities so that a text selected at the instructional level for one member of the group will be at an appropriate level for every member. To arrive at the first group's size, teachers check the fifth or sixth student on their list and decide whether that child's reading ability more closely resembles that of the preceding child, or of the one who follows. Once the first group is determined, teachers continue the process with the remaining names. Figure 5.2 shows a sample of an alternate rank-ordered class list and the resulting guided silent reading groups.

Many teachers tell us about the one or two students whose reading levels are far below the rest of the class. Two children can easily work as a pair. There may be times when the most struggling reader in the class is offered a chance to work alone, receiving lessons that are essentially tutorials. However, before making the decision to work with one student individually while everyone else in the class works in a small group, teachers should consult with the child's parents and the child.

Scheduling the Small-Group Sessions

As previously noted, guided silent reading groups usually do not meet daily, but instead meet every second or third day, depending on the class schedule and size. If the workshop for reading instruction is scheduled for one hour per day, teachers can meet with two groups for twenty to twenty-five minutes. In classes with five guided silent reading groups, teachers might choose to meet every other day with the two groups that struggle most with reading, and every third or fourth day with the remaining three groups. Figure 5.3 shows such a rotation for group meetings over a two-week period.

Figure 5.2 A Sample Alternate Rank Ordering Used to Form Homogeneous Groups

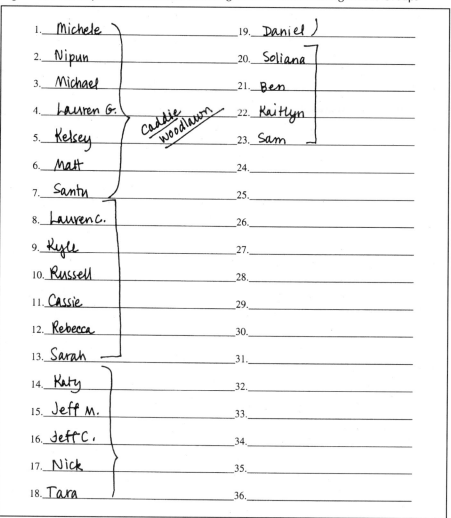

Figure 5.3 A Rotation Plan for Five Groups Meeting During a Two-Week Period

Most Struggling Readers			Most Capable Readers	
Group A	**Group B**	**Group C**	**Group D**	**Group E**
Week One: **Monday**	**Tuesday**	**Wednesday**	**Thursday**	**Friday**
Group A	Group B	Group E	Group B	Group A
Group C	Group D	Group A	Group C	Group D
Week Two: **Monday**	**Tuesday**	**Wednesday**	**Thursday**	**Friday**
Group E	Group A	Group B	Group E	Group C
Group B	Group C	Group D	Group A	Group B

Teachers may worry that they are shortchanging students with infrequent, brief meetings. However, it is important to keep in mind several key features of guided silent reading: (1) students are meeting for a focused session, (2) during the session they are fully engaged in furthering their understandings through discussion and teacher modeling, and (3) they have been given adequate time and guidance to read the book. Because students may read for as long as three hours over a three-day period, they are able to complete a novel or nonfiction trade book in two weeks or less. Sometimes the teaching schedule and class size allow for more frequent group meetings. These are also effective, provided that students have adequate time between meetings to read enough text to discuss.

Selecting Appropriate Text

Because comprehension strategy instruction plays an important role in guided silent reading, students need to work with text at their instructional level. When the text is too difficult, it is impossible for the reader to build enough meaning to learn and anchor problem-solving strategies. When it is too easy, there is no need for intervention and instruction. Therefore, teachers select texts that will provide all students in a group with a balance of comfort and challenge. Such books enable students, like Jena from our earlier example, to read with sufficient ease to notice when an unfamiliar word or concept, a confusing phrase or sentence, or an unexpected event causes their understanding to break down.

Most teachers of guided silent reading have not established a collection of carefully leveled books at the time they begin their guided reading groups. In fact, the process of considering and trying texts already in their school collection is often their first step in developing a set of leveled texts. (For details about leveling books for guided reading and for lists of leveled books, see Fountas and Pinnell 1999.) Teachers also find it helpful to refer to the reading-level estimates on the backs of many trade books. Publishers of supplemental texts in the United States and New Zealand are beginning to develop collections of books especially for guided silent reading at the intermediate grades; a listing of several appears in the Resources section.

Teachers who use guided silent reading are often very successful in matching the texts they already have in their schools to their groups. They rely on past experiences with the texts to determine which will provide a comfortable challenge for a particular group of readers. Although not every match is perfect, teachers who know their book collections and their students generally select appropriate text for their readers, and they become more accurate with experience. They also learn what additional materials need to be purchased to expand their collections to meet the needs of all their readers. When the option of purchasing new materials exists, it is sensible to invest in nonfiction. Publishers are producing wonderful new non-fiction texts for children, about topics that intrigue them and might be part of their social studies and science learning. Because test results show that students need much more practice with nonfiction reading, and because literature circles are an excellent avenue for teaching with fiction, purchasing nonfiction material for guided silent reading brings a sensible balance to instructional programs.

When purchasing new materials is not an option, the types of text used vary according to what is available. Some districts have rich collections of fiction trade books, so novels are used. Other districts depend on literature-based series for reading instruction, and selections are taken from the anthologies. In districts where children's magazines are part of the collection of instructional material, they, too, are used. Teachers have also used selections from publications such as *Parade* magazine and *Reader's Digest*, as well as chapters from science and social studies textbooks, craft direction books, children's hobby and collection guides, and information guides from offices of tourism. Teachers show an impressive resourcefulness in their abilities to assemble rich, varied, and highly appropriate collections of reading material for their students.

Selecting the right text for struggling readers often poses a challenge. The text levels will be below grade level, and in the intermediate grades, this may mean that some readers require rather primary materials. Picture books are a useful alternative for older, struggling readers (Ivey 1999), especially if picture books are integrated into activities that involve the entire class. Teachers who read aloud and think aloud from picture books to demonstrate various comprehension strategies build a respect for easier texts.

When picture books are a valued part of whole-class instruction, teachers can make them a respected part of small-group learning as well. Having students read a number of picture books by a single author as an author study, or read a number of picture books on the same topic as a topic exploration, gives struggling readers opportunities to think more deeply about books that are written at their reading level. Nonfiction or historical fiction picture books and minimally illustrated chapter books often interest older readers. Because the number of struggling readers within a class is often small, many teachers find that they can cater to their interests and choices in book selection, relying on library loans to bring new books to the classroom. The Resources section contains a list of titles that are likely to interest older, struggling readers.

Planning Instruction

After the groups have been formed and the texts selected, teachers identify up to four specific objectives that will become the students' purposes for reading and the focus of their note taking and lesson discussion. Although initially just one or two objectives may be targeted, eventually students learn to read with all four purposes in mind. For example, in time they may read to identify and understand unknown words, to monitor their understanding of confusing parts, to keep track of important information about characters and story events, and to make inferences.

Students use a tool called a "bookmark" for their note taking. The bookmark is merely a sheet of paper folded into quarters and is small enough to serve as an actual bookmark. (See Figure 5.4.) Teacher-librarian Alice Yucht has shared this effective strategy with teachers throughout the state of New Jersey. Although teachers often modify the bookmark to provide enough space for their students' notes, they remain faithful to its original function. The bookmark is a simple means for students to make their own notes; it is not an elaborate study guide of publisher- or teacher-created questions for students to answer as they read.

Each face of the bookmark is labeled with a phrase related to one of the objectives. Because some teachers have found that the quarter-fold does not give students enough space to write notes, they teach their students to

Figure 5.4 Sample Bookmark

"I was confused when . . ." (page number)	"Questions (and their answers) I would ask if I were the teacher . . ." (page number)
"Words that are new to me . . ." (page number)	Bookmark for <u>The Imp That Ate My Homework</u> "When I read . . ., I thought about . . ." (page number)

fold the paper in half and use the resulting four half-sheet faces to take their notes. When students are ready to keep the bookmark safely in their books, they simply fold the paper one more time.

Students are taught to record locations in the text where they noticed themselves thinking about that objective. They note the page number and a few words of quotation, or in the case of vocabulary, the unknown word. Creating the note-taking tool for their students encourages teachers to be organized. To set their students' purposes for reading, they must establish clear objectives. Through these objectives teachers coach students to improve their reading comprehension by monitoring and problem-solving for confusions, and by identifying story elements in fiction, important ideas, and vocabulary in context. They teach their students to self-question, infer, visualize images, and synthesize information within and beyond the text, and to notice (and make notes) when they apply these strategies in their reading. Students learn the importance of monitoring for meaning and of rereading to problem-solve.

Ideas for Bookmarks
Monitoring for Meaning
- "I was confused when . . ." (page number)
- "Some readers might need clarification about . . ." (page number)
- "I stopped reading to think about . . ." (page number)

Summarizing and Predicting
- One-sentence summaries and predictions (page number)

Questioning
- "Questions (and their answers) I would ask if I were the teacher" (page number)
- "Questions I would like to ask the author" (page number)

Making Connections
- "When I read . . . (page number), I thought about . . ."

Creating Visual Images
- "When I read . . . (page number), I could picture . . ."

Identifying and Keeping Track of Important Information
- Story Map (for fiction): Setting, Characters, Problem/Goal, Events, Resolution (page number for each entry)
- Other appropriate graphic organizers: Venn diagrams to compare and contrast, time lines for sequence of events, etc. (page number for each entry)
- Main ideas, headings and subheadings, supporting details (for nonfiction, especially textbooks)

"This section is mostly about . . ." (page number)
"Questions (and their answers) from headings . . ." (page number)

Word Work
- New words (page number)
- Difficult-to-pronounce words (page number)
- Interesting words and phrases (page number)

Fostering Critical Comprehension Skills

The most valuable contribution guided silent reading makes to struggling readers is the opportunity for direct, specific strategy instruction in critical comprehension skills, and the chance to practice those skills with a text they can actually read. It is essential that struggling readers learn to monitor for meaning, to notice when they are confused or comprehension breaks down. Capable readers are well aware of their confusions, and they frequently begin to reread and problem-solve spontaneously, without realizing that they have applied a helpful reading strategy. By contrast, struggling readers are often so confused that they are unaware of just where in their reading confusion first occurred. Struggling readers who do not monitor for meaning also do not use fix-up strategies, such as rereading.

Teachers who begin to read with an eye toward the explicit teaching of comprehension strategies begin to notice places of genuine confusion in their own reading, as well as places they anticipate students will find difficult. These portions of the text can be used to model rereading and other fix-up strategies. In the following example with *The Imp That Ate My Homework* by Laurence Yep, Judy, the fourth-grade teacher referred to earlier, tells students about her confusions and describes the kinds of thinking and strategies she used to clarify her understanding:

> On page 56, when I started to read the new chapter, "The Feud," I noticed myself having to reread and think back and even look back. Did any of you have that experience? [No one said they did.] On page 55, the last line of the previous chapter is Jim talking about hearing the imp: "*Suddenly I heard the imp again. 'Cheat, how can you do this to me?'*" Now, I think that's funny—the imp calling Jim a cheat, after he's caused Jim so much trouble. But then we turn the page and the new chapter starts out, "*Grandpop did a double take. 'So it really was you in that vase,' he said. 'Didn't you learn your lesson last time?'*" I had to read that again to realize that Grandpop can hear the imp, just like Jim does. So, the imp is not just something Jim is imagining.
>
> And the vase, did you remember reading about it earlier? I didn't; I thought, "What vase?" I had to go all the way back to page 10 to find

it. Let's turn to that page, to the part where it says, *"Grandpop squinted as he read the writing on the vase. 'A curse on anyone who opens this vase.' He sat back. 'I wonder if that's what happened to it.'"*

Now back to page 56. Here I find out that Grandpop and the imp have known each other for a long time when the imp says, *"I've been waiting a long time to get out. And when I do, look at what I find. You're an old brokendown wreck."* And it gets even more interesting when I notice Jim realizing that only he and his grandfather can hear the imp. By thinking back, looking back, and rereading, I figured out what was going on.

Teachers should remind students to expect confusions and to reread any time meaning is uncertain. Students can be asked to note parts (including page numbers) that confused them or that they reread. Bookmark pages labeled "I was confused when . . . [page number];" "I reread when . . . [page number]," or "Clarification needed . . . [page number]" encourage students to realize that good readers notice comprehension breakdowns and use strategies to fix them and that they can become good readers by doing the same thing.

Noticing confusions is difficult for most readers, but it is especially difficult for struggling readers. Even if students realize they have lost the flow of meaning, they are often too embarrassed to acknowledge or talk about it. Sensitive teachers in the small-group setting can diffuse the embarrassment by discussing confusions as a normal part of reading and by talking about and demonstrating their own confusions and problem-solving. Bookmark prompts such as those developed by fourth-grade teacher Michelle Knight, "I wondered when . . . [page number]" and "I stopped when . . . [page number]," also help. Praising students who can identify points of confusion is important, too. Variations of "You noticed that you needed to think about it! That's what good readers do!" are effective compliments.

Because most students realize when they don't understand a word, many vocabulary words get listed on the bookmark. Monitoring for vocabulary is a helpful strategy that students can learn to apply with ease and success. To teach students how to do the kind of thinking that is needed to figure out unknown words in context, teachers apply the same think-aloud technique that is useful in so much comprehension teaching. Simply explaining one's own thinking about a word or concept is helpful, as the following example demonstrates. The lesson is again focused on *The Imp That Ate My Homework*:

On page 76, the word *relentlessly* is in the last line of the first paragraph: *"Raising his sword, Grandpop danced relentlessly after the imp."* All of the action that has gone on, on page 73, and even before that, from page 71, lets me know that Grandpop is going after that imp without stopping, and without feeling sorry for him. I'm pretty sure that's what *relentlessly* means. We can check it in the dictionary to be certain, but for now, my meaning makes sense to me. Does it to you? Try to notice when you're thinking about the meaning of a new word you've spotted in your reading. I want you to make a note of it on the vocabulary section of your bookmark. Don't forget to put down the page number, too, so we can look back at the word when we talk about it.

Students are usually so willing to list and talk about unknown words from their reading and to share the contextual clues they used to determine a meaning, that teachers often have to end this part of the lesson before everyone has had a chance to share. Students need to learn that they will not share everything they write on their bookmarks with their group; the lessons would be far too long and tedious if they did.

Teachers can determine how accurately students are noticing, processing, and synthesizing details of the text by providing specific comprehension prompts. Bookmark headings can also help students to identify story elements and important information, recognize text structures (such as cause and effect, problem and solution, and contrast and comparison), summarize and retell parts of the story, and make predictions (see also Chapter 8). When the students' notes reveal that they have either missed or misunderstood these details, teachers can assist by demonstrating the importance of rereading.

Students should also be taught to question what they are reading, to seek answers within and beyond the text, and to create visual images based on their reading. This instruction is best accomplished when teachers model, by thinking aloud, their own application of a particular strategy and then invite students to demonstrate with a think-aloud how they use it (Keene and Zimmerman 1997). The teacher and student think-aloud demonstrations are effective in the small group; because students are able to attend carefully to the teacher, they are less intimidated about sharing, and there is time for every student to participate. After teachers have demonstrated and have had students practice using these comprehension strategies, they can include monitoring for self-questioning and visualizing as part of the bookmarks. Headings such as "When I read . . . [page number], I wondered . . ." and "When I read . . . [page number], I pictured . . ." remind students to apply the strategies. The discussions launched by this type of note taking will center on how the students' comprehension is improved when they think beyond the words they are reading.

Working with Words

Students who struggle with reading may have difficulty with decoding, even when the text is at their instructional level. For some students in the intermediate grades, multiple-syllable words are particularly difficult. Students who can decode *in*, *Tim*, and *date* with ease may balk at *intimidate* and be unwilling even to make an attempt. During the guided silent reading lesson, students reread aloud the passages they have noted on their bookmarks. Even this brief oral reading will reveal whether anyone is having difficulty with decoding, and whether the group requires instruction and practice with multisyllabic words.

Patricia Cunningham (2000, pp. 172–176) has written about her experiences in teaching struggling grade 6 students to use the dictionary pronunciation guide as a coping strategy for decoding multisyllabic words. She found that after repeated practice of the coping strategy, students actually learned to decode the words and no longer needed to use the pronunciation guide. Cunningham's approach can easily be used with guided silent reading groups that require such assistance. First, students are taught how to use the pronunciation guide and provided with some teacher demonstrations and practice. Then a bookmark label of "Words I could understand but could not pronounce . . . [page number]" encourages them to identify words for practice with the pronunciation guide and promotes discussion about the words during the guided silent reading lesson.

Putting It All Together: Components of Guided Silent Reading

Prereading

Teachers meet with each group to provide a good introduction to the text that has been selected for them. (Students who are not meeting with the teacher may be working on a culminating activity for their just-completed reading, working on work board tasks, reading from independently selected texts, or, if their guided silent reading group has already met, reading and taking notes about their assigned text.) The good introduction consists of a discussion of the students' prior knowledge of the topic or themes of the text and a survey of the text (including any pictures) to notice its format and organization as well as excite students' interest. Students might be encouraged to make predictions about the content, or about the demands the text structure might make on them. Teachers establish a purpose for the students' reading by introducing the bookmark that will be used with this text.

If students have not previously used a bookmark, teachers model the reading, thinking, and note taking that they will do. Since learning to note new vocabulary words is perhaps the easiest of the bookmark tasks, it is a good starting point and one that can lead students to understand what to do with other aspects of the text as they read. For young and inexperienced groups, teachers might choose to read aloud the first few paragraphs or pages of the book, stopping to think aloud and make a notation on their own bookmarks when appropriate. This might be followed by asking the students to read on silently for five or ten minutes and make notes while the teacher does likewise. This brief interval of reading is a good time for teachers to consider how many pages of text the students will be able to read before their next meeting.

To determine the range of reading speeds in the group, teachers ask students to record their final page number on a slip of paper at the end of the five- or ten-minute reading period. They then collect the papers and check to see approximately how many pages the slowest reader in the group can read in ten minutes. With this information and a knowledge of the amount of reading time the students will have before their next meeting, teachers can help students set a sensible goal for the number of pages they will read. Most teachers find that goals that slightly exceed the slowest reader's speed are effective.

Before ending the session and sending students off to do their reading and note taking, teachers might describe what they noticed and wrote during the ten minutes, and ask students to share their discoveries as well. At first, this is likely to be a confusing process for many students, and it will take time and practice for them to develop competence. Providing students with a stack of ten sticky notes so they can mark the pages and spots they want to write about on their bookmarks is helpful. Although some students find it easy to alternate between reading and making notes, others find it too distracting. The sticky notes enable them to stop reading just long enough to mark the page; then at the end of their reading session they go back to record their notes. Because the students don't write on the sticky notes, they can reuse them at each reading session. Certain students who struggle with both reading and writing may have difficulty keeping any sort of bookmark. For these students, writing directly on the sticky note, or simply using a sticky note marker with no written notations, can be a helpful modification. Those who need this modification can still participate in the discussion, even without notes, if they can remember what they noticed on the marked page.

As the year progresses and students become more experienced with guided silent reading, they will not require as much preliminary teacher modeling and group practice. At that time the introduction is likely to be limited to three areas: discussion of prior knowledge, predictions about the text's content and structure, and setting purposes for reading (as established by the bookmark).

During Reading

While students read, they are guided by the purposes that have been set for them on the bookmark. As previously described, note taking encourages them to monitor their understanding and become aware of strategies they are using. It nudges them to engage in practices that good readers use automatically and all the time. Students self-question, note confusions and reread to clarify them, recognize unknown words and use context to understand them, and identify important information or story elements to build a fuller understanding of the text. Because the students have been provided with a text that is not too difficult for them (which usually means being able to read with at least 90 percent accuracy; see Chapter 7), they are able to read with confidence and concentrate on the comprehension work. For struggling readers, the guided reading experiences may be among the only opportunities they have to succeed in a reading task that is genuinely challenging.

After Reading

At specified points during the students' reading, as well as after the group completes the text, the students meet with the teacher to discuss their experiences. The instruction that occurs during these times is *responsive teaching*, where teachers ask students to talk about what they noticed as they read and what they wrote on their bookmarks. Because students write down the page number for each entry, they are able to direct the teacher and the rest of the group to the place in the text, and teachers are able to praise, prompt, or instruct the student as the situation requires. Although students sometimes mark similar passages for discussion, interesting conversations often result when the confusions or discoveries are unique. The discussions enhance students' understanding of the text and help them articulate reading strategies that they can also use when reading other materials.

When students have finished reading the chosen text, teachers may wish to assign a culminating activity for them to do as a group, or give them an opportunity to choose one of several options. Any activity that requires students to return to the text to represent it in some new way can be used as a culminating activity. For example, students can create posters that explain their reading and present them to the class as an illustrated book talk, perform skits and raps that highlight important ideas from their reading, and complete graphic organizers such as story maps and Venn diagrams to explain their books. Regardless of what activity they do, the time devoted to group work on the culminating activity is usually brief—a class session or two—and it is the only time that students work in guided silent reading groups without the teacher. More often than not, teachers use classroom management just as much as instructional purpose as the basis for determining the amount of time students should devote to the culminating activity. Groups that finish their reading earlier in the cycle will have more time to complete projects while the teacher continues to meet with groups that have not finished. As a result of the additional time, these groups may carry out more elaborate projects, such as independently reading a new text by the same author or in the same genre for purposes of comparison and contrast. Final projects serve as a useful management technique that keeps even students who have finished their reading actively learning. By the time all groups have completed their reading and their culminating activity, the teacher is ready to regroup students, perhaps for instruction in a format other than guided silent reading, such as literature circles.

Instructional Strategies: Using Literature Circles

Why Students in Grades 3 Through 6 Need Literature Circles

"Literature circles are small, temporary discussion groups who have chosen to read the same story, poem, article, or book," (Daniels 1994, p. 13). When they first begin to use literature circles, students use rotating roles to help them conduct a true discussion. (Figure 5.5 provides a listing of possible roles.) These roles provide students with a specific task that helps them prepare for the discussion. For example, the *discussion director* develops a list of questions for the part of the book the students will discuss, and the *summarizer* prepares a brief summary of the day's reading. The roles also pro-

Figure 5.5 Possible Literature Circle Roles

Role	Function	Comprehension Strategies/Skills
Discussion Director	Develops a list of questions for part of book read	Questioning, identifying importance of information, making within-text inferences
Illustrator	Draws a picture related to the reading	Creating a visual image
Connector	Finds connections between the book, the world, other texts, and self	Making connections; making beyond-text inferences; responding aesthetically to what was read
Summarizer/Predictor	Prepares a brief summary of the day's reading and a prediction for upcoming reading	Summarizing and predicting
Travel Tracer	Keeps track of setting/locale changes	Identifying important information
Investigator	Digs up background information	Creating text-to-text world connections
Vocabulary Enricher/ Word Wizard	Identifies words for discussion: those that are puzzling, unfamiliar, repeated a lot, used in an unusual way, key to meaning	Understanding vocabulary in context
Literary Luminary	Finds special sections of text to be read aloud and describes what makes them special	Understanding author's craft

(adapted from Daniels 1994)

vide each student with a different reading purpose. As students rotate through the roles and share their information in the discussion, they have opportunities to apply a variety of comprehension strategies with particular care. Once they become competent in carrying out a discussion, students no longer need the roles to support them, and their use is discontinued (Daniels 1994).

Literature circles, literature study groups (Peterson and Eeds 1990), literature discussion groups (McMahon 1996), and book clubs (Raphael and McMahon 1994) have been described in a variety of ways by many writers. However, several elements remain consistent in most descriptions: small groups, choice, specific individual responsibility, and developing an understanding of the text through discussion with peers. The intent of literature circles is to give students opportunities to read in the way lifelong readers do and to help them develop into motivated and independent readers.

Literature circles offer struggling readers valuable opportunities: (1) to select books that interest them and (2) to work with more able peers, comparing insights and gaining pleasure and increased understanding by talking about the book. As discussed in Chapter 2, the element of choice is highly motivating to students in the intermediate grades, and no students need motivation in their reading more than those for whom reading is difficult. Children who struggle with reading seldom choose to read; they lack experience with selecting books, and they generally read only when it is required. The choice they must make for literature circle is often their first opportunity to think and decide, "Which book do I want to read?"

Literature circles are especially valuable in classrooms where guided silent reading is part of the instructional program. If students work only with their same-ability classmates, they begin to recognize and think about their ability as it relates to others in their class. When students work for two to three weeks in guided silent reading groups, and then for two to three weeks in literature circles, the groups are fluid and changing. Struggling readers can apply the strategies they are learning in their guided silent reading to their reading of books that might be slightly more challenging. A basic premise of literature circles is that understanding and appreciation of the book that students are reading is enhanced by their conversation with peers. Using both types of small-group instruction provides students who find reading difficult with (1) the specific instruction they need (through guided silent reading) and (2) the opportunity to apply what they've learned in less teacher-directed instruction (through literature circles).

Selecting Appropriate Text

The same collection of books or materials that is being used for regular reading instruction can be put to use for literature circles. In many school districts, sets of theme-related literature and sets for author and genre studies are also available. All of these books are appropriate for literature circles if they are appealing enough to be selected by readers, and if their topics, language, settings, and level of readability make it possible for students to get the main point of what they are reading. Though the students choose what to read, their choice is limited to a selection of books provided by the teacher. The options must include books that are in the readability range of the struggling readers and that appeal to the specific interests and affinities of these students. When the books offered are varied enough to provide something of interest to all students and to expose them to authors and genres that they can identify as personal favorites, literature circles are successful. It is important to keep in mind that although struggling readers need opportunities to learn with text at their instructional level, they also need to learn to cope with text that makes more challenging demands of them. This is particularly true for students whose reading difficulties do not exempt them from the national, state, or local tests that might be required at their grade level. When children will be placed in demanding test settings, we need to prepare them to deal with those demands as effectively as they can. Doing so with text that the students are motivated to read and in situations, such as literature circles, that afford peer (and teacher) support enables students to acquire experience in negotiating more difficult texts without being overwhelmed.

Making the Groups

Most often, teachers present book talks to introduce their students to the range of books that will be available for the literature circles. Book talks generally consist of showing the book, telling a bit about its genre and author, and giving a brief and inviting summary of the story. Because teachers are essentially "selling" the book in their book talk, they find it helpful to highlight both the elements that will make it appealing to particular students and the characteristics of readers who will enjoy the book. The brief, tempting, and informative nature of book talks that most teachers find so effective is illustrated in the following example:

> Those of you who enjoyed Lois Lowry's *The Giver* will really love her new book, *Gathering Blue*. I'm going to read the first paragraph to give you a little taste of it, but I won't give you much more. For those of you who select this book, the excitement is going to be in figuring out how and why the characters you come to know best are brought together, and I won't ruin that for you.

Teachers may present more books than will actually be used to provide a wider range of choice. Giving the students some time to browse through them and decide increases their interest in the book they choose and takes only ten or fifteen minutes. Students select three books they are most interested in reading and turn in those titles to their teacher. The teacher then creates groups that take into consideration student choice, reading ability, and group personality. In some classrooms, it is also important to provide gender and ethnic balance in the groups and to think about English language competency (see Chapter 3). The groups may vary in size, but those that consist of more than five or six children are often difficult for students to manage themselves.

Teachers may opt to incorporate choice in other ways. For example, they might ask students to select three people with whom they would most like to be in a group, and then create groups that allow each child to read with at least one selected classmate. Groups of this type can be balanced for a small range in reading ability and other factors. Each of these groups might be presented with three books that the teacher has selected for interest and readability, and asked to make a group decision about which one they will read and discuss.

Planning and Managing Instruction

As noted at the beginning of this chapter, literature circles meet simultaneously in most classrooms, with the teacher joining one or two groups each day and the other groups meeting for discussion on their own. Although the classroom routine is often such that students read silently for a half hour and then meet with their groups for a half hour, teachers sometimes extend the amount of reading time each day by asking students to read an additional half hour at home. While students complete their in-class reading, teachers frequently model silent reading for part of the time (perhaps ten minutes) and conduct individual reading conferences for the rest. These conferences enable teachers to assist students with any questions they might have about their reading and make quick assessments of the students' oral reading fluency and comprehension (see Chapters 7 and 8). In other classrooms, teachers alternate reading and discussion days; this ensures that students have ample time to read enough to discuss during the literature circle meetings. These children often read silently for forty-five minutes one day and meet together in their groups for forty-five minutes the next. In yet other classrooms, students do all of their reading at home, and all of the class time is devoted to group meetings. Decisions about the amount of time students will spend reading and discussing vary according to how much time teachers have to teach reading. Our experience has been that for most third- through sixth-grade students, half-hour sessions are sufficient for literature circle discussions. Because students must stay engaged and on topic during these discussions, we recommend that they not exceed forty-five minutes. When schedules permit a full hour and a half for reading instruction, teachers often choose to schedule thirty minutes for reading, and thirty minutes for literature circle discussions. The remaining time is spent on word study activities (see Chapter 6), whole-class mini-lessons and read-aloud and think-aloud demonstrations, or other reading and writing work board or center activities.

Sometimes teachers use the group meeting time to roam the room and visit with each group daily. Although this may seem like a beneficial approach, it makes it difficult for the teacher to get a complete picture of how any group operates for more than a few moments. When teachers spend at least fifteen minutes with a group, they are able to carefully observe and make notes about the conversation, and they can intervene with instruction if necessary. Teachers may use the time for think-aloud demonstrations of some of the same comprehension strategies they employ in their guided silent reading instruction or to demonstrate effective discussion techniques (see Keene and Zimmerman 1997).

Since the point of literature circles is to help children use discussion to better understand their reading, teachers need to guide students to consider the sort of questions and statements that will encourage compelling discussion. Many of the same questions that students consider independently as they monitor their understanding during guided silent reading are highly appropriate for literature circle conversations as well (for more on questioning techniques see Chapter 8).

As previously mentioned, many teachers use roles like those listed in Figure 5.5 to help students prepare for and manage a discussion. The roles also provide the students with a reading purpose and help them use specific comprehension strategies while reading, much as the bookmark does in guided silent reading. Roles like that of the *discussion director* also help children learn to pose questions and make statements that lead their classmates into exploration of the literature. After teacher modeling and follow-up practice, students are usually able to conduct their discussions quite independently. They ask questions and share information related to their assigned roles. They seek reactions and input from their classmates and provide them with feedback and further information. By teaching children to ask, "Does anyone have anything more to add?" before moving on to a new speaker, teachers encourage true discussion that involves more than two speakers. The type of interaction that occurs among students as they consider the various inferences and information contributed by each group member leads to an enriched understanding of the text.

Students prepare for each group meeting by completing their reading and by preparing written notes (or a drawing) that allow them to contribute easily to the discussion. Most teachers find it helpful to provide each group with a pocket folder that contains a description of each role and its responsibilities and other directions for the students. Students place their written work in this folder, along with any questions or comments, and return the folder to their teacher after each group meeting. Teachers can then easily review the work and leave notes for the students in response to it. The procedure is a simple but effective management tool that helps students keep everything they need for their meetings in one place.

Teaching children to work together in literature discussion groups is no different from teaching them to do any other cooperative group work: students need to understand their particular roles, realize the importance of being prepared, and know how to interact and work independently with classmates. Many teachers have found it effective to make the shift from whole-class instruction to literature circles by modeling the process with the entire class using the same book. They create heterogeneous groups and determine tasks and roles. They introduce the book to the whole class and assign the roles so that each role is represented in every group and every student has a role. In classrooms where no such group work has gone on before, teachers might use a jigsaw structure (Aaronson et al. 1978; Kagan 1994) to teach each role. For example, here's how fifth-grade teacher Donna Beverly introduced literature circles to her students while they were reading *Number the Stars* by Lois Lowry.

Donna determined that four roles would help the children explore and talk about the novel: discussion director, literary luminary, connector, and summarizer. Because there are twenty-three children in the class, Donna decided to make three groups of five students and two groups of four students. In the groups with five members, two students were assigned the same role. (Struggling readers and non-native speakers often benefit from having another member of their group be responsible for finding and reporting on the same information, especially when they are just learning the process.) After Donna introduced the book to the class with a discussion of the novel's setting and the children's prior knowledge of World War II and the Nazis, she handed the students cards with the name of their assigned roles. As the children began their silent reading, Donna called the discussion directors together for a meeting.

She gave the discussion directors a handout (see Figure 5.6) and explained that their job was to develop a list of questions that would encourage their classmates to think and talk about the reading. Because Donna wanted to make sure that the children focused on inferential rather than literal questions, she included descriptions of the types of questions they might ask on the handout. She encouraged the discussion directors to ask questions that would lead readers to "read between the lines": questions that dealt with comparing and contrasting, cause and effect, lists or sequences of important ideas, or explanations. She also encouraged them to ask questions that would prompt readers to "read beyond the lines." These questions would require classmates to connect ideas from the book with experiences from their own lives, with other books, or with what they knew about the time and place of the novel (their background or world knowledge).

To show the students how to create these types of questions, Donna read the first chapter aloud and demonstrated the process she herself uses. As she came to points of importance, such as the setting, or words that created visual images in her own mind, she thought aloud. For example, "Okay, Ellen and Annemarie are in Copenhagen . . ." (p. 1) and "I can picture Annemarie looking into the soldiers' eyes and then immediately down to the ground, where she sees those *'four tall shiny boots'*" (p. 2). When she finished the chapter, Donna reflected, "It seems that this first chapter helps us to understand that life in Copenhagen has changed a great deal in the

Figure 5.6 A Role Sheet for Discussion Directors

As the discussion director, your job is to develop one or two questions about the section of reading you are going to discuss at the next meeting of your literature circle.

Discussion directors do not ask simple questions. They ask questions that encourage their literature circles to discuss what is important in the reading. When you are the discussion director, these ideas might help you:

1. While you are reading, think about the questions that you are asking yourself.

2. Wait until you have finished reading the whole section you will discuss before you decide on your question or questions.

3. Think about helping your literature circle "read between the lines" with questions that ask them to

   - Compare and contrast.
   - Think about a cause and its effect.
   - Think about a problem and its solution or possible solution.
   - Think about a sequence of events.
   - Think about examples or evidence to support an idea.

4. Think about helping your literature circle "read beyond the lines" with questions that ask them to

   - Make connections between an idea from the book and an experience they've had.
   - Make connections between an idea from the book and another book you and others in your literature circle have read.
   - Make connections between an idea from the book and the things they know about the real world.

three years of the Nazi occupation. That's going to be my first question: *How has life in Copenhagen changed in the three years of the Nazi occupation, and how do Ellen, Annemarie, and their mothers feel about the changes?* I'm not going to ask a simple question like, *How long have the Nazis occupied Copenhagen?* or *What did the soldiers do to scare Ellen and Annemarie?* I'm going to ask a big question that forces us to read between the lines and put all of the information together."

Donna reminded the group that it would be easier to think of big and interesting questions once they had read a big chunk of text. She told them she wanted them to prepare for the next day's discussion with their group by writing in their literature response logs one good question for the next chapter and its answer. That way, they would be ready to ask their question, call on someone from their group to respond, and listen carefully to make sure that person gave a complete answer. She had the students practice calling on each other as the teacher might, and she reviewed polite ways they could respond to group members who answered their questions. She also showed them the pocket folders their groups would use to keep all of their directions and written work organized, and before sending the students back to their seats to continue reading, she asked them to put their role sheets in their group's folder.

After scanning the room to make certain that everyone was on task and reading, she called for literary luminaries to meet with her and spent approximately fifteen minutes teaching them their role. She continued this process until she had met with all of the children and explained each of the four roles with careful demonstration of the thinking they would have to do while they read. She also explained the social skills they would need to do their roles well.

When all of the students were back in their seats, Donna gave each group its pocket folder, now complete with descriptions of all four roles. She showed the students how to place their written work in the folder when they completed their circle meetings. Then she asked the students to take turns explaining their roles to the other members of their group and suggested they refer to their role sheets for help.

While the students talked, Donna circulated among the groups, listening to make sure that each student was able to articulate his or her role. She ended the lesson by reminding the students that the groups would meet the next day to discuss the second chapter and that everyone should be prepared to do their job. Donna planned to have students keep their roles for three days; then she would teach group members another of their jobs. Her goal was to have the children rotate through all four roles during their reading of *Number the Stars*. She knew her class would then be ready to participate in literature circles in which each group reads a different book.

Some students may need more of an introduction to the roles, others less. Like Donna, Steve Blevins, a third-grade teacher, has his students practice literature circles using the same book; however, he finds it helpful to first teach students the roles using the class read-aloud. Each day before the read-aloud, Steve introduces a new role to the class through modeling and discussion and asks the children to consider the role as he reads. After the reading, he provides time for them to prepare for the role and to share their work with the class. For students who can grasp the concepts with a less thorough introduction to the roles, the "fishbowl" technique may be sufficient. When the fishbowl is used, one group demonstrates their roles while all the other children observe, often with the teacher highlighting positive aspects of what the students are doing. This technique is also a great way for teachers to praise and make a model of a group's interactions, efforts, and problem-solving; when teachers witness a dynamic group discussion, they can call the other students' attention to observe the group.

Even with good explanations and practice, managing literature circles can be demanding for some teachers and students. In some classrooms, parent volunteers assist during literature circles, not to provide instruction, but to sit with the children so that they have an adult present to help them monitor their behavior. In most of these situations, the parent volunteers, like student roles, can be phased out of the process once students are engaged in the tasks and discussions and have learned to monitor their own behavior. In some classrooms, time management is a problem. If students are given six to eight weeks to read a novel, their reading is too broken up by conversation and other tasks to remain engaging to them. As a result, they drift from the topic into off-task conversation. By developing and following a schedule in which students complete their reading in three weeks or less, teachers help students maintain their interest and build reading stamina. This is usually accomplished by limiting the amount of written work the students do to the notes they keep in their literature response logs: notes prepared for their roles and any notes taken during the discussions.

Fostering Critical Comprehension Skills

The student roles afford a manageable way for teachers to provide direct instruction in comprehension during literature circles. In teaching children the roles, teachers should be aware, as Donna was in the description above, that they need to describe and demonstrate the *thinking*, as well as the activity, that is required to properly carry out the role. The tasks that students complete as part of their roles also offer teachers an avenue for instruction. Teachers should not regard these tasks merely as activities to keep the students responsible for their work. Rather, they are opportunities for teachers to set a reading purpose for each reader, that will lead each one to apply specific comprehension skills. Figure 5.5 shows the connection between the various roles and comprehension.

The diverse range of roles students can take in literature circles ensures that they will have occasion to learn and apply all the comprehension skills they will use to understand fiction. The listing of roles in Figure 5.5 is varied but not exhaustive; other roles can be created as needed to describe and prompt thinking about everything from the most basic of inferences to the subtle nuances of author's craft. Although inferential comprehension strategies are often difficult for struggling readers to understand, recognize, and apply, the likelihood that they will begin to grasp these ways of thinking increases when they have opportunities to discuss and reflect with peers of varying reading abilities.

Learning and practicing the comprehension skill of returning to the text to support answers and comments is critical for students who are working in literature circles because it is an integral part of all roles. Students who have been engaged in guided silent reading and have learned to monitor for meaning, to reread, and to ask for clarification in response to confusion, can practice these strategies during literature circle. Students who have not internalized these strategies will have to be prompted to use them. One way to encourage students to return to the text is to ask them to supply page numbers for specific citations that support the information they share with their group during discussion.

Working with Words

Teachers often ask students to maintain the same sort of new vocabulary lists in literature circles that they keep for guided silent reading. Armed with page numbers and dictionaries, group members are usually able to work together to use context and definitions to clarify and learn word meanings. Some teachers include the role of *vocabulary enricher* or *word wizard* (Daniels 1994) as one of the rotating jobs to be done independently during the reading. The word wizard identifies unknown words, provides their page numbers, and brings the words to the group for discussion and analysis. The word wizard also facilitates the vocabulary discussion during the literature circle meeting.

If needed, decoding practice can also be provided in the literature circle. Teachers who regularly use word sorts to increase their students' knowledge of how words work can help students apply their new understandings by engaging them in word hunts during literature circles. Students might also be taught to use the Reading Big Words strategy. These and other word-learning strategies are described in Chapter 6.

Putting It All Together: Components of Literature Circle Instruction

Prereading

Before students begin, they need sufficient time to preview their books and their roles, and to set a group schedule. Since the students already have some familiarity with the books through their teacher's book talk and their subsequent browsing, this preview does not have to be elaborate. The book preview generally consists of a study of the front and back covers, followed by predictions. However, students' attention may also be directed to the book's front matter, its date of publication, and its dedication. The table of contents, including any chapter titles, provides students with additional information.

Besides previewing their books, students must also review procedures and be informed of time frames. They need to know which roles they will be using to read and discuss the book, and the number of days they will stay with their roles before rotating to different ones. When the roles are still new, staying with each one for a few days helps the students to learn them. However, once the roles are familiar, teachers often expect students to rotate roles daily; this rotation is important because it guarantees that all students will use a variety of strategies to better understand the book. Students also need to know how often literature circle discussions will be held and what the target date is for completing their circle. Moreover, when the process is new they will have to be reminded of the procedure for organizing the written work they complete as part of their role responsibilities (generally a group pocket folder).

Teachers consider the amount and quality of students' prior experience with literature circles to decide how much assistance they will need before they are ready to read. For students with limited experience, teachers carefully go over the procedures and lead each group through the book preview. When students are somewhat familiar with literature circles, teachers can lead all of the groups in a simultaneous preview by giving directions such as, "For the next three minutes, I'd like you all to study the front and back covers of your books. Talk to each other in your group about what you are finding out." For each bit of information teachers want students to consider as part of the preview, they announce an amount of time the groups will have to focus on the information, and they move around the room to make themselves available to groups needing assistance. For students who are experienced with literature circles, teachers find that they need only provide the books and a group pocket folder containing a list of roles, procedures to follow for written work, a meeting schedule, and the target date for completing the circles.

During Reading

Students read independently and silently, guided by their roles. The texts used in literature circles may occasionally be slightly beyond the instructional level of struggling readers. When this is the case, these students may need to be provided with audiotapes of their texts so that they can listen as they read. Additional means of assisting them may include opportunities to read aloud with a parent or a volunteer or to listen and follow along as an adult reads to them. This type of support is particularly beneficial in the early chapters of a piece of literature and can help the struggling reader establish the setting, the characters, and their motives. Once struggling readers understand the story basics and develop an interest in the unfolding events, they can often negotiate the text without as much support. Their understanding of the story will be further enhanced through the group discussion.

After Reading

At regularly scheduled intervals, students meet to discuss their reading with the other students of their literature circle. As the name implies, the students sit in a circle, their seats pulled together so that they can see and hear each other easily, even though other literature circles are meeting and having conversations at the same time. Each student comes prepared to make a particular contribution to the group's discussion. When students first begin these meetings, they tend to take turns and follow a rather rigid pattern of each presenting their contribution, then moving on to the next speaker. With time, practice, and increased interest in the book they are reading, their conversations become more natural.

Teachers serve as facilitators of the discussions and meet with each group as frequently as the schedule allows but for at least fifteen minutes. During these meetings, they are there mostly to listen and to provide assistance or direction as needed. As described in Chapter 4, many teachers use the time to make notes of their observations and of any teaching points they may have made. They use this information to plan for future instruction and to watch for growing competence in the discussions over time.

Many teachers plan culminating activities for groups to complete when they have finished their books. Very often, the activities lead to brief presentations by each group about their book. These presentation projects serve two purposes: they allow the students an opportunity to focus on the book's highlights and to consider the book as a whole, and they motivate some students in the class to read the books independently for their own pleasure.

Varying Small-Group Instruction for Struggling Readers

Teachers who are capable of using both of the approaches for small-group instruction discussed in this chapter are able to provide readers who struggle with instruction that is specific to their needs without setting them apart from their more able classmates. Guided silent reading provides support for building comprehension-monitoring and for fostering abilities in the comfortable setting of instructional-level text. Literature circles allow children to make choices in their reading material, to apply their comprehension strategies with the support of more able classmates, and to emerge as individuals who are capable of making important contributions to their classmates' understanding of what they read. By scheduling these opportunities for growth throughout the school year, teachers create truly flexible groupings in their classrooms. They also provide the instruction, support, challenge, independence, and success that struggling readers in the intermediate grades need to overcome their reading difficulties.

EXPLORING WORDS

In this chapter we address the word-learning needs of struggling readers and writers in the middle grades. Although these students have likely experienced several years of phonics and spelling instruction, many have acquired only a rudimentary understanding of how our alphabetic writing system works and lack strategic knowledge for reading, writing, and understanding unfamiliar words. Unlike novice readers and writers in the primary grades, who typically approach literacy tasks with enthusiasm and determination, older students who have met with frustration and failure in their reading and writing commonly regard such tasks with apathy or dread.

Background and Issues

Although the ultimate goal of reading and writing is to construct meaning, what children know about words affects their ability to make meaning. When word knowledge is limited, as is often the case with struggling readers and writers, so much attention must be given to figuring out individual words that little energy is left for comprehending text and expressing ideas. We see how truly labor-intensive this process can be when we observe the many pauses that punctuate students' reading and writing as they struggle with words.

Skilled readers process print quickly and efficiently, so they can devote their full attention to meaning. Because they have well-developed sight vocabularies, they are able to rapidly and automatically identify many words. When skilled readers encounter an unknown word, they have little difficulty determining what it is. They are able to apply their knowledge of word analysis strategies and spelling patterns to read the word and follow up by cross-checking the results with the surrounding context.

The approach struggling readers take tends to be more one-sided. Some depend solely on a sounding-out strategy and would forge ahead without pause after "reading" a sentence such as *Let's go watch the game* as though the word *watch* rhymes with *patch*. Others rely on context and may misread *The car whizzed down the road* as "The car went down the road." Although students who rely on context may maintain the overall meaning of a sentence, as in the example above, overuse of this strategy suggests an underlying problem: limited *orthographic knowledge*, or knowledge of spelling patterns (Snow, Burns, and Griffin 1998).

In the primary grades, where text tends to be narrative and most words are within children's speaking or listening vocabularies, struggling readers sometimes compensate for their deficiencies in word knowledge by relying heavily on context and picture clues and using only minimal, if any, letter-sound clues. However, with advances in grade, students read informational text that is rich in content-specific vocabulary with increasing frequency. Because many of the words and concepts are new to students, readers who depend on context discover that it is no longer a sufficient aid to understanding and their reading difficulties become more apparent. All readers need to be able to balance the use of context with a well-developed knowledge of letters, sounds, and spelling patterns.

What Intermediate-Level Teachers Should Know About the Role of Orthographic Knowledge

Orthographic knowledge has been called the engine that drives both reading and writing (Templeton and Morris 1999, p. 103). Children typically come to school knowing many words through spoken language but must learn their printed forms. As they learn to read and write, they begin to associate particular letters and letter sequences with certain sounds. Images that identify an individual word's letters and sounds, as well as its meaning and function (noun, verb, and so on), are stored in memory in a kind of mental dictionary. Reading and writing depend in large part on the strength or quality of how words are represented in memory (Ehri 1998). The more children know about letter-sound relationships, the more complete the stored mental images are and the easier it is for them to read and write words. Because beginning readers and writers lack a full understanding of the spelling system, especially vowel patterns, reading and writing are initially slow processes and often inconsistent. The word *bike*, for instance, may be correctly identified on the basis of remembered associations for just the initial and final consonant sounds of the word (/b/ and /k/). However, because only some of the letter-sound clues are being used, the word may also be misread as *book*, *beak*, *bark*, or *bank*. Children's spellings provide a window that can reveal how complete their stored representations for words are in memory. For example, a child with word knowledge such as the novice reader just described might write the words *bike*, *book*, *beak*, *bark*, and *bank* in an identical manner—BK, demonstrating her attention to the initial and final consonant sounds, but not the vowel.

As children's experiences with print increase and they learn how our English spelling system works, they are better able to recognize and produce words. Letters that recur in various words are perceived as common spelling patterns (*bl*, *sh*, *ai*, and *ake*) and meaning units (*ed*, *ing*, *pre*, and *un*) rather than as individual letter sequences. This "chunking" makes it easier for children to decode and spell words and eventually to recognize and produce them automatically and thereby give greater attention to meaning.

If orthographic knowledge underlies both reading and writing, one may wonder why some students are good readers but poor spellers. Although reading and writing are closely related processes, there are differences between the two that contribute to the seeming contradiction of good reader, poor speller. (1) Familiar words can often be identified on the basis of just some of the letters. By contrast, accurate spelling hinges upon the recall of every letter and its correct order. For example, few of us would have trouble identifying the following word, even though two letters have been omitted: *a com odate*. However, if asked to spell *accommodate* many of us would have to think twice before deciding whether it is spelled with two *c*'s and one *m*, one *c* and one *m*, one *c* and two *m*'s, or two *c*'s and two *m*'s. (2) A particular spelling pattern presented in text has fewer ways of being pronounced than a sound has patterns for representing it. Consider the *ea* pattern in *bead*. As a pattern, *ea* can be pronounced with either a long *e* or a short *e* sound (*deaf*), or in a few instances as long *a* (*great*). By contrast, the long *e* sound can be represented in many different ways, including *he*, *beat*, *deed*, *these*, *thief*, *seize*, *key*, *baby*, and even *ski*. It is little surprise that most people are better readers than they are spellers!

The Importance of Timely Instruction

Activities that foster the development of orthographic knowledge help students read and write more fluently and therefore warrant instructional attention. Although children who experience difficulties may require more direct instruction or may take more time to become confident in their use of new understandings, instruction for them does not need to be radically different than that for normally achieving children (Spear-Swerling and Sternberg 1996). However, it does need to be developmentally appropriate. Like normally achieving students, struggling readers and writers vary in what they know about words and in how this knowledge changes over time. An understanding of how spelling or orthographic knowledge develops is essential to providing students with instruction that is appropriate, namely within their *zone of proximal development* (Vygotsky 1978). When instruction is child-centered and not driven by grade level, students can gain maximum benefit from learning situations; they can experience success while still being challenged. Developmentally appropriate instruction is beneficial for all students but may be a necessity for some if they are to become literate.

What Intermediate-Level Teachers Should Know About How Spelling Knowledge Develops

For more than two decades, researchers have examined children's spellings in an effort to discover how learners acquire a knowledge of the English spelling system (e.g., Gentry 1980; Read 1971; Schlagal 1989; Templeton and Bear 1992). Henderson (1990) synthesized findings from this research and outlined a developmental progression that reflects students' changing understandings of how words work. The progression encompasses five stages and extends from the preschool years through adulthood. Although labels for the stages sometimes differ, the characteristics are similar. A brief summary follows.

Emergent spellers initially write with scribbles and random letter strings, sometimes relying on the letters in their name. They have not yet made the match between speech and print, so there is no connection between the words they try to write and the marks or letters they record. For example, when asked to "read" back the picture caption BN1EF3, the child may reply, "I see my dog!" Toward the end of this stage, as children become aware of the sounds in spoken language, and learn letters of the alphabet, they start to associate letters and sounds. We can see this increased understanding in their writing in the form of attention to initial or initial and final consonant sounds. The caption "I see my dog" may now be written as ICMIDK.

Letter name spellers are beginning to read. Their sight vocabularies are limited as is their understanding of letter-sound correspondences. They use a sound-based strategy to spell words but rely on the names of alphabetic letters rather than their associated sounds. Although this strategy produces recognizable words, it leads to the misuse of many letters. For example, *cap* may be spelled KAP because the letter name *k* makes a /k/ sound, whereas the letter name *c* (/s/) does not. Substitutions are often made for short vowels and for certain consonant patterns that have no direct letter-name match. Spellings such as JRAS for *dress* and SIP for *shop* result. Silent letters and those with difficult-to-discern sounds tend to be omitted (BOT for *boat*, WAT or WET for *went*, and MADR or MATR for *matter*). Struggling readers and writers in grades 3 through 6 often exhibit word knowledge characteristic of this stage and the next.

Within word pattern spellers' growing sight vocabularies and greater experiences with print make them aware that there is more to spelling words than just attending to sound. Although students realize that they must deal with patterns, especially the marking of long vowels, they do so inconsistently (BOET for *boat*, WAIK for *wake*, and SALE for *sail*), and sometimes they even overgeneralize their understandings (TAPE for *tap*). Other vowel patterns in single-syllable words as well as more complex consonant patterns present further challenges (BRN for *burn*, POWCH for *pouch*, RIGE for *ridge*, and BICKE for *bike*).

Syllable juncture spellers use spelling patterns in single-syllable words with confidence but face new challenges with multisyllabic words. Students must learn when and when not to double consonants (*trapped* and *cotton*, but *roped* and *motor*) and how to represent the schwa vowel sound in unstressed syllables. The schwa is a difficult sound to spell because it can be represented by any of the five vowels (*a, e, i, o, u*) as well as vowel combinations; for example, *severe, bacon,* and *mountain*.

Derivational constancy spellers are proficient readers with large vocabularies and well-developed knowledge of spelling patterns. Meaning takes on a significant role at this stage as students learn to make connections between the spellings of words and their meanings. They explore families of words in which the sounds of consonants and vowels change but not the spellings, as in *muscle/muscular, express/expression, define/definition*. Later, they expand their vocabulary knowledge by examining Greek and Latin roots, such as *phon* (sound), *spec* (to look or behold), and *spire* (to breathe), and words that derive from the roots (*spectator, specter,* and *retrospect*).

Because struggling readers and writers in the intermediate grades have often experienced grade-level rather than developmentally appropriate instruction, and an emphasis on rote memorization rather than conceptualization for word learning, they frequently demonstrate inconsistencies in their knowledge of how words work. They may recall the spellings of certain more advanced words but have difficulty correctly representing basic vowel patterns, blends, or digraphs. These "holes" are significant and suggest an instructional situation in which the students did not have adequate time to build a solid foundation before instruction moved on to more abstract issues. Without a firm understanding of underlying concepts, the more complex aspects of spelling become difficult, if not impossible, for them to grasp.

Instructional Strategies: Learning to Recognize and Spell Words

Anyone who has worn a pair of shoes that weren't the right size, slipped into the driver's seat of a car belonging to a much taller or shorter person, or tried on someone else's glasses knows how true the expression "one size does not fit all" is. Because of the developmental nature of learning to spell, the needs of students within a given classroom are also likely to vary considerably, and this must be taken into account when instruction is planned. Although various formats, including whole-class, small-group, partner, and individual, can be used for exploring words, many of the activities we describe in this section are designed for small-group or partner work.

Small-group instruction in word study ensures that students at different stages of spelling development are given timely instruction. This type of focused attention is beneficial for all students because most do not discover how words work on their own; they need guidance to understand where and what to look for. This is especially true of children who are struggling with literacy and for whom focused intervention is critical. Teachers can assist these students by scaffolding their learning through modeling and practice that builds on what they already know, and by planning activities that encourage them to think about words and to form generalizations, rather than merely relying on rote memorization.

During word study, students explore words in and out of context and learn strategies to help them with the words they are reading and writing. Word study activities, such as those described below, should make up only about 15 to 20 percent of the time spent on language arts. Using the instructional framework that was presented in Table 4.1 as a guide, teachers can determine where word study will best fit into their schedules. Word work can be incorporated into the guided reading lessons or literature circles discussed in Chapter 5, into special small-group sessions that target specific needs, or into the writing workshop format discussed in Chapter 9. Follow-up activities might be carried out during the independent reading/writing activities time. To get started, teachers examine students' spellings from informal assessments, such as those described at the end of this chapter, and identify what children already know and what they are ready to learn. The time and effort put into determining appropriate instruction pays off—*all* students can experience success, gain confidence in their word learning, and enjoy exploring words.

Using Analogy

Understanding that sequences of letters often sound the same in different words is a strategy that can make struggling readers' word reading easier and more efficient. *Onsets* are series of letters found at the beginning of a syllable, and *rimes* are the vowel and all the letters that follow it (*b/at, sh/ark, br/ake*). Because every syllable has at least one vowel, all syllables have a rime but may not have an onset, as *at* and *ox*. Most often it is the rime that aids the reading of words. For example, students who can read the word *sing* can probably also read *swing, bring*, and *sting*. Sometimes both the onset and rime are used to decode unfamiliar words, as when a student draws on her knowledge of *drip* and *take* to figure out *drake* in *The male duck is called a drake.*

Although analogy also supports writing, it is less reliable here because of the different ways some sounds can be represented. For instance, knowing how to spell *cake* helps with writing *make, shake*, and *take*, but knowing how to spell *nail* does not guarantee a correct spelling for *pail* (*pale*), *sail* (*sale*), or *tail* (*tale*). Learning to accurately spell words like these homophones requires an understanding of pattern and meaning.

Rimes that are common to many single-syllable words form families of words, like the *ing* family. Because such rimes (see Figure 6.1) are also found in the syllables of longer words, familiarity with them can often help students read and write multisyllabic words. For instance, the word *evaporate* can be broken down into the four rimes: *e, ap, or*, and *ate* (as in *me, cap, for*, and *gate*).

Figure 6.1 50 Common Rimes

-ab	-an	-eat	-ill	-oke
-ace	-ank	-ell	-im	-old
-ack	-ap	-ent	-in	-op
-ade	-ash	-est	-ine	-ore
-ail	-ave	-et	-ing	-ot
-ain	-at	-ew	-ink	-ub
-ake	-ate	-ice	-ip	-uck
-ale	-aw	-ick	-it	-ug
-all	-ay	-ide	ob	-ump
-ame	-eam	-ight	-ock	-unk

Karin Javis, a fourth-grade teacher, introduces her struggling readers to a common rime each week as part of their word study. First, she writes the rime, *ine* for instance, on the chalkboard and pronounces it several times, inviting the students to join in after one or two readings. Then she asks them to brainstorm other words with the rime and records their responses on the board or chart paper. Although the focus is on single-syllable words, the occasional multisyllabic word contribution, as *combine* or *define*, is included as well. Next, word meanings are clarified and the complete list is read aloud in unison. Because the students have heard more words than they have seen in print and because speech may blur the spelling, children sometimes suggest words with similar sounds but a different rime, as when Timmy volunteered *remind* for their *ine* list. When asked what he meant, Timmy replied, "You know, people say I remine them of my dad." Karin responded by writing *remind* on the board and saying, "The word you're thinking of is spelled R-E-M-I-N-D. The second syllable of the word has a rhyming part, but it's I—N—D, as in *kind* and *find*. Perhaps another day we can talk about other words with I—N—D."

Karin culminates the lesson by adding a card labeled *ine* under the "I" heading on their word wall of known rimes. She places the word *mine* directly underneath to serve as an example. Five columns are on the wall, each headed by one of the vowels. Several rimes and word examples are already posted. During the coming days Karin will look for opportunities to encourage the students to use the rime to assist their reading and writing. She may do this by calling attention to an *ine* word encountered in their reading or by asking them to spell a particular word with the rime. Karin realizes that this type of guided practice increases the likelihood of her students using the strategy when they are working independently. To help them internalize their knowledge of this and other rimes they have studied, Karin periodically engages the students in a game of Concentration or Go Fish, using families of words such as *shake/snake* or *slick/trick/pick/kick*.

Comparing and Contrasting Word Features

Although knowledge of rimes can assist students with many words, an understanding of specific spelling patterns is also important, for there are many words, especially those with multiple syllables, with which rimes do not work as well. To help students increase their understanding of spelling patterns many teachers use the strategy of *word sorting*. In this activity students categorize known words according to similarities and differences in their sounds and patterns, and sometimes their meanings or structure. This is unlike traditional approaches, which typically focus on one spelling feature at a time and do not involve comparing or contrasting. For example, one week students might work with long *a* patterns and be presented with words such as *same, eight, great, mail, they*, and *play*, and the next week they might move on to a comparable assortment of long *e* patterns, or perhaps to something totally different, such as contractions. For the child who is struggling with literacy, several problems are inherent in this approach. The multitude of different patterns and the lack of a contrasting sound make it virtually impossible for students to conceptualize what long *a* is and to form generalizations about which pattern to use, and when. The task becomes one of sheer rote memorization. To know "long *a*," students must also know what is not "long *a*"; in other words, how does long *a* differ from other patterns that might be confused with it, such as "short *a*"? Further compounding the difficulties is the notion that the focus the following week will likely be completely different, and the long *a* pattern might not be revisited until the following year. Most important of all is the fact that the student may not be ready to negotiate long vowel patterns at all, but instead may require work with short vowels, blends, or digraphs.

Struggling readers and writers need time to explore features that are developmentally appropriate, and they need to do so in meaningful ways. They also need frequent opportunities to revisit features, so they can deepen and solidify their understandings. Below are some ways to help struggling readers and writers maximize their word learning through word sorts.

Seven Ways to Help Struggling Readers and Writers Make the Most of Word Sorting

1. *Build on what they know.* Use words they can read (about half of which they can also spell), and categories that include known as well as new features.

2. *Keep the sorts simple in the beginning.* Start with two, fairly obvious categories; work up to more, and less distinctive, categories over time. Focus on just sound or pattern; gradually work up to sorting by sound and pattern.
3. *Walk them through the sort.* Model how to attend to particular details within the words.
4. *Maintain their attention on important aspects of the words.* Include an occasional exception or two.
5. *Encourage thinking by asking them how the columns are alike and different and by prompting them to make generalizations.*
6. *Provide time for frequent and varied sorting practice.* This will help them internalize the patterns.
7. *Create opportunities that will require them to apply and extend their understandings through their reading and writing.*

Word sorting has the advantage of actively engaging students, both physically through manipulation of word cards, and mentally by encouraging them to generate and share ideas about the placement of their words. In addition, because word cards can easily be rearranged, students can readily change and fine-tune their ideas as they work through a sort. This is especially advantageous for learners who have experienced frequent failures and who are often fearful of revealing their uncertainty and lack of understanding through a trail of erasures and sometimes torn papers.

When putting together a word sort, it is important to keep several points in mind. For one, use words the students can already identify. This enables them to concentrate on how the words work rather than on figuring out what the words are. It is common practice to include about as many words in the sort that students can already spell as words they cannot. This helps to ensure a "Goldilocks" level of challenge: not too easy, not too hard, but just right. For struggling readers and writers it is especially important to keep things simple in the beginning and plan sorts that involve only two categories. The categories should be fairly obvious and should enable students to build new understandings on the foundation of what they already know. This is easily accomplished by including some known features to contrast with what is new. Once students are comfortable with the new pattern, another can be added so that gradually, over time, the sorting hurdle is raised. The number of categories is built up to perhaps four or even five, and the distinctions among the categories are made less apparent. This form of support or scaffolding for word learning increases student confidence and encourages active participation.

The sorts should address spelling features at the students' stage of spelling development, those that the students are using and misusing, such as OUCH, OWL, and POWCH (*pouch*). Results of an informal spelling

Supporting Struggling Readers and Writers

inventory, such as the one discussed later in the chapter, and a look at students' reading and writing can reveal which features should be targeted. *Word Journeys* (Ganske 2000) presents effective sorting contrasts for spelling features across the stages and includes supplemental words for use in word study activities.

Guiding Students Through a Sort

Words chosen for the compare and contrast activities are written on small cards and then sorted into categories headed by key words. Because the categories are predetermined, usually by the teacher, this type of sort is known as a *closed sort* and is the cornerstone of word sorting. The key words contain a targeted letter-sound, spelling pattern, syllable pattern, and/or meaning unit (such prefixes or suffixes) and set the stage for how all the words in a particular column will be alike. For example, if the short vowels *a*, *i*, and *u* are targeted, the key words might be *bat*, *sit*, and *cup*. All the words with a short *a* sound are sorted under *bat*, those with short *i* under *sit*, and so on. Words such as *stop* and *was*, which don't match any of the key words, are placed under a special category for exceptions, usually identified with a question mark.

Exceptions, when included, are used sparingly, usually just one or two. They serve useful purposes. One, they help students maintain a focus on the important aspects of the word. This is valuable for all students, but particularly for struggling readers and writers who sometimes key in on just a single detail to make their sorting decisions and overlook essential bits of information. For example, in a sort with long *a* and short *a* words, where the long *a* pattern used is *vowel-consonant-e* (VCe) as in *tape*, many students will simply separate the words into two piles, those with a final *e* and those without. Including an exception such as *have* or *was* in the card pile ensures that careful thought is given to how the words sound as well as to how they look. Another advantage of including exceptions is that these words are often high-frequency words. The special attention they receive in a word sort helps students remember them, thereby reducing the amount of outside reinforcement needed. Because exceptions represent an additional element of challenge, they may overwhelm some students if used when a feature is first introduced.

Sometimes a closed sort focuses just on sound or just on pattern, but it can focus on sound and pattern simultaneously. At times, students may be asked to do multiple sorts in a lesson, where they sort the same set of words several times, each with a different aim; for example, they may sort by sound one time and by pattern the next. Sorting by sound and pattern is the most difficult type of sort because students must consider two different aspects of each word before deciding on its placement. However, the emphasis on aural and visual cues makes it a worthwhile goal and one that can be attained, even by students who experience difficulty with literacy-related activities. It should be worked up to gradually when students are showing signs of confidence and success, and it should be preceded by sound and/or pattern sorting with the same set of words, whether that day or earlier.

Figure 6.2 shows multiple sorts that Gail Morris developed for a group of struggling readers in her fourth-grade class. After hearing Gail read aloud *Frindle*, the students begged to read a book by Andrew Clements themselves during guided silent reading. Gail found an easier book that was at their instructional level, *Jake Drake: Bully Buster*. Despite the students' fairly secure understandings of the VCe and short vowel patterns, they repeatedly confused the main character's name, *Jake*, with *Jack* during their reading of the first chapter. This confusion and their need to better understand *r*-controlled vowels, as revealed by Gail's informal assessments, prompted Gail to create a set of words for sorting that included short *a*, *aCe*, and *ar*. Although Gail typically draws words for study from multiple sources, including the children's reading, writing, and various word lists, she was able to get all the words for the sorts in Figure 6.2 from the children's novel.

Whether students sort by sound, pattern, or both, teacher modeling is used to call their attention to the particular details within the words that need to be considered. A "guided word walk" (Ganske 2000, p. 86), works well for this. At the end of the next day's guided reading, Gail "walks" her students through a sound sort by placing cards with the words *sack, bake,* and *hard* in front of them on the floor where they are gathered. Next to the final word, she lays a card bearing a question mark. Because the words are

Figure 6.2 Multiple Sorting, with Words from *Jake Drake: Bully Buster,* a Fourth-Grade Guided Silent Reading Novel

Sorting by Sound				Sorting by Pattern			Sorting by Sound and Pattern			
sack	**bake**	**hard**	**?**	**sack**	**bake**	**?**	**sack**	**hard**	**bake**	**?**
back	grade	smart	want	back	same		class	smart	Jake	are
class	Jake	card		smart	are		back	card	grade	want
fast	same	art		fast	grade		fast	art	same	
	face	are		card	Jake			part	face	
	made	part		art	face				made	
				class	made					
				part						
				want						

Supporting Struggling Readers and Writers

all from the chapter they read and discussed the day before, Gail does not make sure the children can identify the words, nor does she inquire about any of their meanings, as she otherwise would. Instead, she points to the three key words and names them. Before she can explain further, Brandy asks, "Are we sorting by sound or pattern or what?" Gail says they will be sorting by sound.

Craig immediately announces, "This is gonna be a cinch!" Even though the students have previously done several sound sorts, Gail begins by modeling the process: She takes the first card, *grade*, identifies the word, and checks to see which key word it matches—"*Grade/sack, grade/bake, grade/hard; grade* goes with *bake*." She places the card below *bake* to start a column of words. Then she continues in like manner with the next card from the pile, *smart*. Seeing the students' eager faces, Gail holds up the next card, *back*, and says, "Okay, who'd like to try this one? And be on your toes—there could be some tricky words in the stack today. Jeff, here you go." Jeff takes the card and after identifying the appropriate match places it in its column. Gail continues through the cards, allowing the students to determine the appropriate columns. When the *Jake* card is held up, James volunteers to place it. He starts to name the word *Jack*, but quickly changes his mind as he holds the word under the *sack* column and says, "Oh, that's right; this word is *Jake*, because it's got an *e* at the end, just like *bake*."

"How would *Jack* be spelled?" Gail asks.

"J-A- . . . C-K," James declares.

"Good thinking, James! You're on your toes. Now how about this word," and Gail holds up *want*. Several hands shoot up.

Gail hands the card to one of the volunteers, saying, "Randy, you haven't had a turn; show us where you think it goes."

Randy takes the card and thinks aloud. "Well, this one's tricky; some people might think it should go under *sack*, but that would make it sound like somebody crying . . . 'waant.' I don't think it fits any of the columns. I think it belongs here," and he places the card below the question mark card.

"You're right, Randy. You paid close attention to sound; good job."

After all the words are sorted, Gail asks the students to read through each list and to generate ideas to explain why certain words are grouped together (such as, "The words under *bake* all have the long *a* sound, and it's spelled with *a-consonant-e*"). Through discussion, Gail and the students clarify and confirm or reject the hypotheses.

Because the sound sort was completed with ease, Gail decides to go ahead and have the children sort the same words again, this time by sound and pattern. She gathers up the cards, leaving just the key words and question mark, and tells the group what she has in mind. Because this will be the students' first attempt at sorting by sound and pattern, Gail plans to model with several words before she invites the children to join in. She will correct any mistakes they make, in her usual way, by immediately moving the word to its appropriate column and saying something such as, "No, *are* goes in the oddball column. Even though it sounds like *hard*, it has a different pattern, and this time we're sorting by sound and pattern." When all of the words have been sorted, she will again ask the students to form ideas about the characteristics of each column of words.

Opportunities to Internalize the Features

Struggling readers and writers need frequent sorting practice to internalize the patterns under study. It is this deep understanding of how words work that facilitates students' reading and writing of words with similar patterns. Although practice may simply mean sorting the words under key words, a number of variations serve to add interest and maintain students' enthusiasm. Once students have a clear understanding of how to categorize a particular set of words, they may engage in *speed sorts*, in which they attempt to sort their fastest but with accuracy. Often individual goals are set and several trials completed with a stopwatch to reach the goal or to break a previous personal record. Care should be taken to help struggling readers and writers set attainable goals and to provide them with ample practice time. *Picture sorts* and *blind sorts* are other variations. They encourage students to focus on sound, which is especially important since phonological awareness plays such an important role in learning to read and write. In a picture sort, pictures are substituted for all or some of the words. Besides making it so learners must consider similarities and differences in sound, pictures enable novice older readers to learn about beginning consonant sounds, short vowel sounds, and rimes without being hindered by their limited sight vocabularies. Blind sorts encourage a balance between visual clues and auditory clues, because students must determine the correct placement of a word after hearing it read but before it is shown. Usually partners at the same stage of spelling development work together and take turns reading and pointing to the appropriate key word. If desired, instead of pointing to the correct column, students can write the words under column headers on a piece of paper as their partner reads them aloud. A final sorting activity, the *open sort*, adds variety and an element of mystery to the task. In this activity students determine their own categories. When everyone is finished, students and teacher try to figure out the categories that each person used. This activity is not only motivating but can also provide the teacher with useful insights about the students' approach to words. For example, do they design categories based on what has been studied, or do they focus on less pertinent details, such as word length, placement of the vowel, or how the word begins?

Applying What Has Been Learned

Word hunts return students to text they have been reading or writing and encourage them to apply their understandings about words. Using a story, poem, content-area material, or other text, students search for examples of words with the particular patterns they have been studying. These, as well as any exceptions, are recorded, sorted, and discussed. The recording may be done on word cards, in notebooks, or on chart paper. Initially, it may be helpful to limit the number of features that struggling readers and writers search for at one time. If three or four categories have been used in the sorting, the group may first hunt for one pattern, then another, until all have been explored; or individual students or pairs of students may hunt for different patterns and pool their results at the end. Once struggling readers and writers understand the process and have had guidance in searching for all of the categories at once, they can complete word hunts collaboratively, with a partner or in small groups. Several groups can hunt for words simultaneously while the teacher circulates, prompting and encouraging appropriate categorizations. Because word hunts involve application of learning, students should have a clear understanding of the spelling features that are targeted.

Reading Big Words

Struggling readers and writers enjoy the opportunity to apply their knowledge of letters and sounds, spelling patterns, and meaning units to tackle multisyllabic words. Collaborative efforts enable them to combine their understandings and learn from each other. Even students with very limited word knowledge can make contributions. One student may draw attention to a single consonant or blend, another to a rime, vowel pattern, or meaning unit. Prepare for the activity by selecting a word from math, social studies, science, or the current read-aloud that is in the students' listening or speaking vocabularies. Write it on the chalkboard or overhead transparency, and invite students to point out recognizable parts of the word. Here are connections one group of students made with the word *interested*:

David: The *ed* at the end shows something happened in the past. We could cover that part up for now and just look at the rest. [*Teacher puts her hand over this part of the word.*]

Jen: The *in* at the beginning is the same pattern that's in *win* and *in*.

Josh: I know you can divide a long word between consonants, like the *n* and *t*, to break it into smaller parts, so *t-e-r* is probably another chunk.

Evan: *E-r* is in a lot of words like *her*.

Marcy: And *t* sounds like /t/, so that chunk is /ter/.

Kamika: The last part has the same spelling as the end of *best*, *e-s-t*.

Teacher: Can you put all the parts together now? [*Uncovers the* ed.]

Students: In-ter-est-ed . . . inter-ested . . . *interested*!

Teacher: Good job! These same types of strategies can help you read many other big words.

Even when students' contributions don't quite match the actual pronunciation, getting close can often help them figure out the word. For example, thinking that the second syllable of *captain* has a long *a* sound because of the *ai* pattern may still trigger the correct word in students' memories, especially when they can use the context of the sentence to double-check.

Because students will encounter big words in their reading, teachers should consider how and when to intervene with assistance. Jumping in immediately and providing the word or, if in a small-group setting, encouraging other members of the group to do so, is probably not the best approach. This neither builds the reader's confidence nor allows the reader to exercise what he knows to try to read the word. Instead, teachers should be prepared to wait a few moments (three to five seconds) while the student attempts to decode the word; then, if necessary, the reader can be prompted to use a helpful strategy. For example,

Teacher: Remember, Josh, if you need to break a longer word into chunks and you see three consonants in the middle like this word has [*athlete*], be sure you keep the two together that make a team when you divide the word.

Josh: Oh, like the *th*. So I should split the word between the *h* and the *l* [*covers up* lete]. The first part is . . . *ath*, and [*uncovers* lete] the second part is *lete* . . ., so the word must be *athlete*.

Teacher: That's right!

Although it may be tempting, interventions during students' reading should not digress into a ten-minute mini-lesson; this would be too distracting. During students' reading or rereading, interventions should be brief, just long enough to get the student back on track. Later, after the passage is completed, or the following day, a mini-lesson might be planned to reinforce the strategy that required cueing. Errors that don't alter meaning may be allowed to pass without correction, unless they are a frequent problem.

The Slate Game

This activity is used to reinforce students' understanding of spelling features at the letter name stage: blends, digraphs, and short vowels. The use of slates to write words makes this activity particularly motivating, even for sixth graders. Students and teacher sit in a circle. The teacher dictates a single-syllable word and everyone, including the teacher, writes it down. Then the teacher says, "Show me," and all turn their slates around. Students check their accuracy against the teacher's, while the teacher notes which students had difficulty. Misspelled words, such as FAP or FALP for *flap* are decoded and discussed. If desired, students can use the following point system to keep score on their slates: one point for a correct beginning element (single consonant, blend, or digraph), one point for a correct short vowel, and one point for a correct final element (single consonant, blend, or digraph). For additional challenge, teachers may include a few "alien" words. These are syllables taken from multisyllabic words, such as *seg* from *segment*, or real words that the children may not yet be familiar with, such as *shod*.

Teachers can teach students a number of strategies to help them spell the words.

1. Before writing the word, say the word carefully by stretching it out like a rubber band. Draw a line on the slate for each sound you hear. Be sure your word has at least that many letters. For example, "f-l-a-p" needs four lines and "sh-i-p" three.

2. Think of a word that rhymes with the one you are trying to spell. If you can spell that word, the new one may have the same spelling pattern.
3. Identify an easy-to-spell word for each short vowel (for example, *cat, bed, lip, hot,* and *cup*). Be sure you can name the vowel sound in each. Use these key words to help you choose the right vowel. Compare the vowel sound in the word you are trying to write with that in each key word until you find the closest match. If necessary, peel away other parts of the word and isolate the vowel sound: *grip* ⟶ *ip* ⟶ *i.*

Using Context

Sometimes struggling readers have difficulty with both letter-sound knowledge and the use of context clues, as the child who reads *Pete hit the big red ball* as "Pet hit the big red bal." *Cloze* passages encourage students to use context to figure out unknown words. The procedure is easy to carry out. A short passage of text is selected and copied or summarized on the chalkboard or a transparency. Several words are deleted, and students are guided to figure out the missing words by using the sense of the surrounding sentences. Students who have difficulty with this may be given banks of words from which to choose their answers; including three words in each bank usually works well. When an aim of the cloze activity is to help students learn to cross-check their use of context with letter-sound clues, the beginning part of each omitted word can be provided. This limits students' answer possibilities to words that fit the meaning of the sentence and begin with the appropriate letter-sound. Carol O'Meara, a sixth-grade teacher, has been regularly using the cloze technique to help one of her struggling readers, Scott, learn to balance context and letter-sound clues. In the following example, Carol and Scott work with an upcoming passage from Phyllis Reynolds Naylor's *Shiloh,* a book Scott is reading for guided silent reading.

Before Scott arrived, Sharon summarized on the chalkboard a portion of the story he was about to read. Then she deleted several key words, leaving only their onsets. Next, she placed a sticky note over the top of each blank, covering up even the onset.

Marty's mom walked over to the ☐ of the pine tree. She undid the wire that keeps the fence ☐ , so she could get in. She crouched ☐ in the pine ☐ , and Shiloh started to ☐ up on her with his front paws. He licked at her ☐ .

Later, when she met with Scott, she asked him to carefully read the paragraph and try to figure out the hidden words. Initially, Scott thought the missing words might be *back, shut, down, needles, jump,* and *face.* The first blank gave him considerable trouble; after vacillating between *back* and *side,* he finally shrugged his shoulders and said, "It could be either; you can't tell," and then opted for the former word. Sharon asked Scott to reread the paragraph aloud. She knew that some of his selections were incorrect, but overall, the words he had chosen made good sense in the paragraph. She praised his efforts at using context clues and then peeled away the sticky notes so Scott could see the beginning of each word.

Marty's mom walked over to the tr_____ of the pine tree. She undid the wire that keeps the fence cl_____, so she could get in. She crouched d_____ in the pine n_____, and Shiloh started to l_____ up on her with his front paws. He licked at her f_____.

She encouraged Scott to reconsider his choices in light of the additional information, saying, "It looks like you may have many of them right. See if the letter-sound clues can help you with the ones that obviously don't fit."

Immediately upon looking at the first blank, Scott said, "Oh, it must be *trunk.*" After careful consideration of the next blank, he changed his response to *closed* and then quickly added, "but *shut* means the same thing." He stuck with his original choices of *down, needles,* and *face,* but couldn't think of a different response for the next-to-last blank. As a further help, Sharon added the word's final letter, *p,* to the end of the blank. "Oh, it must be *leap!*" Scott said.

"You did a good job of putting the clues together, Scott!" Sharon noted and ended the session by reminding him of how valuable it is to use both context *and* letter-sound clues when reading and by telling him they would try another passage the next day.

Instructional Strategies: Learning to Understand Words

As we noted earlier in this chapter, struggling readers in the intermediate grades are likely to need instruction that helps them to better understand spelling patterns and enables them to build a repertoire of decoding strategies. They also need help learning new concepts and the words that represent them; this is especially important considering that the conceptual load in content-area studies increases in the intermediate grades. Students must be able to read and understand many words they do not use in their speech to comprehend the informational text. According to the National Reading

Panel (2000), "reading vocabulary is crucial to the comprehension processes of a skilled reader" (p. 4-3). Good readers, who tend to read a lot, already know many words and understand many concepts. As they read and encounter new ideas, words, and expressions, they are able to relate this new information to existing understandings, and their vocabulary grows, making it easier for them to comprehend even more difficult text. The cycle is different for children who experience difficulty in reading. Their reading is often slow, laborious, and even frustrating, and their vocabulary knowledge may be limited. Because reading likely provides little enjoyment, they are apt to read less and be exposed to fewer new ideas and concepts. Rather than increasing, their reading ability may be further impeded, leading to a downward spiral of reading failure.

To realize the detrimental effect that encountering numerous unfamiliar words can have on students' comprehension, read the following paragraph and try to identify this well-known piece of literature in this "meatier" form:

> A female of the Homo Sapiens species was the possessor of a small, immature ruminant of the genus Ovis, the outermost covering of which reflected all wavelengths of visible light with a luminosity equal to that of a mass of naturally occurring, microscopically crystalline water. Regardless of the translational pathway chosen by the Homo Sapiens female, there was a 100 percent probability that the aforementioned ruminant would select the same pathway.

Although readers may have previously heard all, or nearly all, of the words in the paragraph, most are probably unclear about some of the concepts associated with them. Furthermore, few readers probably make a regular practice of using words such as *Homo Sapiens, ruminant, Ovis, wavelengths, luminosity, microscopically crystalline* and *translational* in their reading, writing, or speaking. The paragraph's concentration of unfamiliar words makes it difficult, if not impossible, to connect ideas and understand the whole. The task is even more daunting for anyone who has never experienced Mother Goose rhymes, for those who are familiar with the rhymes might be able to recognize the text as "Mary Had a Little Lamb" by figuring out just a few key phrases. Without such background knowledge, a topic discussed in Chapter 8, the paragraph may never make sense.

Thus, it is essential that teachers engage struggling readers in activities that foster vocabulary development. Wide reading is one such activity. As previously discussed, struggling readers need encouragement and opportunities to read, read, read, both in school and out of school. They learn words through this reading, as well as through their everyday speaking, listening, and writing experiences. Although wide reading should be

Supporting Struggling Readers and Writers

encouraged and facilitated, struggling readers need more than just time to read. They seem to have difficulty gleaning the meanings of words from context (McKeown 1985) and benefit from having new words and concepts that are critical to their learning taught directly to them. They also need instruction and practice in the use of specific strategies, such as those described in the previous sections of this chapter, so that they can continue to learn new vocabulary on their own.

Which Words Should Be Taught?

Many social studies, science, and math texts highlight new vocabulary in the teachers' and students' texts. The number of new words and concepts can be staggering—as many as twenty to twenty-five in a single chapter! Teachers need to be selective when deciding which words students should "know." Words should be taught because they are crucial to understanding the content, not just because they are identified as new.

Support for the meanings of new words that aren't taught may be provided in the form of a handout that lists the new word or concept and its page number, followed by an easily understood synonym or explanatory phrase to which students can refer as they read. Also, teachers can use On-the-Spot Elaboration to extend students' understanding of some of the words. This simple technique, which is especially beneficial to English Language Learners, can easily be incorporated into read-alouds and discussions. When a concept or word is encountered that is likely new to at least some of the students, the teacher merely provides an immediate, short explanation. For example, "Today you will be reading about the earth's *crust*, its outermost layer," or "I want you to *paraphrase* what the king said about the colonists' actions; in other words, tell me in your own words what he said."

How Should Words Be Taught?

Traditionally, vocabulary instruction consisted of a weekly list of words distributed to students with the expectation that they look up the meanings, use each word in a sentence, and prepare for a quiz at week's end. More often than not the words had no relation to each other and generally were not even connected to what was being learned in the classroom. Although the length of the list might vary depending on the teacher, student response to the practice tended to be similar. Some were overwhelmed by the task, and others were annoyed at having to put so much effort into learning words they figured they would probably soon forget, even if they passed the test. Instead of this type of passive learning, students need to be actively involved when learning new vocabulary (Allen 1999; Stahl 1986). There are many ways to accomplish this, including discussion, real-life experiences and simulations, mapping activities, drawings, and games.

1. *Active involvement through discussion.* Teacher read-alouds afford wonderful opportunities for struggling readers to immerse themselves in the rich vocabulary and interesting language of children's literature. Relieved of the obstacles presented by limited word recognition ability, poor readers can think about and enjoy reading material that is more advanced than they are able to read on their own. During the read-aloud, new concepts and interesting words can be puzzled over, savored, discussed, or investigated in the dictionary. For example, Terry Behr has been reading *Harry Potter and the Sorcerer's Stone* (Rowling 1997) to her fourth-grade class. In the story Harry has just put on the sorting hat to find out which house dormitory he will be assigned to, when he hears a voice in the hat thinking aloud as it makes a decision. It muses that the decision is a difficult one and then recalls several of Harry's attributes, including courage, a good mind, and talent. The hat further observes that Harry seems to have a "nice thirst" to prove himself. At this point in her reading, Terry pauses and thinks aloud, "'. . . and a nice thirst to prove yourself.' *Thirst* is a word we usually use when we want a drink of water. A 'thirst to prove yourself' doesn't sound like water. I wonder what the sorting hat means here. Can anyone help?" Terry looks around, noticing a few puzzled looks and several hands poised to volunteer an answer. "Jay, what is your idea?"

Jay briefly explains, "The hat probably means that Harry *really* wants to prove himself, just like when you're thirsty for water, you feel like you just have to have it."

"That makes good sense, Jay, and what an interesting way for the author to say that Harry seems to have a desire to prove himself."

This type of vocabulary discussion often occurs during Terry's read-aloud. Not only does it ensure that everyone understands the meanings of difficult words and phrases, but it also enables Terry to model how good readers monitor their understanding as they read. Struggling readers' participation in the discussion as either listeners or speakers helps them acquire new understandings and extend and deepen their existing knowledge of words.

2. *Active involvement through real-life experiences and simulations.* Some topics of study lend themselves to field trips, classroom visits by a local expert, or in-class simulations. These types of experiences can make the abstract concepts that are presented in reading material much more concrete for struggling readers. For example, a trip to a nearby water treatment plant may help students to realize what *filtration, sedimentation,* and *purify* mean. A supporting hand on the back of a standing fellow student can serve to demonstrate the real meaning of a *flying buttress.* Such real-life

Supporting Struggling Readers and Writers

experiences and simulations, or skits, create memorable moments for students and make it easier for them to recall and use the words later.

3. *Active involvement through mapping activities.* It is best to engage struggling readers in semantic maps using a whole-class or small-group format and teacher guidance. This collaborative effort enables struggling readers to increase their own understanding of a concept by drawing upon the knowledge of their peers, and helps them connect ideas to what they already know. To begin the activity, the teacher chooses a concept important to material that is about to be read. As the group shares their ideas about the concept, the teacher makes a visual representation of the discussion on the board or chart paper. Robin Davies, a sixth-grade teacher, has decided to do a web for *justice*, a concept she considers important for the students' reading of their next social studies chapter (see Figure 6.3).

1. First, Robin writes the word on the board and draws an oversized box around it. She informs the students that they will be reading about the justice system in the United States.

Figure 6.3 Concept Map for Justice

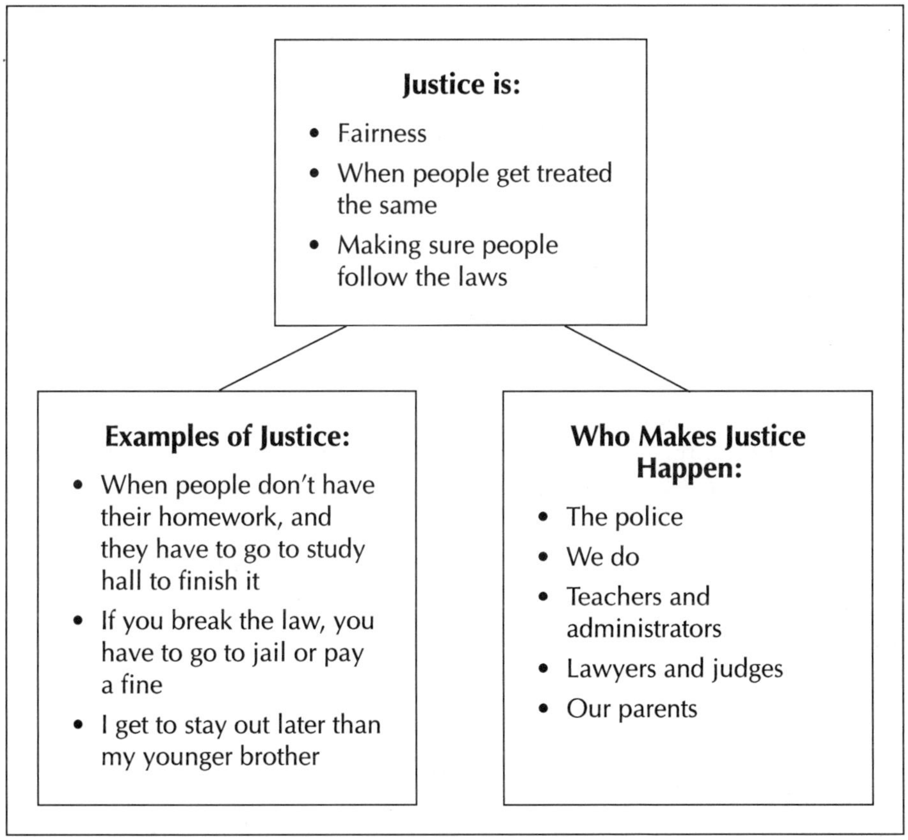

Justice is:
- Fairness
- When people get treated the same
- Making sure people follow the laws

Examples of Justice:
- When people don't have their homework, and they have to go to study hall to finish it
- If you break the law, you have to go to jail or pay a fine
- I get to stay out later than my younger brother

Who Makes Justice Happen:
- The police
- We do
- Teachers and administrators
- Lawyers and judges
- Our parents

2. Then she invites students to tell what they think *justice* means and records their responses under the word, inside the box.
3. Because some of the responses are examples of justice, Robin makes a new box for this information and then asks the students to share other examples of when they've seen or experienced justice and adds these to the recorded information.
4. Finally, Robin asks the students to consider who they think is responsible for bringing about justice, and she completes the map on the board by creating one more box for this new information.

Sometimes teachers reuse the same categories when mapping different words or concepts. These might include relations such as synonyms, characteristics, antonyms or opposites, examples, the word's meaning, or students' personal connections.

4. *Active involvement through drawing.* Phrases that form idioms also need to be taught. Because the individual words in an idiom do not literally represent the meaning of the phrase, idioms such as those in the sentences that follow can be difficult for students to grasp, especially English Language Learners (see Chapter 3).

My brother gets in my hair.
The teacher called him on the carpet.
I'm in the doghouse.
Don't make a mountain out of a molehill.
Maybe we should play a game at the party to break the ice.
Money always burns a hole in my sister's pocket.
You've lost your marbles!

Despite their trickiness, idioms provide fun learning opportunities. As an aid to remembering their meanings, students in the intermediate grades seem to particularly enjoy drawing comparison pictures labeled at the bottom with the idiom. One illustration shows the literal interpretation of the phrase and the other the actual meaning. For example, one picture for *my brother gets in my hair* might depict a youngster with a brother entangled in his or her hair. The other would represent the brother as a pest. Collections of such comparison drawings are often bound into class books or displayed in hallways. Because idioms are such fun and so common in everyday speech and the language of books, it usually takes little encouragement to get struggling readers and writers to try spicing up their writing with such phrases.

Students can also draw comparison pictures for homophones, words that sound the same but have different spellings and meanings (such as *cellar* and *seller*); for homographs, words that are spelled the same but have

Supporting Struggling Readers and Writers

different pronunciations and meanings (such as *desert the army* and *cross the desert*); and for the different meanings of a particular word (such as *an index in a book*, and *your index finger*). Such activities not only serve to reinforce word meanings in a way that most students enjoy, but also provide an opportunity for some struggling readers who may be very capable drawers to demonstrate expertise.

5. *Active involvement through games.* Students need many exposures to words and their meanings before the words become part of their vocabulary. Games such as Concentration are well suited for reinforcing vocabulary. Vocabulary words are written on one card and a synonym, definition, or sentence example (with a blank drawn where the word belongs) is recorded on another card. Students randomly place eight or ten card pairs facedown in front of them and take turns drawing cards and trying to make matches. Most card games and many television game shows can be adapted to reinforce vocabulary learning. Because students find the games engaging, they are eager to play again and again, and each time their understanding of the words is strengthened.

Celebrate Words

Teachers can encourage all students to learn and use new vocabulary by calling their attention to unusual and interesting words during read-alouds and by applauding particular words that students include on their bookmarks during guided reading or in their role as word wizard during literature circles (see Chapter 5). A chart or bulletin board area might be devoted to "exotic words," out-of-the-ordinary words that have captured students' interest. Students can be asked to tell where they found the word (story, conversation, billboard, and so forth), what it means, and why it's special to them. Among the many finds on a fifth-grade exotic words board, and the student's reason for posting it, are

> *humdrum* ("way it sounds")
> *quay* ("way it's pronounced")
> *audiophile* ("I am one")
> *regurgitate* ("its meaning")
> *rojo* ("because it's Spanish)
> *cosmopolitan* ("it's a really fancy word")
> *filet mignon* ("it looks really weird")
> *tittered* ("I'm going to use this one in my story")

Teachers can also engage students in I've Got a Word; What's Your Word. In this activity the teacher writes a sentence on the chalkboard or an overhead transparency, underlines one of the words, and invites students to come up with a synonym for it. The teacher's word may be an overworked word, such as *said*, or an unusual word, such as *ponder*. In the former instance, students generate words that are less familiar, such as *commented, uttered, proclaimed, announced, shouted*. By contrast, when a word such as *ponder* is used, students are more likely to suggest more common words, such as *think* or *consider*, but may offer *contemplate*.

Assessment Strategies

Appropriate instruction hinges upon informed teachers. Observation is one means for teachers to learn about their students' word learning. As children engage in reading, writing, and word study activities, teachers capture insights about the students' discoveries and use of strategies by taking anecdotal notes. To make their instructional decisions, they then consider this information in conjunction with information gained from more structured forms of assessment, such as spelling analyses, the Names Test described in the Strategy Bank, and running records (see Chapter 7).

Spelling Analyses

To plan effective word study experiences, teachers need to know which spelling features students are ready to explore. Invernizzi, Abouzeid, and Gill (1994, p. 160) suggest that appropriate features are those the student is "using but confusing." For example, consider the words *rain, float*, and *fright*. Syllable juncture spellers write words like these correctly. They already know how to use long vowel patterns in single-syllable words. Since there is no confusion, instruction focused on this feature would not benefit them. By contrast, letter name spellers show only confusion; they tend to omit long vowel markers entirely (MAK for *make* and AT for *ate* or *eight*). Their lack of experimentation is a strong indication that they are not ready to study this feature. Students at the within word pattern stage are. As spellings such as TAKE, SAME, TRANE for *train*, and WAYT for *wait* reveal, they have some knowledge of how the feature works but not a complete understanding.

Once teachers become familiar with how spelling knowledge develops, they can examine children's spellings to see what is being used but confused and plan instruction accordingly. A wealth of information about students' spelling competence can be gained by comparing invented spellings from their daily writings with those from a dictated word inventory. Children's writings afford valuable insights about their ability to apply their knowledge of words in live writing situations, where spelling is just one of many concerns. However, the number of inventions in spontaneous writing is sometimes limited, and interpreting the errors for meaningful instruction can be difficult and time consuming. Dictated word inventories (Bear et al. 2000; Ganske 2000; Schlagal 1992) are quick and easy to administer and yield information that can guide teachers' instructional planning.

Spelling Inventories

Figure 6.4 shows a student's performance on the letter name list of the *Developmental Spelling Analysis*—DSA (Ganske 2000). The DSA includes a separate list of twenty-five words for each of the stages: letter name, within word pattern, syllable juncture, and derivational constancy. Each list focuses on different spelling features and different words. The scoring system enables teachers to examine a student's ability to spell individual features as well as entire words, thus making it possible to recognize understandings that are just developing. As Figure 6.4 illustrates, correctly spelled words receive a score of two, words that are not correct but that have a correctly spelled target feature are awarded a one, and those with an incorrect feature are given a zero. Answer cards make it easy to score the items and analyze performance.

Figure 6.4 Jessi's DSA Performance at the Letter Name Stage

Answer Sheet: FORM A   Name _Jessi_

Stage ___L N___ +12   Date _Mar. 31_

1	1. Jat _jet_		0	16. gab _grab_
1	2. shep _ship_		2	17. chop
2	3. bet		2	18. fast
2	4. got		2	19. dish
2	5. cap		0	20. Wat _went_
2	6. drum		2	21. win
0	7. bop _bump_		1	22. fad _fed_
1	8. moch _much_		0	23. drip _trip_
2	9. with		1	24. rob _rub_
2	10. map		0	25. fet _fit_
2	11. hop			
0	12. pah _plan_			
2	13. that			
1	14. sled _slid_			
0	15. mod _mud_			

From *Word Journeys* by Kathy Ganske. Copyright © 2000 by The Guilford Press.

Jessi is a third grader who reads with support at a late first- to early second-grade level. She spelled twelve of the twenty-five words correctly on the letter name stage list. Her responses reveal a growing but incomplete knowledge of the letter name features. Jessi demonstrated a strength in her use of beginning and ending consonants. She correctly represented the feature in each target word: *got, map, win, fed,* and *rub* (as well as in other list words). However, when the initial or final element was a blend, Jessi had difficulty. Incomplete blends are evident in her spelling of *plan, grab, bump,* and *went* as PAN, GAB, BOP, and WAT. Jessie also had trouble with *tr.* When *t* or *d* is followed by *r* it makes the sound you hear at the beginning of *jet* and *chop.* Because several different letters and letter combinations can produce this sound, sound-conscious spellers at this stage often confuse them, as Jessi has in her spelling of DRIP for *trip.* Short vowels proved challenging as well. Jessi's uncertainty over which vowel to use is apparent not only in her spelling of the targeted short-vowel words (*bet, cap, hop, mud,* and *fit*), but throughout the list.

What implications do these assessment results have for instruction? Given Jessi's solid grasp of initial consonants, her teacher Ms. Graves decides to build on this strength and begin by having Jessi compare words and pictures with single consonants to those with blends (for example, *p* and *pl* or *g* and *gr*). Then she plans to have Jessi contrast several different blends, such as *pl, sl, gl,* and *cl.* Next, to help Jessi sort out the use of short vowels, Ms. Graves intends to introduce families of words that have the same vowel, such as *ip* and *it.* She has chosen word families as a starting point because vowel sounds are more stable in rimes than they are alone (compare the sound of short *a* in *cat, that, hat,* and *bat* with *clap, ran, dad,* and *pat*). After families of different vowels have been explored, the focus can shift to the short vowels themselves. For example, words with short *a* and short *i* might be contrasted. This type of systematic approach will help Jessi discover the regularities of English spelling and strengthen her reading and writing.

Darrell, a fifth grader who reads with support at the third-grade level, responded to words from the DSA at the within word pattern stage and correctly spelled eighteen of the twenty-five words. An analysis of his performance on the five targeted features reveals a firm understanding of the vowel-consonant-e pattern (as in *grape* and *smoke*) but some confusion with other patterns.

VCe	R-Controlled Vowels	Other Long Vowels	Complex Consonants	Abstract Vowels
5/5	3/5	4/5	3/5	3/5

Although Darrell correctly spelled other long vowel patterns in four out of five words (for example, *might* and *steep*), he had difficulty with the feature in *least* (LEEST). Long vowel patterns were also a problem for him in words with *r*-controlled vowels. He accurately spelled *girl, short,* and *hurt,* but misspelled *glare*/GLAIR and *fear*/FEER. Complex consonants and abstract vowels presented further difficulties for Darrell as shown by his spelling of BRIG for *bridge* and SKRAP for *scrap,* and by his correct spelling of *couch, yawn,* and *point* but his inaccurate rendering of *frown*/FRAWN and *stood*/STOUD.

Based on these results, where should word study instruction begin? Other long vowel patterns are a good first choice. Darrell has already learned much about this feature but will benefit from opportunities to solidify his understandings. His teacher plans compare and contrast activities that focus on long *e*. She gives Darrell a stack of cards to sort that includes words with short *e*, a feature Darrell already knows, as well as words such as *sheet, feet, keep* and *heat, leap, feast*. First, Darrell categorizes the words by sound (short *e* and long *e*), then by sound and pattern (short *e*, long *ee*, and long *ea*). Inclusion of the word *bread* in the sort as an exception encourages Darrell to think carefully about the words as he sorts them. The following week his teacher may include more words like *bread* in the sort to help Darrell realize that numerous short *e* words are spelled with this pattern.

Daily Writing

Darrell's writing can also be analyzed to reveal information about his spelling strengths and weaknesses. As Figure 6.5 shows, he spelled numerous high-frequency words correctly, such as *said, was, many,* and *have*. His use of short vowels is a strength, as is his spelling of words with VCe. Some of the using but confusing of patterns that characterizes Darrell's inventory results is not evident here, because words with those patterns were not used. For example, *ow* in *know* is the only long vowel pattern he used besides VCe. Darrell has errors in several multisyllabic words, but the issues in these are more complex and would not be addressed at this time. The influence of dialect can be seen in his spellings of EVNEN for *evening* and WEN for *when*.

Darrell's spelling ability in his *Freckle Juice* response can also be analyzed by applying the *index of control* formula devised by Laminack and Wood (1996). Although described by the authors as "time-consuming" (p. 48), the formula enables teachers to estimate how well students correctly spell words in their writing. The index is determined by dividing the number of different words that a writer spelled correctly by the number of different words he used. Of Darrell's 104 words, 65 are different, and 52 of these are spelled correctly. His index of control is 52 divided by 65 = .80 x 100 = 80 percent. Darrell used a variety of words and demonstrated control over 80 percent of them. A word of caution in interpreting the percentage

Figure 6.5 Darrell's Log Entry for Freckle Juice by Judy Blume

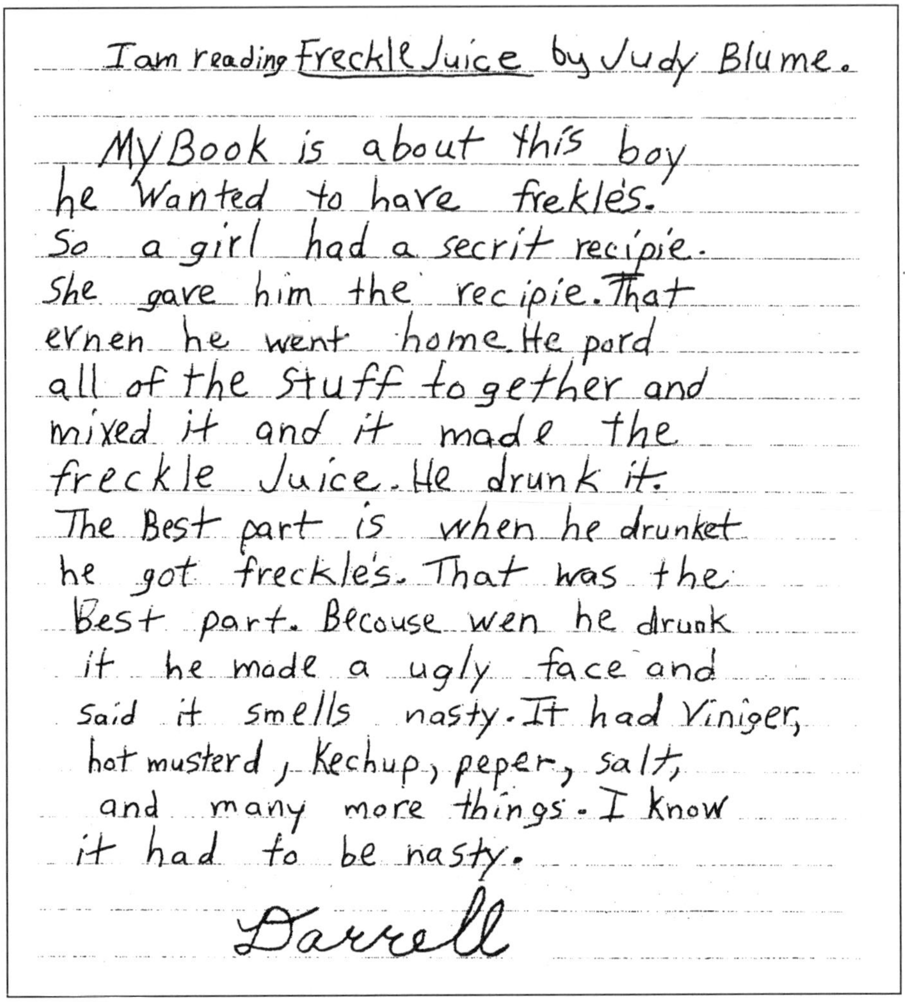

I am reading <u>Freckle Juice</u> by Judy Blume.

My Book is about this boy he wanted to have frekles. So a girl had a secrit recipie. She gave him the recipie. That evnen he went home. He pord all of the stuff together and mixed it and it made the freckle Juice. He drunk it. The Best part is when he drunket he got freckle's. That was the Best part. Becouse wen he drunk it he made a ugly face and said it smells nasty. It had Viniger, hot musterd, Kechup, peper, salt, and many more things. I know it had to be nasty.

Darrell

scores: High percentages sometimes result when students play it safe and limit their choice of words to those they know. By contrast, students who freely express themselves and construct spellings for words they don't know may exhibit a low index of control.

It is important that teachers be sensitive to where struggling writers are in their spelling development so they can set realistic expectations for accuracy in daily writing. If correctness is stressed above all else, the students are likely to avoid risks and write little. Follow-up editing with a partner or a spell-checker (available through most school supply stores) can aid struggling writers when accuracy is deemed necessary, as it is in published pieces of writing. Difficult-to-spell words that will be used frequently during a unit of study should be recorded in a notebook or on a wall chart for easy reference (see Chapter 9). Also, when reviewing the spellings in writ-

Supporting Struggling Readers and Writers

ing of students like Darrell, teachers should be careful to notice and point out to students what they are using correctly. For example, although a spelling of REVALUSHUN for *revolution* is far from correct, it does show attention to beginning, middle, and ending sounds and reveals an understanding, though perhaps tacit, that every syllable needs a vowel.

Learning how words work is a challenge for some students. Too often we have responded to their limited understandings by providing them with grade-level instructional fare and pushing them onward. Without a solid foundation, struggling readers and writers end up with a mishmash of understandings that don't allow them to make sense out of our English spelling system and expand their knowledge of words. It is time to provide more student-centered instruction, instruction that takes into consideration what students know and what they are ready to learn, instruction that encourages students to think about words and motivates them to read and write.

7 FOSTERING READING FLUENCY

In this chapter, we explore an important but often overlooked aspect of reading—fluency. Students in the intermediate grades generally read silently in school, a mode that reflects real-life reading situations. Although silent reading tends to be faster and can facilitate students' comprehension, struggling readers are likely to be hindered in their silent reading by a lack of fluency. As their oral reading reveals, some of these students are still learning to decode words. Others who have crossed this hurdle nonetheless still read hesitantly and with no expression, ignoring punctuation marks. Why some readers have difficulty becoming fluent and what teachers can do about it are the subjects of our discussion.

Background and Issues

It's DEAR time and after short conferences with several students who are sprawled on the floor or in their chairs, a fifth-grade teacher makes her way across the room to the Book Nook, where Tucker, a struggling reader, has been reading for the past twenty minutes. "What did you choose today?" she asks with a knowing smile and then adds, "I saw your quick beeline over here. I knew you must have a rare find in mind." Tucker returns the smile and holds up a hot-off-the-press copy of the class literary magazine *Writing on a Magic Carpet*.

"Checking out your story?" she asks. "It turned out really well!"

"Yeah, it's great! My mom's gonna really be proud of me. Now I'm reading Chelsea's story, 'Rapunzel Continued.' It's good . . . funny! Just listen to this part here, where Rapunzel talks about her Prince Charming—only his name is Charles." Tucker begins reading at a moderate pace but cautiously and with little expression [the slash marks indicate his phrasing]:

"'*For in / stance, / today he was wearing trousers / that went down / to his knees. / Underneath / he was wearing tights. / I mean / I don't even wear tights! / He was wearing / silly brown shoes / and a huge overcoat / even though it wasn't cold. / He looked . . .*'" Tucker pauses and asks, "Is this word *ridiculous?*"

"That's right, Tucker. Good reading! That's a big word."

"I thought it was; it makes sense," he remarks before finishing, "'*He looked ridiculous.*'"

"Chelsea's Rapunzel story is a funny one; I know you'll enjoy it. By the way, Tucker, I liked the way you concentrated on reading smoothly and remembered to pause at the ends of sentences and at commas. That helped me to picture how the prince looks. I noticed that Chelsea used an exclamation mark at the end of this sentence [*she points to the mark*]. How do you think Rapunzel would say those words?"

"Probably in a way that shows it's *stupid* wearing tights, because she said he looked ridiculous. Like this." Tucker repeats the sentence, this time with expression.

"I bet you're right. That sounded just like talking. Enjoy the rest of the story!"

Reading fluency, as defined by Harris and Hodges (1995) in *The Literacy Dictionary*, is "freedom from word identification problems that might hinder comprehension in silent reading or the expression of ideas in oral reading" (p. 85). Although accurate and rapid identification of words is an essential aspect of fluency, the way ideas are expressed is also important. Besides being able to automatically recognize words, readers must be able to use appropriate phrasing and appropriate expression, or their comprehension may suffer. In our everyday conversations we chunk words into meaningful phrases, vary the rise and fall of our voices, stress some words but not others, and punctuate our speech with pauses to convey our thoughts and feelings. In a similar way, suitable use of phrasing, intonation, stress, stops, and fast and accurate word identification helps readers comprehend and enjoy text. For many school children fluency is a serious weakness (Pinnell et al. 1995). Allington (1983a) noted that struggling readers typically lack fluency, and even though the skill can be taught it is often neglected during reading instruction. He offered six hypotheses to explain why some children achieve fluency but others do not:

1. Some children are exposed to fluent reading through adult role models; some are not.
2. Good readers tend to be given encouragement to read with expression; poor readers more often have their attention directed to figuring out individual words.
3. Good readers have more opportunities to read and therefore get more practice with connected text.
4. Good readers spend more time reading text that is easy for them; poor readers are more often confronted with text that is too difficult for them.
5. Good readers engage in greater amounts of silent reading, which gives them more experience.
6. Good readers seem to view reading as a meaning-making and enjoyable experience, whereas poor readers see the process far more as one of decoding and blending.

Several implications for fostering the fluency of struggling readers in the classroom may be drawn from Allington's hypotheses. Struggling readers need to experience models of fluent reading; they need many opportunities to orally and silently read text that is not too difficult so they can learn to read expressively, increase their sight vocabularies, and discover reading as a pleasurable, meaning-making activity. Struggling readers need teachers who are knowledgeable of strategies and techniques that encourage fluent reading.

Instructional Strategies That Foster Fluency

Modeling

Read-Alouds

Because struggling readers' experiences with text have so often translated into work rather than fun, a primary objective of the read-aloud should be to engage these students, as well as the rest of the class, in a reading experience that is rewarding because it is meaningful and enjoyable. To make sure students can devote their full attention to the reading and lose themselves in the story, it is a good idea to ask them to set aside competing desk activities, or have them gather on the floor. Then, supplied with a good book, an awareness that reading too fast is not good modeling, and a willingness to risk feeling silly by taking on the voices of characters in the story, teachers are ready to model fluent reading. In addition to showing that reading is expressive, the modeling will demonstrate that good readers read in phrases, not word by word, and that the phrase reading, pauses, and changes in voice inflection that signal various types of punctuation facilitate the meaning-making process. Teachers can easily evaluate the success of their modeling by noticing how engaged their students are during the reading. Books such as Roald Dahl's *The BFG*, Louis Sachar's *Holes*, or Margie Patalini's *Piggie Pie* are a joy to read and captivate students' attention when read fluently.

Fluent reading should be modeled every day, but it does not have to be done with a lengthy chapter book. Poems and picture books work equally well when time is short. Book talks can also to be used to model fluent reading. Rather than just telling about a book to introduce it, teachers might read aloud a highlight as well. This direct connection with the text has the added advantage of creating a strong enticement for students to read the entire story. For example, few older struggling readers (as well as proficient readers who haven't already read the book) can resist Beverly Cleary's *Ramona Quimby, Age 8* after listening to a description of Ramona's horror in "The Hard-Boiled Egg Fad," when she discovers she has just cracked a raw egg on her head. Listeners' cries of "Ooooh" and "Yuck!" and the encouragement of classmates to "read that one" send students scrambling for the book and more of Ramona's humorous escapades.

The start of a new guided reading book opens up another possibility for modeling fluent reading; teachers sometimes read the first few pages or entire first chapter aloud to students. Because struggling readers can follow along, they are able to see the many ways the print cues meaning. This approach also smooths students' transition into the story and is likely to enhance their understanding when they read on themselves.

Choral Reading

Choral reading is reading aloud in unison. It, too, enables struggling readers to hear fluent reading, and allows them to participate without feeling self-conscious about making mistakes. Because they don't have to fear the embarrassment of being corrected, struggling readers are more willing to take risks, and this increases their confidence (Tierney, Readence, and Dishner 1995). This type of support reading is especially beneficial for students who are not yet fluent with English; they may join in as they feel able to do so.

Poetry is a good choice for choral reading, since it is meant to be read aloud. Books with predictable text also work well because their rhyme, rhythm, and repeated phrases make it possible for poor readers to anticipate what is coming and keep up. The process is easy:

1. Make the selection available to students, either by providing them with individual copies or by writing the text on a chart or transparency.
2. Begin the session by reading the piece aloud to students while they follow along.
3. Then reread the poem and ask students to join in, or read individual lines and have the students echo them.

Through successive choral readings the students will become comfortable with the text and teachers can fade out whenever possible.

Sometimes teachers vary the format of choral reading by having groups of students or individuals alternate in reading different parts of the story or poem. Paul Fleischman's *Joyful Noise: Poems for Two Voices* and *I Am the Phoenix: Poems for Two Voices* were written with this purpose in mind. Other poems such as Ernest Thayer's "Casey at the Bat" or John Ciardi's "Mummy Slept Late and Daddy Fixed Breakfast" can be read in a format that is shared by a whole class. Some teachers even "take the show on the road" and have students perform the pieces for other classes, at a parent meeting, or over the intercom as a part of morning announcements. Students are usually more than willing to suggest favorite poems for choral reading. In addition, a selected list of recommended poems and poetry anthologies is included in the Resources section.

Using Appropriate Text

As we noted earlier, good readers tend to read text that is relatively easy. This likely has several positive benefits, including the fostering of fluency, understanding, a sense of success, and enjoyment. All of these, but especially the last two, are apt to leave readers with a desire to engage in reading again and again, for we generally choose to do things that we find fun and feel we are good at, and we tend to avoid just the opposite. There are times when struggling readers must face text that is overly challenging, and we must teach them strategies to cope with these situations (see Chapter 5); however, nearly all of their reading should be done with text that is appropriately challenging, or even easy. A common criterion for determining fairly easy text is no more than one error in about every twenty words of running text, or 95 percent accuracy (Adams 1990). When text is too difficult, with less than 90 percent accuracy, fluency and understanding are hindered, and reading becomes a drudgery that is dreaded and often dropped. A simple running record like the one discussed in the last section of this chapter enables teachers to estimate text appropriateness. The five-finger technique presented in Chapter 2 lets students quickly determine whether a particular text is likely a good match.

Teachers who routinely give struggling readers books to read that are too hard because they are concerned that the students will feel "different" or because they fear easier reading material will not interest them do these students a disservice. An analogy may serve to illustrate this point: putting a novice skier on an expert slope does not build the skier's confidence or skill; it merely increases the skier's anxiety and sense of his own limitations. Although in decades past, engaging text for older novice readers may have been rather limited, this does not hold true today. Many adult sports and newsmagazines now have counterparts for young people. Whereas picture books formerly targeted children in preschools and the primary grades, today many are written with older students in mind or have themes that appeal to readers in the intermediate grades. In addition, a wealth of engaging chapter books is accessible to students with limited reading abilities. These are often part of a series and carry the added benefit that once a student finishes a book another is waiting on deck, ready to be read. This is especially valuable for struggling readers who sometimes have difficulty choosing books (see Chapter 2). Informational texts, including biographies and those with content related to social studies, science, and even math are becoming increasingly available for older, less capable readers. The Resources section includes a list of favorite, high-interest/low-vocabulary books for older readers.

Multiple Readings of Text

Read-alouds, and the literature circles and guided silent reading lessons discussed in Chapter 5, help students discover reading as an enjoyable, meaning-making activity and foster positive attitudes toward reading.

Techniques that encourage struggling readers to reread meaningful text (such as choral reading and the activities described in this section) have further advantages and should be incorporated into the reading routine. They enable students to practice phrasing and expression, enhance their understanding through multiple readings of the same text, and build new sight vocabulary in a way that evolves naturally from the reading. As Darrell Morris (1992) points out in the following analogy,

> Just as a traveler going down a winding road for the second or third time begins to notice specific houses along the way, children on their second or third trip through a text will begin to focus on specific words—committing them to memory. (p. 123)

As students' sight vocabularies increase they are able to identify words more rapidly and easily and, in turn, read more fluently.

Rereading activities can be carried out in a variety of formats and with different fluency-developing aims in mind. For example, one time the emphasis might be on expressive reading of dialogue or on attending to punctuation; another time students might strive to increase their overall rate or to read more in phrases. Students may sometimes practice several aspects of fluency at once. Whatever the choice, student engagement and success should be considerations. Whereas primary-grade students often delight in reading the same text again, older students, even if beginning readers, may be reluctant to do so.

Readers' Theater

This strategy offers an enjoyable way to incorporate performance into practice reading, but without the major commitment of putting on a full-fledged play. Some teachers provide students with a prepared script. *Plays*, a wonderful monthly magazine ordered by most community and some school libraries, is brimming with scripts. Other good sources of scripts include books and Web sites such as those listed in the Resources section. Other teachers prefer to use a short story or a scene from a chapter book. When the latter route is chosen, if there is enough dialogue, the actual text can be used with the speaking parts highlighted. Students read aloud the characters' speeches, and a narrator reads the descriptive parts, usually omitting the "said" phrases. Although gestures, emotion, and character interpretation are important aspects of readers' theater, there is no movement around a stage or room. Instead, students sit in front of the class on chairs (stools work well) and expressively read their parts.

Students can also write their own scripts based on an original text. This approach combines writing with dramatic reading and means that additional speaking parts can be added or narrative sections condensed, when necessary. Since the process needs to be modeled, teachers often write one or more scripts collaboratively with the whole class, using the overhead. This helps students learn how dialogue is written down and is good preparation for small-group script writing. (See also Paired Script Writing, in the Strategy Bank.)

Sometimes readers' theater episodes are created from students' social studies, science, or math material. Either trade books or textbooks can be used as sources of information. Informational picture books should not be overlooked, as these are often the best source of all. They usually include all the basic concepts being studied but without excessive detail that can confuse students; plus, the text is likely to be more accessible to struggling readers and therefore will make it easier for them to participate. In social studies, groups of students might write short skits that interpret a historical event and depict possible conversations among people of the times. In science, students might write interviews between reporters and "people on the scene" to describe the effects of earthquakes or volcanoes or to announce a scientific discovery. Readers' theater in math might consist of a dialogue between a math teacher and her students as she teaches them how to carry out a particular operation or how to work with fractions.

Regardless of the type of material used for readers' theater—whether prepared script, text right from a story, the students' own scripts, or a teacher-created dialogue—students need many opportunities to practice

reading their parts individually and with the other characters before they perform. This practice helps students increase their fluency. Tape-recording the reading can provide students with feedback about their speed, pauses, and expression as they prepare to perform the work for others. If the recording is made during one of the final practice sessions, it can be placed in a class or library listening center after the presentation for students' continued enjoyment.

Visiting Readers

This strategy is particularly motivating and encourages poor readers to practice reading easy text. In many schools upper-grade classrooms form "buddy" partnerships with primary-grade students. On a regular basis, the older students assist their younger buddies with activities; these often include read-alouds and story dictations. Because the read-aloud necessitates that everyone, even skilled readers, prepare an easy text, poor readers aren't embarrassed by reading a "baby book" over and over.

One of Joanne's former schools developed a Visiting Reader project in which older students from all of the intermediate grades read to younger students. Although some teachers include more capable students in the project, in most cases the readers are those students who need practice reading below-grade-level texts to improve their fluency, comprehension, or word recognition. Students who read and speak too quietly to be heard, who are shy and need opportunities to shine at the center of attention, or who need to learn to help others are also encouraged to participate.

The school librarian facilitates the project. Her access to and familiarity with the collection of picture books, as well as her knowledge of how to help children select books, have greatly contributed to the program's success. In fact, her involvement has proved to be even more valuable than expected. Those who work with the project have found that as reluctant readers come to know the library and librarian better, they become more interested in going there and selecting books and, in turn, less reluctant to read. Also, as the librarian gains a keener understanding of the children's interests and reading abilities, she is better able to help them select books. Being introduced to topics and authors that lead to successful visiting reader experiences has helped many of the children learn to choose their own books.

Once students have selected their books they meet regularly as a group to learn techniques for reading aloud. They are taught to read in phrases and with expression, and they learn to use pictures to understand the author's intent and to match an appropriate voice to a character. They are taught how to handle the book so the listener(s) can see the pictures. They are encouraged to ask for help with words they cannot identify and usually do so willingly, knowing a misread will cause embarrassment.

Students also gain experience in the important skill of finding the main idea as they learn how to introduce the book to their listener(s). Teachers at the school use the phrase "This book is mostly about . . ." as a starter to help visiting readers focus their listeners on their reading purpose. It provides an effective and easy opening and is the phrase most frequently used for main idea questions on their standardized tests. Students are directed to read the book silently to determine what it is about and are taught that this may take more than one reading. Thus, they also learn that multiple readings make it easier to understand the story.

After their initial group meetings, most of the students' work on the project is done independently. They practice reading aloud alone, with a partner from the group, to their teacher(s), and to family members at home. They also learn to practice while recording themselves and to listen to the tape to determine what parts of the book might need additional attention. When they are ready, students meet with the younger children and read for about ten to twenty minutes. The session consists of the following three components and visiting reader roles:

- *Before Reading.* Show the cover, read the title, tell what the book is mainly about (including a statement of the main idea), invite predictions, and show and read the dedication page.
- *During Reading.* Read the story aloud, be sure the pictures are visible, and answer any listener questions.
- *After Reading.* Ask listeners how they liked the story, talk about favorite parts, reread passages at listeners' requests, and respond to any questions.

Dictated Experience Stories

Although use of this strategy is often associated with students in the early grades, it is appropriate for older students as well, especially for those who lag severely behind their peers or who are just learning English. Like the techniques already described, dictated experience stories involve repeated readings of text. However, another benefit of this strategy is that the text comes from the students' own experiences and therefore reflects their natural language. The personal quality of the experience story can motivate otherwise reluctant readers to reread the accounts. Also, older struggling readers often find the topics themselves more interesting than those that are in the easy texts they are able to read. When using dictated experience stories with students, follow these general steps:

1. Encourage students to suggest a topic or, if necessary, provide one.
2. Discuss the topic (creating a web of the ideas may be helpful; note any specialized vocabulary related to the topic).

3. Record students' dictated sentences on the chalkboard, chart paper, or a transparency, making changes in the content only when needed for clarity.
4. Read the text aloud, and point to individual words if students are still learning to make connections between speech and print.
5. Reread the completed account, using choral reading.
6. Provide students with their own copy of the story for practice rereading with a partner or independently.

As individual students reread the text, teachers can check to see which new words the students are able to identify in isolation and add these words to the students' collections of known words—their word banks. Students might record word-bank words in a notebook, or they might write them on small cards and keep them in an envelope. Because cards can be manipulated, the latter approach has the advantage of enabling students to use their word-bank words in a variety of activities, including the sorting activities we described in the previous chapter, and to review them through card games such as the one described below. These types of reinforcement help students solidify their recognition of the words so that the words become part of their sight vocabularies.

Garth Ferguson's fifth-grade students often ask to follow up the guided reading lesson with a quick game of "Oh No!" The game is played by two to four students and requires at least thirty to forty sight-word cards. The cards are randomly placed facedown on a playing surface, along with one or two cards labeled *Oh No!* A time limit is set for the game (usually five to ten minutes), and play begins. Students take turns drawing a card and reading the word. If the word is correctly identified it is placed in a pile next to the player; if it is not, the player returns it to the playing area and scrambles it with the remaining cards. In either case, it is then the next player's turn. If a player draws an Oh No! card he must return any cards he has accumulated to the playing area, with the exception of the Oh No! card. Once drawn, this card is set aside. The cards are then rescrambled, and the game resumes with the next player. Play continues in like manner until the timer goes off. At this point, players count their identified words. The player with the greatest number of cards is the winner.

Paired Repeated Reading

This approach to repeated readings (Koskinen and Blum 1986) requires minimal teacher direction once students have learned the procedure. Working with a partner, students read short self-selected passages of text several times with the goal of improving their fluency. Self-evaluation, partner support, and feedback encourage students to be engaged and help them learn to monitor their own reading. Because the passages are short, the entire activity can be completed in ten to fifteen minutes. Since students do not work with the teacher, modeling of the process is critical to the success of this strategy. First, students learn the role of the reader, then they learn the role of the listener, and finally, they perform the procedure under teacher supervision. After they have been introduced to the strategy and have had an opportunity to practice it, students are usually successful in completing the activity on their own. Here's what they do:

1. Each student chooses an interesting short passage from an easy text (about fifty words work well), making sure to end at a complete sentence, and reads the selection silently.
2. While one partner reads his chosen passage aloud, the other listens attentively, helping with words if asked to do so.
3. The reader self-evaluates the first reading by considering such factors as speed, smoothness, expression, and attention to punctuation, and circles the rating for Reading #1 on a teacher-provided handout like the one shown in Figure 7.1.

Figure 7.1 Paired Repeated Reading Evaluation

Reader _____ **Date** _____

Passage Used _____

How well I read:

Reading #1:	great	good	so-so	not very good
Reading #2:	great	good	so-so	not very good
Reading #3:	great	good	so-so	not very good

What I did best in my reading today is

Today I listened to _____ **read.**

Reading #2: Here's how my partner's reading got better:
_____ My partner read more smoothly.
_____ My partner read with more expression.
_____ My partner knew more words.
_____ My partner stopped more for punctuation.

Reading #3: Here's how my partner's reading got better:
_____ My partner read more smoothly.
_____ My partner read with more expression.
_____ My partner knew more words.
_____ My partner stopped more for punctuation.

Based on P. S. Koskinen and I. H. Blum. 1986. "Paired Repeated Reading: A Classroom Strategy for Developing Fluent Reading." *The Reading Teacher* 39 (2): 70–75.

---

4. While the partner listens attentively, the reader rereads the passage, striving for improvement, and self-evaluates this reading.
5. The listener provides feedback about the second reading by telling the reader one way this reading showed improvement over the first and by checking the appropriate category under Reading #2 at the bottom of his own handout.
6. The reader, striving for further improvement, reads the passage a third time and makes a final self-evaluation.
7. The listener again provides positive feedback by sharing a comment with the reader and marking the checklist for Reading #3.
8. The students change roles and follow the same procedure.
9. The teacher collects and reviews the evaluation sheets.

If students are accustomed to working with a partner during word study or writing workshop they likely know the expectations for cooperative work, including acceptable voice volume, the need to start promptly and stay on task, and how to take turns. They probably also know how helpful a partner can be. However, if partner work is new to students, guidelines will have to be discussed and perhaps practiced. Most students enjoy getting positive feedback, and this serves as a motivation for doing paired repeated readings. Because they value their partner's comments, students often choose short passages from sources other than their current reading material, passages that they will be sharing with others, such as an excerpt from a writing piece or a readers' theater trouble spot.

Timed Repeated Readings

The purpose of this technique (Samuels 1979) is to improve reading rate and fluency. However, because word reading becomes easier with successive readings and requires less attention, comprehension is also enhanced and confidence is built. The strategy consists of having students reread short, meaningful passages of text to reach a personal reading rate goal. In general, goals in the range of 80 to 100 words per minute are reasonable. The passage used should be of interest to the reader and at a difficulty level that ensures at least 90 percent accuracy. A 50- to 200-word section of the text is marked off for practice. As the child reads, the teacher or other adult (aide or parent volunteer) keeps track of the time. A stopwatch works well for this. The rate of the first unpracticed reading, and later practiced readings, is graphed in words per minute (wpm) on a chart; if desired, space may be added for recording the number of errors. Let's consider the example in Figure 7.2.

Jeremy is a fourth grader who struggles with fluency. To help him and two other students with similar needs overcome their difficulties, Margo Lopez, their teacher, decided to have the students complete timed repeated

Figure 7.2 Graph of Timed Repeated Readings

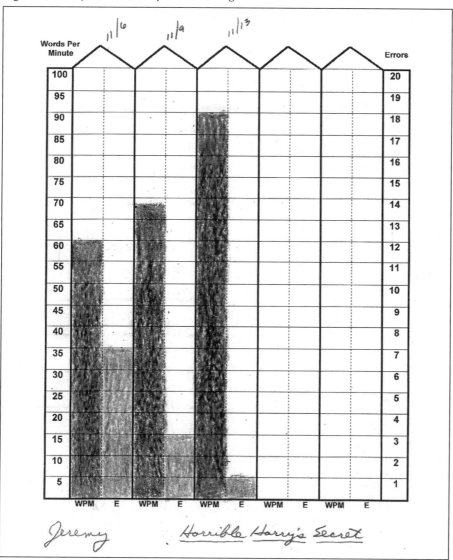

Jeremy   Horrible Harry's Secret

readings twice a week. Margo enlisted the aid of Mrs. Price, a parent volunteer who helps out two days a week, so she could carry on small-group instruction while Mrs. Price monitored the timed readings. To enable the children to keep track of their progress, Margo created work folders for them by stapling a blank graph to each inside cover. After the process was explained to the children, they were handed their folders and were ready to begin. For his first set of trials, Jeremy chose a relatively easy book, *Horrible Harry's Secret* by Suzy Kline, and set his goal at 90 words per minute with one or no errors. Jeremy and Mrs. Price chose a section of text with 80 words and Jeremy began to read. Mrs. Price timed Jeremy's reading and kept track of his errors by placing a mark on a sheet of paper every time he misread a word, left out a word, added a word, or needed her help to figure out a word. When Jeremy had finished the passage, Mrs. Price calculated his reading rate using the following formula:

$$\frac{\text{(total words in the passage)} \times 60}{\text{time in seconds}}$$

The formula works like this: If a passage consisted of 110 words and was read in one minute, ten seconds, which converts to 70 seconds, the rate would be figured by multiplying 110 x 60 and then dividing the result by 70; in other words 6,600 ÷ 70 = 94 wpm.

The results of Jeremy's unpracticed first reading are shown in Figure 7.2. He read at a rate of 60 words per minute [(80 x 60) = 4,800 ÷ 80 = 60] and made seven errors. Although Jeremy's accuracy is not recorded as a percentage, he read 73 of the 80 words correctly, or 91 percent (73 ÷ 80 = .91), revealing that the book chosen is at an appropriate level of difficulty.

After coloring in the graph, Jeremy put his book in the folder and returned it to Margo's desk. During the following days, after completing his work, Jeremy reread the passage several times. His next timed reading with Mrs. Price showed that he had increased his rate to 68 words per minute and decreased his errors to three. Eager to reach his goal of 90 words per minute with one or no errors, Jeremy continued to practice the passage during the independent reading/writing activities time (see Chapter 4) after completing his other tasks. On this third timed attempt Jeremy reached his goal for both rate and accuracy and was pleased with his improvement. Mrs. Price congratulated him on his progress, stapled a new blank graph over the first one, and told Jeremy they would choose a new passage the next time she came, one of similar or slightly greater difficulty, perhaps even another from the Horrible Harry book.

Because students are generally motivated by the challenge of reaching their goals, they, like Jeremy, are usually willing to put in the practice that this technique requires. However, because practice is so important, it helps to remind students that athletes and musicians must also continually practice to be fast and accurate in their movements. Over time, as students use this strategy, teachers should notice them reading more fluently even on their unrehearsed passages.

Teaching Phrasing, Expression, and Attention to Punctuation

Most students know how to chunk parts of a sentence together and automatically do so when they read so that the language sounds natural. They may have gained this understanding from their own experiences with reading or from listening to others read to them. By contrast, many struggling readers read in a choppy fashion that breaks apart meaningful phrases. They need to be taught to make their reading flow. The previously described technique of choral reading helps struggling readers learn phrasing, because they read along with others. Teachers can also draw examples from text the students are reading, show them how to break the sentences into chunks, and help them see that certain breaking points lead to reading that is easier to understand than do others.

As part of learning to use phrasing appropriately, students need to learn that punctuation marks such as commas, semicolons, parentheses, and dashes signal the end of a phrase and require a pause in reading. For example, consider the following sentence from Louis Sachar's *Holes*:

> It was a little surprising, he thought, that X-Ray was the leader of the group, since he obviously wasn't the biggest or the toughest. (p. 53)

This sentence is part of a passage in which the main character in the story is reflecting on his fellow campmates. The commas provide a clue to many of the phrase breaks; readers must determine any others.

To assist struggling readers, teachers might write a sentence like the one above on the chalkboard without the commas and read the sentence in one breath, without any breaks. When asked, most students will be quick to point out that the reading didn't sound right. Teachers can then add the commas and show the phrase breaks with slash marks, letting students know that a comma is a clear signal that a phrase is ending. Other possible phrase breaks may be discussed and tried; slashes may be added to the sentence to show the final decision, as illustrated below.

> It was a little surprising, / he thought, / that X-Ray was the leader of the group, / since he obviously wasn't the biggest / or the toughest.

Teachers may also demonstrate phrasing with sentences that have no interior punctuation and by using an entire paragraph. After working as a whole group, students may determine phrasing with a partner and alone.

Sometimes children attend to punctuation and read in phrases but with no expression. Reading that is done in a monotone is likely to be more focused on words than meaning. To help her students read more expressively, third-grade teacher Debbie Walters tape-records an upcoming portion from the class read-aloud, or other text, that includes a lively exchange of dialogue. She then provides the students with a copy of the sentences and asks them to read the sentences the way they think the author intended. She reminds the children that periods signal a drop in the voice, question marks a rise, and that exclamation marks can be used with either a drop or a rise, but must show strong feeling. After a few practice trials, she plays the recording for comparison, and the class discusses similarities and differences. Students then pick favorite parts from their current reading material, rehearse the passages with expression, and share the results with the group. Periodically during the year, Debbie repeats the activity with a new segment of text drawn from the read-aloud. Students enjoy the challenge of anticipating the kind of expression that Debbie will use on the tape recording and of trying to match or even top it. Debbie also incorporates paired repeated reading into her routine to help students monitor their progress with this and other aspects of fluency.

Engaging in Silent Reading

Although many struggling readers need oral reading practice to improve their fluency, they also need to be encouraged to read silently. As we pointed out at the onset of this chapter, silent reading not only tends to be faster, but also facilitates comprehension. Unfortunately, in many classrooms a practice that has been labeled as "outmoded" in *The Literacy Dictionary* (Harris and Hodges 1995, p. 222) still prevails as a common approach for reading text, particularly content-area texts. *Round-robin reading* is the practice of calling on one student after another to read aloud a passage from a text that is frequently being read by the whole class. Despite the fact that students are reading passages aloud, often a paragraph, this activity does not promote fluency. The practice is akin to asking students to give an impromptu performance for classmates, for the text they are being asked to read is being read for the first time. Those who have experienced round-robin reading often have similar reactions to it, including

"I hated it!"

"It made me uptight. I spent all the time before my turn counting up paragraphs so I could find my part and see if I knew the words."

"I was so concerned about making an embarrassing mistake when I had to read that I hadn't a clue what anyone else was reading about."

"I didn't worry about the words, because that wasn't a problem for me, but I didn't like it. It took some of the kids forever to get through their paragraph, and some you couldn't hear very well. I usually read ahead a ways and just sat there and waited, thought about something else."

Teachers need to give students time to read silently (see Chapters 2 and 5), but they also need to provide varied reading materials. Although textbooks are one resource for teaching subject-area content, there are many others, including chapter books, picture books, Internet sites, and magazines. When other resources are integrated into the children's studies, struggling readers can learn about topics by reading silently and with confidence at their instructional or independent level. They can become fully engaged, in the "flow" (Csikszentmihalyi 1990), and experience reading as an enjoyable and meaning-making activity.

Assessing Fluency

Disfluent readers are seldom difficult to identify. Their slow, word-by-word, labored reading, which is often delivered in a monotone, sends a clear signal. Rather than bringing to mind thoughts of a smooth limousine ride, disfluent reading is more likely to evoke images of an old ramshackle automobile jolting its way down the road in stops and starts. It is easy to detect a lack of fluency, but it is less easy to determine students' progress in developing fluency. Fluency can be evaluated using techniques such as running records, which are described below, and the Diagnostic Fluency Assessment (Martinez, Roser, and Strecker 1999), included in the Strategy Bank. The former examines students' accuracy in identifying words and the strategies they use to do so. The latter, based on earlier work by Zutell and Rasinski (1991), considers five aspects of reading: *rate, accuracy, fluidity, phrasing,* and *expressiveness*.

Running Records

This form of assessment devised by Marie Clay (1985) and first used in the Reading Recovery tutoring program is common in classrooms. Running records help teachers evaluate fluency and make it possible to quickly and regularly check on the match between reader and text. As a student orally reads a passage of text, the teacher uses a marking system and a copy of the text to keep track of the student's reading behaviors. Teachers make a mark for each word the student reads correctly, usually a check. Other marks indicate errors or *miscues*, self-corrections, words the student does not know, and sometimes repetitions and pauses. Some teachers record the behaviors on a separate sheet of paper; others find it easier to mark directly on a copy of the text or next to it, as shown in Figure 7.3. Although recording on a separate sheet is likely to require a little more practice, it has the advantage of enabling teachers to take running records any time, with any child, using any text. (See Johnston 2000 for a self-tutoring guide to running records.) Regardless of the approach, it is a good idea to tape-record the first few trials and check recording accuracy by replaying the reading. Teachers who find it difficult to keep up with a child's reading even after practice may choose to mark only the miscues rather than check off every correctly read word. Figure 7.4 shows examples.

Teachers calculate the percentage of correctly read words and use this information as well as their analysis of the miscues to document progress,

Figure 7.3 Results from a Running Record

Text	Running Record
Lizzy had tried all day to get Leo down. She	✓ ✓ ✓ ✓ ✓ ✓ ✓ ✓ ✓ ✓
knew the roof was no place for a cat, but now	✓ ✓ ✓ ✓ ✓ ✓ ✓ ✓ ✓ ✓
that the skies looked like it could storm, she was	✓ ✓ ✓ ✓ ✓ ✓ ✓ ✓ ✓ ✓
really worried.	✓ $\frac{scared}{worried}$

Text	Running Record
That morning Leo had chased a squirrel up an	✓ ✓ ✓ ✓ ✓ ✓ $\frac{squ\text{-}squire}{squirrel}$ R ✓ ✓
oak tree near the back porch. He often did this,	$\frac{old}{—}$ ✓ ✓ ✓ ✓ ✓ ✓ ✓ ✓
but today instead of climbing back down, he had	✓ ✓ $\frac{insisted}{instead}$ $\frac{on}{of}$ ✓ ✓ ✓ ✓ $\frac{—}{had}$
leaped onto the porch roof.	✓ ✓ ✓ ✓ ✓

Text	Running Record
At first Lizzy thought she could coax Leo back to	✓ ✓ ✓ ✓ ✓ ✓ $\frac{call}{coax}$ ✓ ✓ ✓
the tree. Now she wasn't sure. So far he had just	✓ ✓ ✓ ✓ ✓ ✓ ✓ ✓ ✓ ✓ ✓
ignored her and gone even higher. For what	$\frac{ig\text{-}ing—}{ignored}$ ✓ ✓ ✓ ✓ ✓ ✓
seemed like the millionth time she called,	✓ ✓ $\frac{a}{the}$ $\frac{million}{millionth}$ $\frac{times}{time}$ ✓ ✓
"Come here, you silly cat. Come down,	✓ ✓ ✓ ✓ ✓ ✓ ✓
PLEASE!" Just then big drops of rain began to fall.	✓ ✓ ✓ ✓ ✓ ✓ ✓ ✓ ✓ ✓

plan instruction, and determine whether the text is "easy," can be handled "with support," or is "too difficult." Text that struggling readers can read with 90–97 percent accuracy tends to be sufficiently challenging without being overwhelming; it is at their instructional level and can be read with support. There are few miscues, and some of these are likely to be corrected by the reader without assistance. Easy text can be read independently; almost no errors are made. This type of text builds readers' confidence. By contrast, text that is read with less than 90 percent accuracy is too difficult. The many miscues detract readers' attention from making meaning and cre-

Figure 7.4 Recording Oral Reading Miscues

Type of Miscue	Marking on a Copy of the Text	Marking on a Sheet of Paper
Miscues That Count as Errors:		
Substitution	. . . she was really ~~worried~~. [scared above worried]	$\frac{scared}{worried}$
Insertion	. . . an ^old^ oak tree . . .	$\frac{old}{—}$
Omission	. . . he had ~~leaped~~ . . . [had underlined/barred]	$\frac{—}{had}$
Teacher Gives Word	. . . he had just ignored her . . . [ig-ing— T above ignored]	T / ig-ing— / ignored
Other Miscues That Provide Helpful Information:		
Self-correction	. . . had chased a squirrel up . . . [squ-squire ✓ above squirrel]	✓ / $\frac{squ\text{-}squire}{squirrel}$
Repetitions	. . . had chased a squirrel up . . . [repetition arrow back to "had"]	had . . . squirrel [with repetition arrow]
Pauses (about one slash per second) [Anna made none.]	Example: That /// morning Leo . . .	/// morning

ate frustrating experiences for students, reinforcing their sense of being poor readers and perpetuating the notion that reading is not fun. Students need text that is easy or that can be read with support and that is of interest to them.

By analyzing and categorizing running record miscues, teachers can identify strategies students are using and determine appropriate instruction. For example, one student's miscue analysis might reveal an over-reliance on a particular strategy, such as letter-sound clues or context, and a need to learn how to use other sources of information. Another's, like Anna whose running record is shown in Figure 7.3, might demonstrate a balanced use of strategies. Although Anna made ten scorable errors in her reading of the 119 words, most of the miscues did not significantly affect meaning (or syntax, sentence structure), as her substitutions of *scared* for *worried* and *call* for *coax*, and her omission of *had*. Despite Anna's good use of context clues, limited letter-sound knowledge hindered her ability to recognize words and read fluently. Not surprisingly, the less familiar and more complex multisyllabic words, such as *squirrel, instead,* and *ignored,* were the most troublesome for Anna. Instructionally, she would benefit from learning how to break longer, unfamiliar words into smaller parts and from learning to apply her knowledge of spelling patterns to decipher them (see Chapter 6). Anna should also be encouraged to continue using context to make sense of what she reads.

For many struggling readers acquiring fluency is a major step toward becoming a skilled reader. However, we need to keep in mind that fluent reading does not guarantee comprehension. Some children can recognize words efficiently but still not understand what they are reading. These "word callers" are missing out on the real purpose of reading—making meaning (Stanovich 2000). Strategies that foster comprehension have been described in Chapter 5. They are also the focus of our next chapter.

IMPROVING READING COMPREHENSION

Reading comprehension has been called the essence of reading (Durkin 1993), essential not only to academic learning in all subject areas but to lifelong learning as well. Improving students' comprehension abilities is arguably the most important challenge teachers and students face in the middle grades. In this chapter, we explore some of the issues associated with helping students improve their comprehension abilities and offer numerous suggestions for instruction. This chapter was written with the assistance of Cindy Mershon, Elementary Supervisor of Language Arts, West Windsor–Plainsboro Schools, New Jersey.

Background and Issues

Janine Nicholls glances through several student portfolios. The marking period will end soon, and she is experiencing a feeling of dread as she contemplates the grades she must give her fifth graders. In this district, teachers give a single letter grade for each subject area. In addition, most teachers write a brief statement about overall progress on the back of the report card. As Janine looks at her students' work samples, however, she is struck by the fact that the letter grade tells very little about the nature of the students' reading abilities or about the problems some of them are experiencing. For example, four students who are having difficulty in nearly every aspect of the curriculum face a major obstacle—each has a severe problem with reading comprehension. Gordon is so inept with word recognition that he loses control of the meaning of sentences as he laboriously tries to apply his weak decoding strategies. Lucia, on the other hand, is an excellent decoder. She moves rapidly through material, but often misses important ideas. Paulo, a newcomer to English, is making steady progress. But his progress is also very slow, and he sometimes gets frustrated and gives up. Sandra, an enthusiastic student, appears to be a rather competent reader. She loves chapter novels and enjoys swapping them with her friends. Unfortunately, Sandra tends to approach all kinds of reading material in the same way that she reads novels. Thus, her comprehension of content-area material falls far short of what is expected of a fifth grader.

Janine has been working with the reading specialist and attending workshops to learn more about how to help the students she finds perplexing. She is pleased that some signs of progress are evident. As she looks through Gordon's folder, she sees samples of work on word building and structural analysis that she planned exclusively for him. Lucia's folder includes some written retellings designed to help her think about and reflect on the materials she reads. Paulo needs encouragement. He is a bright boy, whose English-language acquisition and background knowledge need time to catch up to the demands of fifth grade. Janine has recommended some high-interest/low-reading-level books for him to read at home. A list of those he has read is in his folder, along with a brief comment from him about each. Sandra's needs are very typical of intermediate-grade students. Work on specific strategies that deal with various types of texts, including content-area text materials and math word problems, is an objective that Janine has established for the entire class. Sandra, along with a few others, needs some additional, small-group instruction in this area.

Janine smiles wryly as she thinks about the complexity of teaching and of her students. She quietly concludes to herself, *Helping my students become better comprehenders may be the most important accomplishment of the year. Their progress in every aspect of the curriculum depends on it.*

A Look at Good Comprehenders

When teachers such as Janine examine the difficulties that poor comprehenders demonstrate, they draw upon what is known about good comprehenders: what they seem to do with effortless ease and competence. For example, good comprehenders usually recall key information in a text. They have the ability to use information from various parts of a text to infer meanings that are not explicitly stated. In other words, they not only remember the facts that are directly stated, but also read between the lines.

Good comprehenders have a sense of how texts work. They understand the elements of narratives, such as the characters, setting, problems, problem resolution, and so on, and they use these structural components to make predictions and draw conclusions about the plot. They recognize that expository texts also have structures that help guide the reader. They use these structures—found in informational textbooks, math word problems, maps, and graphs—as a framework for remembering, understanding, and acting on the content presented.

Making sense is of primary importance to good comprehenders. The term *active reading* is often associated with them. It refers to their tendency to interact mentally with a text, to make sense. They think with the text as they read—agreeing, disagreeing, questioning, and responding in a variety of ways. When things do not make sense, good comprehenders experience discomfort and have strategies to apply to overcome their confusion.

Good comprehenders tend to approach what they read purposefully. They are flexible readers and know that they must adjust the way they read to fit their purpose and the type of text they are reading. They know that whether they are reading a story, a grocery list, or a chart in a science textbook, each deserves attention in a different way. Moreover, they have sufficient vocabularies and background knowledge to bring to a text, enabling them to determine the meanings of material that may be new or challenging to them. They integrate print and nonprint information in books, magazines, and electronic media to understand and make use of texts.

Vocabulary and background knowledge are critically important to good comprehension and to students' writing abilities. Vocabulary instruction that requires students to use words in meaningful ways, both orally and in writing, provides them with access to the word meanings and conceptual understandings of the materials they read (see also Chapters 6 and 9).

Both direct, firsthand experiences and literary experiences expand background knowledge. At least two types of background knowledge influence students' reading and writing abilities. Knowledge about the world is the first of these. The kinds of information that students accumulate through life experiences and through books and other media contribute to a store of knowledge that influences what they bring to the printed page and what understandings they construct. A second type of background knowledge involves what students know about texts and how they are constructed. Students who have been exposed to a variety of types of texts learn to have certain expectations for stories as opposed to poems or informational books. They learn to approach a chapter in a social studies textbook differently from a mystery story or a recipe. These kinds of expectations help guide the reader and influence the effectiveness and the efficiency of the reading.

Comprehension Challenges for Struggling Readers

By examining the characteristics of good comprehenders, we can better understand how to address the instructional needs of students who require help in this area. Needless to say, an ongoing emphasis on vocabulary and concept development and building background knowledge is critical. However, direct instruction in using specific strategies for comprehension is also useful.

A recent review of instructional strategies for reading comprehension revealed a strong core of research-based strategies that have demonstrated effectiveness (Report of the National Reading Panel 2000). Some are useful when used alone, but many are more effective when used as part of a multiple-strategy approach. The general types of strategies are

1. *Comprehension monitoring.* Readers learn to be aware of their understanding of the material.
2. *Cooperative learning.* Students learn reading strategies together.
3. *Use of graphic and semantic organizers* (including story maps). Readers make graphic representations of the material to assist comprehension.
4. *Question answering.* Readers answer questions posed by the teacher and receive immediate feedback.
5. *Question generation.* Readers ask themselves questions about various aspects of the story.

6. *Story structure*. Students are taught to use the story's structure to help them recall story content and answer questions about what they have read.
7. *Summarization*. Readers are taught to integrate ideas and generalize from the text information.

We devote the remainder of this chapter to descriptions of specific strategies for improving reading comprehension and offer the following tips for their use.

Select two or three strategies that apply to an area of need and work on them over an extended period of time. Make sure that the initial materials used to practice the strategy are easy enough for students to apply what they are learning. Use the techniques described in Chapter 4 to scaffold student learning. Begin with examples and demonstrations of the strategy. Invite student participation with teacher guidance. Only after students display some understanding and competence should they be expected to move on to independent application. Remember: For the struggling student to succeed, the task must be made as transparent as possible. When most students seem to have command of a strategy, move on to another one or a combination of strategies. Continually look for opportunities to point out ways students can apply what they have learned to their daily work. This application is important for obvious reasons—if transfer of learning does not occur, then the strategy instruction is useless.

Instructional Strategies

Using Text Features to Activate and Build Prior Knowledge

A quick browse through a library or local bookstore reminds us that we know a great deal about many topics and little or nothing about many others. Our lack of understanding about certain topics is of no consequence unless we need to use the knowledge, for example, to comprehend new information through reading or listening. Then it matters a great deal, for prior knowledge facilitates understanding. Many of the struggling readers we observe in classrooms have limited background knowledge for topics they must study in their content areas; this makes it difficult for them to integrate new information with old and, in turn, recall it later.

Even when students know quite a bit about a topic, they may not realize that their information is relevant to what they are reading and studying and, as a result, fail to "bring it into action." The "Mary Had a Little Lamb" example described in Chapter 6 illustrates what happens to readers when they are unclear about the content of the text. Because we did not alert readers to the fact that the paragraph was a nursery rhyme variation, most probably turned to other understandings, perhaps those related to science or history, in an effort to make sense of the difficult text.

For struggling readers, it is critical that we not only activate their knowledge of topics they must read about and study, but also be aware of situations in which they have little or no background knowledge so that we can build essential understandings before they begin reading. The time spent doing this may be the most important part of the lesson; without it struggling readers have little chance of understanding what they are reading. Teachers might read a picture book or a short article on a topic to be studied to build prior knowledge. They might generate class discussions to brainstorm and group ideas, call students' attention to pictures as sources of information, and encourage students to pay heed to text features such as headings and subheadings. Techniques like these make students mindful of the important information they know about a topic and help them acquire basic understandings that will support their reading and thinking.

Brainstorming and Grouping Ideas

Fourth-grade teacher Gia Bartoli is ready to begin a unit on earthquakes and volcanoes. After announcing the new unit, Gia breaks her twenty-four students into six groups of four, making sure that each group includes students who are likely to have greater and less prior knowledge of the subject. She hands each group eight note cards and tells the students they have five minutes to share with their group members what they know about earthquakes and volcanoes. She asks them to write on a separate note card any word or concept that they think is important and will be in their reading. At the end of the five minutes, Gia draws the students' attention to a pocket chart containing the words *Earthquakes* and *Volcanoes* and one at a time invites students from each group to talk about their words. As they share, they tell what the word is, why they think it is important, and which category it belongs under. Here are a few of the results:

Earthquakes	Volcanoes
San Francisco	lava
tremor	ash
fault	Mount St. Helens
aftershock	Pompeii
Richter scale	crater
plates	eruption
	Kilauea
	plates

Sometimes Gia records the children's brainstormed words in a web drawn on the chalkboard rather than using the pocket chart. One aspect of the

Supporting Struggling Readers and Writers

pocket chart that Gia likes is that all of the words are included; duplicates are placed behind previously identified words. This enables Gia to see which concepts or words the children deem most important or know the most about. For example, although Kilauea and Richter scale have only one card each, the word *crater* appears on six cards, stacked behind each other. Also, the word *plates* stirred up some debate as the students discussed their ideas about the role of plates in earthquakes *and* volcanoes and finally placed the word in both categories. This activity also has the advantage of exposing students with limited background knowledge to at least some of the concepts twice: once during their small-group discussion and again when the groups bring their ideas together.

Pictures as Sources of Information

The old saying that "a picture is worth a thousand words" is worth recalling when we consider how to help students build and make the most of their prior knowledge. Whether informational or fictional text, the pictures in books are valuable tools that can focus students' attention on important information and aid their understanding as they read. Pictures can make otherwise abstract concepts more concrete. However, struggling readers in the intermediate grades may need help in learning to "read" them, especially in their content-area texts. Rather than considering an illustration as a good source of information and one to be examined, students' primary reaction is frequently a cursory glance accompanied by a thought such as, "Oh, good, less text to read here."

To help students learn to use the illustrations of expository text to gain information, teachers might select a picture from the text students will be reading or from a related source: picture book, calendar, art print, and so forth. They then think aloud about what they see and describe their reactions to the picture. After this type of modeling, teachers show students an illustration and engage them in a similar process. For example, as part of a unit on slavery, a teacher might have students examine one of the powerful paintings from Julius Lester's *From Slave Ship . . . To Freedom Road*. Students are given time to study the representation, to think about what they see, and to consider what the image reminds them of or how it makes them feel. Then using the Think-Pair-Share strategy described in Chapter 2, they discuss their ideas with a partner and then as a whole class. This sort of approach enables students to acquire understandings that will help them make connections as they read and study about the topic. If carried out repeatedly, students will likely apply the strategy to gather information when they work independently.

Teachers of primary-grade students often do a "picture walk" with children before reading a book to them. This act of paging through the book and examining the pictures fosters interest in the book and helps the children connect what they know to what the story might be about. These purposes are equally valid and valuable when texts that have a lot of pictures are used with older students, particularly struggling readers. Barbara Vaski, a fifth/sixth-grade teacher, found this to be true for a group of her students. After several unsuccessful attempts to excite the students about reading, Barbara found an author that appealed to them—Paul Fleischman. Their reading of a mystery called *The Half-a-Moon Inn* during guided silent reading first sparked their interest. Fluency practice with another of his books, *Joyful Noise: Poems for Two Voices*, increased their motivation. At a recent school book fair Barbara noticed a picture book written by Fleischman—*Westlandia*. Although Barbara had read about using picture books with older students, as yet she had not tried the technique. Because the students had enjoyed the author's other two works, Barbara thought they might like this picture book. The pictures were certainly engaging; there was an element of the mysterious about them—a strange-looking alphabet, plants of enormous size, kids playing some peculiar game on stilts. After reading *Westlandia*, the story of a summer project that turns into the founding of a new civilization and of friendships, Barbara was convinced that it was a good choice. Not only was the story rather unique, but also it would make a wonderful follow-up to the class's recent study of ancient civilizations. She bought enough copies for the small group and planned to introduce the book the following week.

For the picture walk, Barbara decided to use just her copy of the book and limit the picture previewing to three of the fifteen double-page illustrations, plus the front cover and inside spread of the unusual alphabet. As soon as she showed the cover with its young hero dressed in rather primitive clothing, standing atop a gigantic tulip-like plant while a neighbor stares out a window at him, the students demonstrated their enthusiasm:

Jamal: Cool! Look at this guy!

Jason: What is Wes-lan-dia? Oh, and hey, look; this book is by Paul Fleischman!

Barbara: That's right. The book is called *Westlandia*, and who or what Westlandia is, is something you will discover as we read the story. Because pictures are an important part of this book, we're going to take a careful look at a few of them before we read. Perhaps they will provide a clue about Westlandia. What else do you notice in this picture?

Sandi: This boy, whoever he is . . . maybe he's Weslandia . . . you know, Wes, for short . . . anyway, he reminds me of Johnny Appleseed. Look how he's dressed, and see, he's even got a little bag, like Johnny Appleseed carried. I read a biography about Johnny Appleseed last year; but that wasn't his real name; it was Chapman, or something like that.

Barbara: Those are good observations, Sandi. What do you think he uses the pouch for?

Terry: Maybe he has seeds in there, and he grows those humungous plants.

Barbara continued with the next set of pictures, calling the students' attention to details and asking them to explain their thinking when necessary. After the students had a chance to look, reflect, and comment on each of the five pictures, Barbara asked them to predict what they thought would happen in the story by recording their ideas in their response logs. Meanwhile she distributed the books and reflected on the effectiveness of the picture walk. The pictures had definitely motivated the students and caused them to make connections to some of their experiences. Sandi's early comment about Johnny Appleseed was unusual for two reasons: (1) she usually had to be drawn out to participate, and (2) this was one of the few times Barbara had heard her connect a previous reading experience to the current text. Jamal, too, had made a text connection when they examined the picture of the game. What was it he had said? Something like, "as weird as that quiditch game in the Harry Potter book you're reading." Barbara was pleased with the picture walk introduction and knew she would use it again.

Text Features as Sources of Information

When students are confronted with a task of reading expository text, few first look through the book or chapter at such features as the table of contents, headings, subheadings, and captions; more often than not, they simply dive in and start to read. This approach is much like starting out on a journey without first consulting a map to see how you will get there, a method few travelers would choose. Text features such as the table of contents, headings, and subheadings provide a blueprint or outline of the author's plan for presenting information and signal which concepts are especially important. For example, *A Look Around Rain Forests* by Ed Perez includes the following topics in its table of contents, providing students with a clear idea of the kind of information they will gain from reading the book:

What Is a Rain Forest?
Different Kinds of Rain Forests
Rain Forests Have Tops and Bottoms
More Rain Forest Creatures
People of the Rain Forests
Why Rain Forests Are in Trouble
What Kids Can Do
Glossary
Index

Students need to be made aware of the importance of these aspects of the text and the ease with which they can be used. They should be taught to routinely survey the features before beginning to read.

Like most informational texts, *A Look Around Rain Forests* has a glossary and an index; students need to know where these are and how to use them. *Penguins*, by Stacy Savran, a book in the Smart Start Reader series, has no table of contents and no index or glossary, but it does have headings and a wealth of photos that students can preview to see where their reading journey will take them and to glean bits of information that will make comprehending the text easier when they read it.

Text that has an abundance of pictures, graphs, and diagrams can present problems for the reader: knowing which caption goes with which image can be confusing. Many students need guidance to be able to navigate their way around. Captions are not always placed directly below the illustration; sometimes they are next to it, above it, or on a facing page. Reader-friendly texts place an arrow or other symbol with the caption to direct the reader's attention to the appropriate illustration.

Using Text Structures to Assist Understanding

When children set out to read a book such as *The Big Bug Book* by Margery Facklam, they are confronted with a very different task than when they sit down to read a story such as *Cinder Edna*, a fractured fairy tale by Ellen Jackson. Not only does the content of the two differ but also their structures, and both content and structure count in the meaning-making process (Just and Carpenter 1987). Narrative text structure, which typically consists of *setting, characters, problem/goal, events/plot*, and *resolution*, tends to be quite consistent from story to story. By contrast, expository text structure differs from text to text and even within a text. The list of patterns generally includes *description, sequence, compare and contrast, cause and effect*, and *problem and solution*.

Teachers can help students more easily comprehend text by familiarizing them with the various text structures and by teaching them to use the structures to organize information. Think-alouds and graphic organizers, like those shown in Figures 8.1 and 8.2, are useful for accomplishing these goals.

Although good readers may not need guidance in understanding how narrative texts are structured, poor readers are likely to. They are better able to answer questions and recall what they read when they receive instruction in not only content, but also story organization (National Reading Panel 2000). Story maps, such as the one pictured in Figure 8.1, help students focus on the important elements of the story and anticipate what might happen next. Because narrative text structure is similar from story to story, teachers can keep a ready supply of blank story plans on hand

Figure 8.1 A Story Map of *Westlandia* by Paul Fleischman

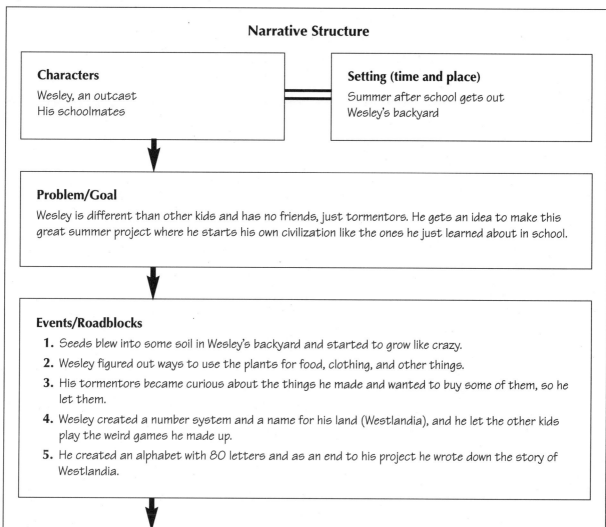

Narrative Structure

Characters

Wesley, an outcast
His schoolmates

Setting (time and place)

Summer after school gets out
Wesley's backyard

Problem/Goal

Wesley is different than other kids and has no friends, just tormentors. He gets an idea to make this great summer project where he starts his own civilization like the ones he just learned about in school.

Events/Roadblocks

1. Seeds blew into some soil in Wesley's backyard and started to grow like crazy.
2. Wesley figured out ways to use the plants for food, clothing, and other things.
3. His tormentors became curious about the things he made and wanted to buy some of them, so he let them.
4. Wesley created a number system and a name for his land (Westlandia), and he let the other kids play the weird games he made up.
5. He created an alphabet with 80 letters and as an end to his project he wrote down the story of Westlandia.

Resolution

When Wesley created the civilization in his backyard, all the kids thought the things he did were cool, and it made them want to play with him and be his friend. By September, he had tons of friends and a land named after himself.

for students to use with their reading (and writing). Initially, struggling readers will need to complete the plans with teacher prompting and support as the story is read and discussed. After adequate practice, students can independently fill out the sheets as they read. Story plans guide students' understanding as they read and provide a framework to help them retell or summarize afterward.

Figure 8.2 Graphic Organizers for Informational Text

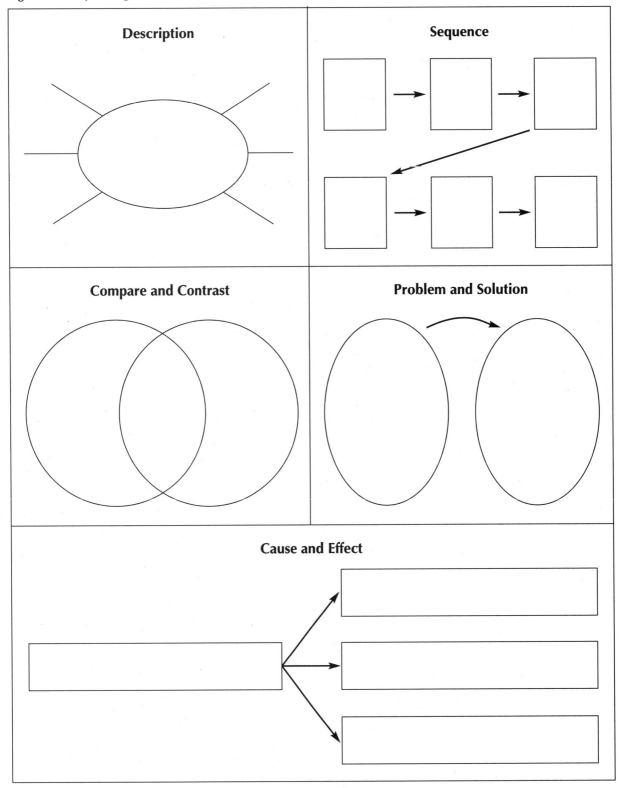

Supporting Struggling Readers and Writers

Because expository texts can have different structures, teachers will need to model each pattern separately and do so numerous times. A teacher who wishes to demonstrate the use of informational text structures with a think-aloud might do the following:

1. Choose one of the structures to focus on.
2. Select a short passage of text—sometimes just a paragraph—that illustrates the structure.
3. Think aloud while reading the passage to the class; draw students' attention to words that signal the targeted structure, and share thoughts that come to mind as a result of noticing the structure. For example, while reading a paragraph from *Observing the Sky* (p. 44) by Carole Stott, a teacher might share thoughts like the following:
   "It says that planets look like stars when you first look at them. The way this sentence is worded—*'planets look like stars'*—makes me think this paragraph is going to compare stars and planets. [Reads on] It's clear that the two are being compared: Here, where it says *'Planets follow different paths from stars,'* I know that *different* is a word that signals a compare-and-contrast kind of text. I wonder how the paths of stars and planets differ. [Reads on.] These last two sentences make it even more clear that the author is comparing and contrasting stars and planets. She used the words *differently* and *but*, and they give me more evidence. So, stars seem to move together, and one that moves *differently* could be a planet."
4. After the modeling and any further reading, the teacher might help students to use a graphic organizer, such as the one for Compare and Contrast displayed in Figure 8.2, to record information.

Story maps and informational text organizers make it easier for students to make sense of new information and remember it. They can be applied before, during, or after students' reading. When used before the reading they activate students' prior knowledge, provide a structure for organizing information, and encourage purposeful reading and prediction-making. If applied during the reading, they help students make sense of new information and enable them to see connections between events and concepts. Graphic organizers that are used after the reading assist students in verifying predictions and in providing more detailed responses; their structure also makes review, retellings, and summary-writing easier.

Words and Phrases That Signal Informational Text Structures

Descriptive: *for example, characteristics are, includes, such as, also, for instance;*

Sequence: *first, second, third, finally, next, before, after, then, later, now, on* (date);

Compare and Contrast: *similarly, by contrast, same, different, however, but, instead, although, on the other hand, more than, less than, least, most, other;*

Cause and Effect and Problem and Solution: *because, as a result, therefore, since, reasons why, if . . . then, nevertheless, thus.*

Helping Struggling Readers Monitor Their Comprehension

All of us who have worked with students who are not successful readers have experienced a conversation similar to this one:

Student: I didn't get this.
Teacher: What part of it didn't you understand?
Student: I didn't understand any of it.
Teacher: How much of it did you read?
Student: I read all of it.

The important lesson in this sort of conversation is that some students define reading as "looking at every word on the page that you assigned me." Very few of us who read easily would continue reading in confusion. Instead, we would identify the part of the text where comprehension initially broke down and then use strategies (perhaps rereading, looking back to earlier parts of the text, and considering or even checking resources for word meanings) to regain our understanding before we continued to read. By contrast, students who view reading as "looking at all the words" or "trying to say all the words" miss the critical point that prompts readers to monitor for meaning, namely that "This is going to make sense to me as I read it; I will be informed or entertained."

Students must be able to monitor for meaning to apply the comprehension fix-up strategies we teach them, such as rereading, self-questioning, or summarizing. Because monitoring is so critical to comprehension, it makes sense that in our work with struggling readers we teach it repeatedly and in different ways. In Chapter 5 we discussed ways that guided silent reading and literature circles can be used to help students learn to monitor their understanding; others follow.

Helping Struggling Readers to Answer Questions

Who the weak comprehenders are in a given class is usually no secret. Their inability to answer the questions they are asked about text makes them easy to identify. Years of classroom experience and research have demonstrated that teaching students how to answer questions is a valuable way to help them learn to think about and better comprehend their reading. However, simply asking questions is not enough; it will not have the effect of improving comprehension. If the goal teachers have in questioning their students is to *teach* rather than to *assess*, they need to consider (1) the quality of the questions they ask, (2) the feedback they give to student responses, and (3) the explicit instruction they provide students in how to answer questions. The problem that arises when questions are primarily used to assess rather than to teach comprehension skills was identified more than two decades ago (Durkin 1978–1979), yet it persists in many classrooms today. Questioning without appropriate planning and follow-through is not instruction; it is, at best, assessment.

Asking Quality Questions

Questions are often categorized by type: literal, inferential, or application. High-quality questions engage readers in thoughtful reflection about their reading. Some require that readers return to the text to reconsider the ideas presented by the author; this is true of most inferential questions. Others, including some inferential questions and all application questions, require readers to think beyond the author's ideas and use their own prior knowledge. In many of the classrooms we visit, the bulk of teachers' questions are literal questions that require little reflection about or beyond the text. Students are generally able to answer these questions with quickly stated details they remember from their reading. Those who are not able to answer—generally, students for whom reading is difficult—receive little guidance in how to rectify the problem; they merely receive feedback that their response is incorrect. To provide high-quality questions, wise teachers plan them in advance of the teaching and use all three types.

Some of the planned questions should be of the literal variety—questions that require students to "read the lines" and give an answer that was provided explicitly in the reading. For example, a teacher preparing questions about Patricia MacLachlan's *Sarah, Plain and Tall* might ask, "From what state has Sarah come?"

Most of the questions teachers ask should be inferential questions—questions that require students to "read between the lines." "What are Sarah's reasons for leaving her home?" is an example of one type of inference question. Although the answer to this question is provided in the reading, it is implicitly stated, and students must link ideas from a number of sentences to figure it out. Another type of inference question requires students to create an answer that is not provided in the reading, such as, "What advice would you have for Sarah as she makes her decision?" This question requires students to use information from the text, along with their own prior knowledge. Some of this type of inferential question should be "real questions" for which teachers do not have an answer.

Application questions are those for which students must "read beyond the lines"; these, too, should be part of the plan. "How would you feel about leaving your home to live in a place where you knew no one?" is an example of an application question. Students rely on their own prior knowledge to answer this type of question, with no assistance from the text. Again, these questions are genuine. Teachers will be interested in students' answers not just to determine whether or not students "did the reading," but to understand more about their students' ideas, feelings, and responses to the text.

Providing Immediate, Appropriate Feedback

When teachers ask students questions, they must provide immediate and appropriate feedback for their questions to be instructional. Very often, teachers ask questions to assess their students' understanding of a text but fail to follow their students' answers with a response that makes the exchange instructional. In our classroom observations, we have watched teachers respond to an incorrect answer by turning to a second and even third child for the correct one. The student who answers correctly is told, "That's right," but there is no explanation of why.

What is appropriate feedback? A response that is directed to the student who gave the answer, rather than away from that student and toward another, is a good start. When a student's answer is correct, appropriate feedback specifically explains why the answer is a good one. It reaffirms the student's thinking and may provide helpful information for students who were not thinking of the correct answer. If the student's answer needs some refining, a prompt encouraging the student to think in a slightly different way may lead to the correct answer. If the student's answer shows confusion or faulty reasoning, a think-aloud demonstration, complete with checking back to the text, can offer essential feedback and guidance.

Explicit Instruction About Questions and Answers

Question-Answer Relationships (QARs) (Raphael 1986) is a teaching strategy for explicit demonstrations of literal, inferential, and application questions and the types of thinking required to answer them. The language of QAR is "kid friendly." Figure 8.3, QAR at a Glance, provides a graphic representation of the concepts and language involved.

With direct instruction and practice, students learn that a literal question such as, "From what state has Sarah come?" and an inferential question such as, "What are Sarah's reasons for leaving her home?" are both *In the Book* questions, in the language of QAR. They learn that these questions require them to remember exactly what the author said or return to the text

Figure 8.3 QAR at a Glance

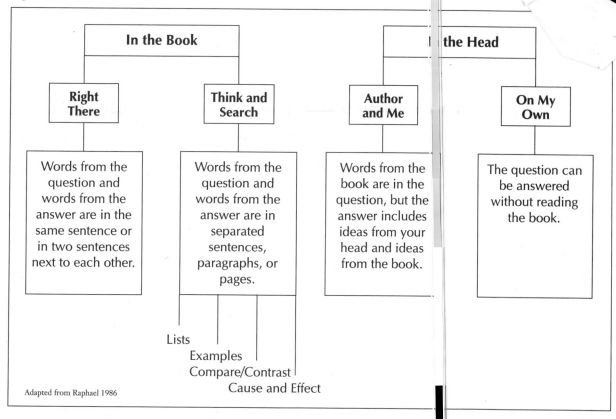

Adapted from Raphael 1986

to find what the author said. They also learn an important difference between these two types of questions. The literal question is *Right There.* Words from the question and words needed for the answer are in the same sentence or contiguous sentences. By contrast, the inferential question requires a *Think and Search* answer. Words from the question and words from the answer are spread throughout sentences and paragraphs, and may in fact be separated by pages.

QAR also helps students understand that for some questions they are asked about their reading, they will not find an answer in the book. For many struggling readers, this is new and startling information. Students' indignant responses to a correct answer that was implied in the text—"Where did they say that in the book? I didn't see that in the book!"—indicate that they are unaware that some questions require answers that are *In the Head.* We also see this lack of awareness from students who select an incorrect multiple-choice answer because it includes words from the text, words that do not appear in the correct answer.

QAR allows us to teach students that inferential questions such as "What advice would you have for Sarah as she makes her decision?" require language and ideas from their own heads to be correctly answered. We can further teach them that the same is true of application questions such as, "How would you feel about leaving your home to live in a place where you knew no one?" The language of QAR also helps students to understand the difference between the two questions. The inferential question is called an *Author and Me* question, and students learn that they need ideas from the text as well as their own ideas and words to answer it. In contrast, the application question is called an *On My Own* question, and students learn that they could answer it even if they had not read the text.

Introducing QAR to Students

When Penny MacMillan introduces QAR in her third-grade classroom, she uses a short text and creates examples of each of the four types of questions. This year when her students were reading Arnold Lobel's *Fables*, she selected the one-page fable "The Ducks and the Fox" for her introductory lesson. She prepared the following questions:

> *Right There:* Why doesn't the second Duck sister want to find a new way to the pond?
>
> *Think and Search:* What differences of opinion do the two Duck sisters have?
>
> *Author and Me:* Which of the two sisters are you more like, and why?
>
> *On My Own:* When do the routines we have for doing things help us, and when do they hurt us?

For the fables unit, some of Penny's students read silently and independently; others read silently while listening to a tape of Penny reading the fable. A small group of students sat with Penny and followed along in their books while she read aloud to them. After ten minutes of reading time, she called all of the students back to their seats for the lesson.

Penny started the lesson by saying, "Today we're going to talk about questions and answers related to our reading. When I ask you a question about something you've read, like the fable, the information you need to answer my question can come from two different places." On the overhead, Penny placed a covered-up graphic display of the QAR categories (a simpler version of Figure 8.3). As she introduced the concept of *In the Book* questions, she uncovered that portion of the graphic, saying, "Sometimes I ask you questions that have answers you'll find in the book, like, 'Where were the Duck sisters going when they had their big adventure?' Tell your partner the answer to my question, and listen while your partner tells you. Then check the book to see if I'm right when I say that the answer is there."

Penny briefly engaged the students in conversation to determine that everyone agreed the sisters were on their way to the pond when the Fox jumped on them and that the answer was in the book. Then, displaying the *In the Head* part of the figure, she continued, "Sometimes I ask you questions that have answers you won't find in the book, like, 'What is a *routine*? What does the word *routine* mean?' You have to use your head, what you know, to find the answer to that question. Tell your partner the answer to my question, and listen while your partner tells you. And again, check the book to see if I'm right when I say that the answer is not there."

The students were excited to talk about this question. Some said they knew what *routine* meant, so it didn't matter that there was no definition in the book. Others argued that the book helped them to figure out what *routine* meant, so it was "sort of in the book," though they agreed with Penny that the answer to her question wasn't exactly there. Penny kept the students in this conversation, asking them to explain their points and to define the word. She wanted to be certain that all of the students could articulate or agree on a definition for *routine* along the lines of "something you do the same every time you do it." She also needed to be sure the children understood that the word was not defined in the text, but that the combination of the tale and the statement that followed it, "At times, a change of routine can be most helpful" (p. 5), could lead them to their answer.

"You're way ahead of me!" Penny said. "You're ready to hear about all the different kinds of question-and-answer relationships I have in store for you." She showed her students the entire illustration on the overhead, and told them, "Today, we're going to talk about the two kinds of questions that have answers in the book. In the next few weeks, you'll have many chances to learn about all of these QARs."

As Penny and her students continued, the following dialogue ensued:

Penny: Sometimes when I ask you a question that is definitely in the book, words from the question and words from the answer are in the same sentence, or in two sentences that are right next to each other. We call that kind of question a *Right There* QAR. Work with your partner to try this one: "Why doesn't the second Duck sister want to try a new way to the pond?" Decide on the answer, and decide, is it *Right There*? Use your books to help you.

[*The students work together with their books for about a minute.*]

Penny: Emily, what did you and Pat decide? Why doesn't the second Duck sister want to try a new way to the pond?

Emily: She says she likes the old way.

Penny: Can you find her exact words in the book?

Emily: Yes.

Penny: Will you read it to us? We'll all read along silently.

Emily: *"I really do not want to try a new way. This road makes me feel comfortable."*

Penny: I agree with you, Emily; that's the reason the second sister won't try another route. Do you agree with me that it is *Right There*, because words from the question I asked and words from the answer are in the same sentence, or in two sentences next to each other?

Emily: Yes. It's two sentences together.

[*Before moving on, Penny checks to see that the class agrees on the answer and the type of question that was asked.*]

Penny: Okay, we're ready to work on the other kind of QAR that has an answer that's in the book. With this kind of question, the answer isn't *Right There*. You have to *Think and Search*. See how the name tells you just what to do? For this kind of question, you have to use information from sentences that are not right together. You have to look for the answer, think about it, and put it all together. Ready for a try?

[*Various positive responses are heard.*]

Penny: Once again, work with your partner, and use your book to answer this question: "What differences of opinion did the two Duck sisters have?" And also decide, did you *Think and Search* to get the answer?

[*The students work together with their books for about two minutes.*]

Penny: Jesse, what differences of opinion between the two Duck sisters did you and Martin notice?

Jesse: Well, the first sister, she wants to find a new road to the pond, but the second sister, she doesn't want to, so that's one, and . . .

Martin: Yeah, and we also found that the first sister didn't like the Fox, and the second sister did, so . . .

Jesse: We found two differences.

Penny: It sounds to me like you guys had to think and search to find your answer.

Martin: We definitely did!

Penny: Other partners, thumbs-up if you talked about how the sisters disagreed about trying a new road and about whether or not the Fox was okay, the same as Jesse and Martin did.

[*The students show thumbs-up.*]

Penny: You all did a good job of using the book to think and search, and that's why everyone had a complete answer. Let's put our two index fingers over the two spots in the book where we got our information for our complete answer. Can you all see that there is some space between those two bits of information? I can tell from your fingers that you all know where you got your information. As you can see, sometimes we have to do some thinking and searching to find the right answer. Now, let's take a few minutes to talk about some things that you won't find in the book, some ideas that I know you have in your heads. How did you like this fable? What did it show you?

Penny's lesson affords some important insights about introducing this strategy to students:

1. *Know the strategy, and be prepared to teach it.* Penny was ready to use and demonstrate the entire QAR strategy. She knew that she would not explain and demonstrate all four question types in this lesson. Nonetheless, she was able to respond to the students' *Author and Me* concerns by defining the word *routine* through context clues. Penny has long-term goals for this strategy in her classroom, and she will devote many lessons to helping her students understand and use it with a variety of text types.

2. *Let the students show you what they understand.* Penny gave the students an opportunity to use the strategy with the guidance and support of her questions and explanations. Through their practice she was able to observe and determine how much they understood. Penny uses this information to decide what to teach next.

3. *Integrate the strategy instruction with content goals.* The questions Penny asked her students in this lesson were questions she wanted them to think about as part of their general comprehension of their fable reading. She devoted time and attention to providing explicit instruction about answering questions, because she wants to make her students aware of ways to think about their reading that will improve their comprehension. She introduced her students to QAR within the context of a lesson that is a regular part of her curriculum. Penny will continue to integrate QARs with her teaching of social studies, science, reading, and even math over the next month. She plans to use short passages of text so that the lessons can be completed in less than twenty minutes, and as in the fable lesson, will give specific explanations of the question types. The overhead figure will be used until she has fully introduced QAR. At that time, she may post the image on each wall of the classroom, so that she and her students have easy access to the QAR language. Penny knows that once her students have internalized the language of QAR, she can use it as part of the immediate instructive feedback she gives when they answer her questions about their reading. Feedback and guidance such as, "You found one part of the answer for this question, but you need to think and search to find the rest," or "This is not a *Right There* question" is helpful to the student who knows the strategy.

Students who know about QARs have a strategy they can apply in their regular classroom reading and in standardized testing. When students are able to approach a multiple choice or open-ended question by asking themselves, "What kind of a question is this?" they are on their way to thinking strategically about the sources of information they need to consider to determine an accurate answer. Also, as they build a solid understanding of

the types of questions that can be generated from text, they become better able to ask and write effective questions of their own.

Helping Struggling Readers Generate Questions

All comprehending readers question themselves as they read. We wonder throughout our reading about the connections and inferences we make, about what will happen next, and about anything that doesn't make immediate sense. Readers who don't think while they read do not generate self-questions. We must show them how to create questions and then put them in situations that require them to come up with good questions about their reading.

The most direct and effective way for teachers to help students do this is by demonstrating self-questioning through think-alouds. Many teachers have found that reading aloud short but intellectually challenging picture books allows them to pause and think aloud about the questions that they themselves generate as they read. Teachers who are aware of their own comprehension monitoring are able to do this with ease. However, catch-

Supporting Struggling Readers and Writers

ing yourself in the act of thinking about a question requires practice, even for teachers.

With repeated modeling of the think-aloud, students begin to monitor and question their own understanding as they listen to the teacher read. Asking the questions is far more important than answering them. The questions readers ask themselves seldom have a single correct answer, and they often lead to more and deeper questions. Sometimes we find answers to our questions as we continue reading, but sometimes we lose interest in certain questions as the text continues or discover that we will have to wait until the text is finished to ponder them.

Fourth-grade teacher Jean Anderson has been impressed with her students' increasing understanding that good readers generate questions while they read. During the past school year, Jean's reading of *Mosaic of Thought* (Keene and Zimmerman 1997) inspired her to combine think-alouds with picture book read-alouds to demonstrate specific comprehension strategies. Here's how she modeled the technique of self-questioning while reading *Knots on a Counting Rope* by Bill Martin, Jr., and John Archambault.

Jean read aloud from the first page of the book, "*I promise you nothing, Boy. I love you. That is better than a promise.*" Then she thought aloud, "I am wondering: Is love better than a promise?" She read on to the fourth page and thought aloud with another question, "Why does the boy keep saying *no* to the way the grandfather is telling the story?" When she read aloud from page 16, "*Will I always have to live in the dark?*" she thought aloud again, "What is it like living in the dark?" On page 17, Jean read, "*I see the horses with my hands, Grandfather, but I cannot see the blue. What is blue?*" and she asked, "Will the authors tell what I think they have been showing about the boy?" Jean did not ask any of these questions to encourage her students to give answers. She was simply demonstrating the questions that entered her mind as she read and thought her way through the text.

As Jean comments, "Some of my students really didn't have any questions occurring to them while they read, and it was hard for them when we started. But we've been talking about our questions, and I've been demonstrating. Now even the students who didn't know what we were talking about when we started have questions to share. They are thinking while they read now."

Learning to Summarize Information

Getting the "big picture" can be a momentous task for the struggling reader who often has difficulty organizing and recalling even limited amounts of information. Nonetheless, summarization is a critical tool for reading comprehension. Readers who are able to synthesize information and see the big picture are better able to recall the information. This is important, whether for communicating with others, or being able to connect future new understandings with current ones.

The process of summarizing, which usually involves writing, can and should be taught. It includes three components (Hidi and Anderson 1986):

1. Including and excluding information: for example, selecting the main idea and supporting details, but deleting extraneous and redundant matter.
2. Condensing information by generalizing: for example, instead of "He boiled, fried, or roasted the food," the information could be summarized as "He cooked the food."
3. Putting the information into a written format.

Despite the limited number of components, the process is not an easy one, especially for struggling readers and writers. However, by scaffolding students' learning and moving from teacher modeling to repeated guided practice, students can over time become competent in their use of this strategy. Graphic organizers like the story maps and informational text organizers (see Figures 8.1 and 8.2) discussed earlier are valuable aids for summary writing. Students gather and "filter" information *as* they read rather than leaving all the work to *after* they read. This makes the task more manageable. Once the text has been read and the graphic is complete, students use their recorded ideas and transform them into a written summary. For example, information from a story map might be summarized by writing three short paragraphs: a beginning (characters, setting, and problem), middle (events/plot), and end (resolution). Information from an expository graphic organizer might be written in paragraphs corresponding to the parts of the graphic; for example, students could write a separate paragraph for each event they have listed on a sequence organizer.

Besides the graphic organizers previously discussed, teachers sometimes find it helpful to use a graphic like "What's the Big Idea?" shown in Figure 8.4, which was completed during a reading of John Reynolds Gardiner's *Stone Fox*. After each chapter, or designated section of text, students write down the big idea for that portion. When they are finished with the entire text, they read through all the big ideas and decide what they think the overall big idea is. As with any summary writing, this type of integration of information takes practice, time, and teacher support. The type of collaboration that occurs during small-group discussions is valuable and helps to maximize student participation.

In addition to the preceding suggestions for teaching students to summarize, here are a few more considerations to keep in mind:

Figure 8.4 What's the Big Idea?

What's the Big Idea?

1. Grandpa is sick, but little Willy is determined to make him better.

2. Little Willy works hard to harvest the potatoes, but that doesn't help Grandpa.

3. Winter is coming, and little Willy and Searchlight get ready for it.

4. Clifford Snyder, the tax man, comes and threatens to take the farm, and Willy finds out that's why Grandpa's sick.

5. Everybody tells little Willy to sell the farm, but he plans to get the money for the taxes by winning a race.

6. Willy uses his own college money to enter the sled race, but it will be hard to win against Stone Fox because he really wants to win, too.

7. Willy meets up with Stone Fox and gets slapped for petting one of his dogs.

8. The day of the race comes, and when Willy starts he is nervous but thinks he can win.

9. Little Willy takes the lead and keeps it, but Stone Fox is close behind.

10. Searchlight dies, but Stone Fox lets little Willy carry her over the finish line.

What's the big idea?

Willy's determination helped him to save the farm and Grandpa. If you're determined enough, you can do just about anything.

---

1. Narrative text is likely to be easier for students to summarize than informational text and, therefore, is a good starting point.
2. Starting the teaching/learning process with short selections of text is also easier.
3. Asking students to retell what they read, whether orally or in writing, can also help some students ease into summary writing. Although certain students may have a tendency to tell *everything* and may not

do the necessary deleting and condensing, retelling will at least allow teachers to ascertain that students understood what the text was about. To provide support for including important elements in the retelling of stories, teachers sometimes ask students to use a guide sheet such as the one in Figure 8.5.

4. Learning to summarize is a difficult process that warrants teacher patience and recognition of the small strides that students make toward adding this technique to their repertoire of comprehension strategies.

Figure 8.5 Story Retelling Frame

Story Retelling Frame

Title: _____

Author: _____

Retold by: _____

This story takes place _____

_____

The main character in the story is _____

who _____

A problem happens when _____

_____

After that, _____

_____

Then, _____

_____

The problem is solved when _____

_____

The story ends with _____

_____

Supporting Struggling Readers and Writers

IMPROVING
WRITING

Process writing and its inherent difficulties intimidate many struggling writers. In this chapter we describe the components of a
writing workshop that can empower these students to achieve success.
We stress the importance of a supportive classroom environment in
helping struggling writers overcome their resistance to writing and
present instructional strategies that teachers can use to scaffold students' learning in ways that foster self-assurance and writing proficiency. This chapter was co-written with Russ Walsh, Director of
Language Arts, Montgomery Township Schools, New Jersey.

Background and Issues

Writer's Block
I'm staring at this blank paper,
Because I have nothing to say.
"Write what you know," says the teacher.
I guess I know nothing today.

Even the most effective teachers of struggling writers acknowledge one immutable fact: Writing is hard work. This statement will surprise no one who has ever tried to write, for everyone on occasion has struggled with getting words down on paper, whether it was a college admissions essay, an analysis of a poem, a book critique, a research paper, or some other writing task. At times, we have struggled with composing chapters for this book. Sitting at our computers, we have had to contend with issues of audience, purpose, clarity, style, deadlines, punctuation, and spelling. All of this struggling, and we are experienced writers who know a good deal about the topic.

If those of us who are experienced, knowledgeable, reasonably successful writers can admit that writing is hard work, it should come as no surprise that children who have little experience, limited knowledge, and a three-, four-, or even five-year history of failure to achieve in writing will be resistant to it. The teacher's first job, then, is to accept that some students will naturally be reluctant to write and to view this unwillingness as a teaching challenge and not as recalcitrance.

The second thing all successful teachers of struggling writers must accept is that writing is risky business. Writing makes demands of the student that few other school activities make. When children commit words to paper, they create a more or less permanent document exposing all that they know and do not know about the written form of language. For any student, this can be a little intimidating. For a student who struggles with sentence construction, word choice, spelling, grammar, and mechanics, the risks can be overpowering. The successful teacher of struggling writers recognizes the risky nature of writing and works to provide an atmosphere where children are comfortable taking risks.

Once teachers accept the difficulties inherent in the writing process and realize the effects these difficulties can have on children who struggle with writing, they are ready to think about instruction that will help struggling writers overcome the difficulties and succeed. Teachers need to develop a repertoire of strategies that will encourage struggling writers' developing abilities and enable them to learn to use the various forms of written language effectively and confidently. These strategies provide a framework of support that makes the task of writing a little less difficult and a little less risky for the struggling writer.

The Writing Instruction That Every Child Needs

The focus of this chapter is, of course, on the struggling writer; however, for most teachers in most classrooms these students do not exist in a vacuum. They are but one element of a heterogeneous classroom that includes some skilled writers, some writers who are beginning to develop competence, and some struggling writers. Over the past twenty years we have learned a great deal about what good writing instruction looks like for all students. Before teachers modify their teaching to meet the needs of struggling writers, they must first be sure they are providing the kind of writing instruction that is beneficial to all students. All students need

1. *Instruction that is rooted in the writing process.* (Graves 1983; Calkins 1994; Murray 1986). The idea of writing as a process is based on the way real writers produce real texts. Although different authors sometimes label parts of the process differently, it is generally agreed that it consists of prewriting, drafting, revising, editing, and publishing. By teaching students strategies for each component of the process, we help them produce richer, more fully realized, more accurate writing.

2. *A predictable structure to the writing instruction.* This structure should include time for direct input from the teacher through mini-lessons, extensive time to write, opportunities for conference time with the teacher and with peers, and opportunities to share what has been written (Calkins 1994). Instruction should occur daily, and it is best if it can occur at the same time each day. Some schedules may not allow for five writing workshops a week; three should be a minimum. A typical writing workshop period of 45–60 minutes might look like this:

- Short, focused mini-lesson   10–15 minutes
- Independent student writing,
  peer and teacher conferences   25–35 minutes
- Sharing time   10–15 minutes

This type of structure allows for lots of teacher input in the form of directly taught mini-lessons and lots of student input in the form of active engagement in writing and collaborative learning. Students spend the bulk of their time in what researchers have consistently noted to be a key to improved writing performance—actual time spent writing. The structure also provides teachers with the time and opportunity to meet individually with students. This is essential to working successfully with struggling writers.

3. *Writers need ready access to the "tools of the trade" and instruction in how to use them.* Some space in the room should be designated as the Writing Center, and it should be stocked with the materials a writer needs. The center might include the following:

> A coffee can full of pencils
> Yellow paper for rough drafts
> White paper for final drafts
> Blank paper for illustrations
> Editing checklists
> Colored pencils for editing
> A word wall of frequently misspelled words
> Dictionaries, thesauruses
> Stapler, stencils, and other materials for publishing books

Mini-lessons provide an ideal framework for teaching students how and when to use materials from the Writing Center and how to care for those materials.

Establishing a Supportive Classroom Environment for Struggling Writers

In modifying the classroom environment to meet the needs of the struggling writer, the teacher must begin with unconditional acceptance and provide tools and structures to help the writer focus on the writing task.

Unconditional Acceptance

A struggling writer in the intermediate grades enters the classroom carrying a heavy load of emotional baggage. This baggage may include low self-esteem, feelings of intellectual inadequacy, frustration, parental pressure to perform, years of writing failure, task avoidance behaviors, and fear. In addition, the child may be carrying some external baggage provided by previous teachers, child study teams, child psychologists, and parents. This baggage may take the form of labels, such as lazy, learning disabled, ADHD, or developmentally delayed.

The first thing this child needs upon entering the writing classroom is to feel "safe." Only the child who feels safe can park the accumulated baggage at the classroom door and begin to take the risks that are necessary to produce writing. This means that the initial writing efforts of this student, no matter how meager and flawed, must be accepted unconditionally (Avery 1999). The teacher must focus solely on what the student is doing well and heap praise upon the learner for what has been accomplished.

We are not suggesting false praise, merely that teachers sheath their editor's pens for a while and focus on what the child does well. Perhaps the child has written only a few words on the page. In this case unconditional acceptance means praising the student for taking the risk to get some words down and then responding specifically to the message the student is attempting to communicate. The praise must be specific and focused. Vague responses of "good job" or "nice work" will not suffice. Suppose a struggling third-grade writer has produced this text: *I like to plae sokker*. An attitude of acceptance might produce the following conversation:

Teacher: Read your story to me, Michael.
Michael: I didn't write much.
Teacher: I am pleased to see you took the opportunity to write. Please read it to me.
Michael: *I like to play soccer.*
Teacher: I see from your writing that soccer is something you enjoy.
Michael: I play for the Tigers.
Teacher: The Tigers, huh?
Michael: Yeah, we're pretty good.
Teacher: So the Tigers are a good team.
Michael: Yeah, we won our last game six to one.
Teacher: You won by five goals!
Michael: I had two goals myself.
Teacher: Wow! You had two goals! That sounds like quite a game.

At this point, Michael might take off and tell the story of his two-goal game, and it might be tempting to try to get him to write down the story. However, right now the teacher is more interested in sending a message of acceptance of what Michael has written and demonstrating an interest in him as a student and person. How teachers can help students like Michael move from oral storytelling to written stories is discussed later in the chapter; at the moment, the teacher wants Michael to make the writing decisions. Therefore, after a discussion about the two-goal game, the teacher might end the conversation this way:

Teacher: Michael, that was sure an exciting game for you. Is there anything I can help you with in the story you have written?

Michael: I am not sure I spelled *soccer* right. [*He had spelled it* SOKKER.]
Teacher: *Soccer* is a tricky word. Let's look at it. You have it almost perfect.
The first two letters are correct, and I can see that you know that
many words that end in the /r/ sound are spelled E-R. You also know
that the letter in the middle is doubled. In this case, the doubled letter
is *c* even though it sounds like a *k*. So, *soccer* is spelled S-O-C-C-E-R.

In this scenario, the teacher has followed the child's lead to find out
what help was needed. In the discussion, the teacher focused on all the
things Michael knew about spelling the word and suggested that the part
he did not know was "tricky." Because Michael chose the word *soccer* as a
focus, this discussion may be considered part of that early unconditional
acceptance. What the teacher is saying to Michael here is, "I accept your
assessment of what is important for you to know at this point." Knowing
how to spell *soccer* may actually free him up to write more. It is not unusual
to find struggling writers who are overly concerned with surface correctness in a first draft. The teacher chooses not to focus on the word *play*,
which was also misspelled, because Michael did not initiate a discussion of
the word. Perhaps Michael will now write more, and perhaps he will not.
The important thing here is that the groundwork has been laid for future
positive interactions with writing. The seed has been planted that the classroom is a safe writing environment and this increases the likelihood that
Michael will be willing to take risks with his writing in the future.

Sometimes students write nothing at all. For example, here is what
happened to Russ Walsh when he introduced the writer's notebook
(Fletcher 1996) to a group of fifth-grade children:

After reading a story and talking to the children about the many possibilities open to them for entries in their writer's notebook—observations about the world around them, thoughts, feelings, dreams—I
sent the children back to their desks to do an initial entry in the notebook. I moved around the room, answering questions, clearing up
confusions, when my eyes fell on one girl at the far side of the room.
She was alternately picking up her pencil, staring at the blank book in
front of her, putting the pencil back down, and staring off into space.
I walked over and asked, "How's it going, Angela?"

No sooner were the words out of my mouth than Angela's eyes
began to well with barely contained tears. "I don't know what to
write," she sobbed. Seeing the frustration in Angela's face, I felt I first
needed to validate her feelings. The following dialogue took place:

Russ: That is very frustrating, isn't it. It happens to me all the time.
Angela: It does?

Russ: Sure. Every writer gets stuck for something to write sometimes. Here's what I do: I just write whatever comes into my head without even thinking, until I think of something I want to write about.

Angela: But I can't think of anything to write about.

Russ: Then just write that. Just write, "I can't think of anything to write about," until something else comes to mind.

Angela: OK, if you say that's all right.

Russ: I say it's all right.

At this point, I left Angela and noted that she had begun to write. At the end of the writing workshop she came up to me, thrust her writer's notebook out and said, "Well, here it is." This is what Angela wrote:

> *I don't know what to write. I don't know what to write and Mr. Walsh said it was ok if I wrote this. So—I don't know what to write.*

Sometimes children think that their writing has to be about momentous things. Big ideas. Exciting trips. Fantastical stories. Angela couldn't think of anything momentous enough to write about. Our conversation gave Angela permission to just write what she was thinking. This was such a revelation to her that she declared that an authority had given her permission right in her journal entry. Part of unconditional acceptance is allowing kids to express their feelings in writing without judgment as to appropriateness.

Tools for the Struggling Writer

Earlier in the chapter we mentioned some of the writing tools that every student needs. In addition to these, struggling writers may need some personal tools at their seats to help with writing, particularly with spelling. These might include an index card or bookmark listing high-frequency words for quick reference (see Figure 9.1). When needed, a meaning clue can be added in parentheses; for example, *there* (place). The card can be laminated and, if desired, taped to the student's desk, or kept in a library pocket attached to the inside back cover of the writer's notebook. A personal dictionary containing frequently used words with space for adding more words is also helpful. These dictionaries, which are commercially available, include spellings only and provide struggling writers with a quick and easy tool to check spellings. Handheld spell-checkers, which can be purchased through many school supply companies as well as at various stores, are another effective aid to have at hand during the editing phase of the writing process; two or three are usually sufficient for an entire class.

Figure 9.1 A Bookmark of Selected High-Frequency Words

100 Commonly Used Words

about	friend	only	time
after	from	other	to
again	girl	our	too
all	give	out	two
also	great	over	up
always	have	people	us
an	here	really	very
and	house	said	was
are	how	saw	we
back	I	scared	well
because	into	school	went
been	just	see	were
but	know	she	what
by	let	some	when
can't	like	than	which
come	little	that	who
could	many	the	why
didn't	more	their	will
does	most	them	with
done	next	then	work
down	now	there	would
every	of	they	write
family	off	things	years
first	once	think	you
found	one	this	your

(front)   (back)

Struggling writers often have difficulty with organization. Valuable writing time can be lost as students search for notebooks, drafts, and homework. A writer's folder is useful in helping students to stay organized. The folder is typically created from a file folder or two-pocket folder and might contain the following items:

A list titled "Things I Can Write About"
A writer's notebook
A list identifying the title and genre of completed pieces
Rough drafts of work in progress (each dated and the pages numbered)
Spelling aids, such as personal dictionaries

To reduce the number of items the students must keep track of, teachers often staple the lists of writing ideas and completed works to the inside of the folder covers. Nonetheless, teachers need to be diligent and regularly check on these students' folders to make sure they have ready access to the materials.

Status of the Class: A Framework for Structure

As children develop their pieces during writing workshop, they are likely to be at different phases in the process at any given time. One student may be working on a first draft that is several pages long; another, whose piece is just a page or two in length, may be polishing the final draft or considering what to write about next. This variation is to be expected; in true writing workshops, where students write about meaningful topics, all students will not complete their prewriting one day, their first draft the next, and so on. To help monitor and track students' progress and help struggling writers stay on task, teachers often use a simple organizational technique called "status of the class" (Atwell 1987). At the beginning of writing time, the teacher asks students to take out their writing folders and think about what they will be working on that day. As the teacher calls the roll, students tell where they are in the writing process: brainstorming an idea, first draft, editing, final draft, conferencing, and so on. The teacher records the students' responses on a status-of-the-class sheet, usually in abbreviated form and often with a comment (for example, *D-1 "The Tournament"* or *Conf. Poem*). The sheet is nothing more than a six-column grid, with the students' names written down the left-hand column, and the days of the week as headings for the other five columns. When students are prepared, teachers can complete a status of the class for twenty to twenty-five students in five minutes or less.

From Oral Language to Written Language

The greatest ally struggling writers in the intermediate grades have for becoming skilled and confident writers is the oral language ability they have developed and practiced daily over their eight to ten years of life. Although written language is not talk written down, talk does provide a scaffold for all successful writing. The wise teacher of writing will use the powerful resource of oral language to help the struggling writer build a bridge to written language. But how is this to be done?

First, of course, the teacher must engage the student in conversation. Let's look at an example from a fourth-grade classroom.

Russ had just read the picture book *I'm in Charge of Celebrations* by Byrd Baylor to the class. The book is the story of a desert dweller who declares personal celebrations (celebrations other than traditionally recognized holidays) based on the natural phenomena that she has observed on her travels in the desert. After reading the story, Russ listed several of his own personal celebrations on the chalkboard and invited the children to do the same. All of the children were able to name at least one or two celebrations. Russ then asked the children to choose one and do a ten-minute quickwrite about their own celebration. Most children got straight to work, but not Greg. The teacher had told Russ that this student had great difficulty getting words down on paper. This day was no different. He sharpened his pencil, wandered over to take a peek at the classrooms' pet salamanders, and then came up to Russ and asked, "Can I go to the bathroom?" The following conversation took place:

Russ: Having trouble getting started, Greg?
Greg: Yeah, I don't know what to write about.
Russ: Well, let's look at your list.
Greg: I only could think of two.
Russ: Let's see them.

Greg took Russ over to his desk, where he had written two words on his celebration list:

1. *Rainbow*
2. *Oshun*

The story had mentioned a rainbow, so Russ decided to ask Greg about that.

Russ: The story talks about a rainbow. Did you see something like that?
Greg: Well, it wasn't a triple rainbow like in the story, but I'm pretty sure it was a double rainbow.
Russ: Sounds neat. Tell me about it.
Greg: Well, I stay for EDP [Extended Day Program] every day because my dad works late. He came to pick me up and we went outside and it was real dark, like it was going to rain again. Anyway, we were driving home and we went over the hill on Grandview Road when we saw it.
Russ: What did it look like?
Greg: Well, it was a weird rainbow. It was real fat and real bright; not like most rainbows that are sort of shimmery and don't last long. This one was short, fat, and bright. You could see every color in it. And the weirdest part was that it had a black cloud behind it, a real dark black cloud that made it look even brighter. My dad pulled the car off the side of the road and we just sat there and looked at it for a couple minutes.

Russ: Greg, that sounds like something to celebrate.

Clearly, Greg had a great story here; the question was how to help him convert this oral story into writing. Greg seemed to have forgotten about the bathroom, an indication that he was willing to try to write something. Russ considered several possibilities, keeping at the forefront of his decision-making his knowledge of the student's ability and the nature of the writing assignment.

Using Greg's situation as an example, here are the available options for scaffolding the move from oral to written language. They are arranged from least supportive intervention to most supportive intervention.

1. If Russ is confident that Greg can now write this story after having told it aloud, he can simply say, "Greg, you have a wonderful story for a celebration there; go ahead and write it down."
2. If he feels that Greg needs a little more support than this, he might "say back" the story. In the Say Back strategy, Russ would merely restate the story so that Greg could hear it before he begins to write. It is a form of oral rehearsal for the writing activity.
3. If Russ is worried that Greg's writing is blocked because of too great a concern about spelling, he might choose to write down a few key words from Greg's story. In this story, the words *shimmery, bright, Grandview Road, weird*, and *cloud* might be chosen. Writing these words for Greg not only helps him with spelling, but also provides some reminders about key details in the story.
4. If the concern about Greg's writing extends beyond spelling to concerns about organization, Russ might help Greg build an organizational web for his story. By asking a series of questions related to the structure of the story, he can help Greg organize his thoughts. For this story he might ask

   • What is this story about?
   • How does the story begin?
   • What happened next?
   • Then what happened?
   • How did the story end?
   • Why would you say this story is a cause for celebration?

   As Greg answers the questions, Russ constructs a web (see Figure 9.2) for him to use in writing his story. Here, too, key words are recorded that help with spelling and memory.
5. Finally, if the interventions above do not enable Greg to get words on paper, Russ could have Greg dictate part or all of the story. As he

Figure 9.2 Web for Greg's Story

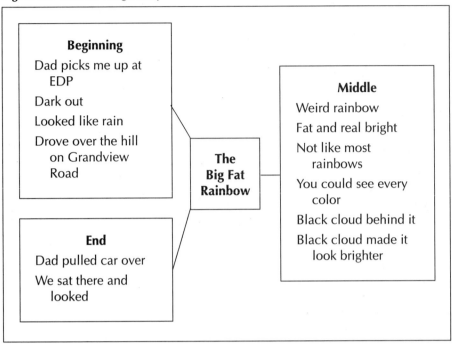

dictates, Russ takes down exactly what Greg says, so that it remains his story (see also Chapter 7). Teachers must use their best judgment as to whether to write down the entire story or turn the pencil over to the student after getting a good start. The key here is helping the child learn that what is said can be written down and that what the student says is worthy of being written down.

By using one of the strategies above, the thoughtful teacher can help a struggling learner build writing skills on the foundation of oral language.

Instructional Strategies

Strategic Writing Instruction

Writers need a variety of strategies to help them move productively and successfully through the writing process. These strategies are similar for all writers: skilled, average, and struggling. For the struggling writer, however, instruction in these strategies must be insistent, consistent, and persistent. Collins (1999) has suggested an instructional design for teaching struggling writers to take a strategic approach to writing.

Supporting Struggling Readers and Writers

1. Identify a strategy worth teaching.
2. Introduce the strategy by modeling it.
3. Help students try out the strategy in a writer's workshop.
4. Help students move toward independence in the use of the strategy through repeated practice.

This focused and systematic approach should be applied to all the instructional strategies discussed below. As with all the other strategies we have described in this book, teachers should pay particular attention to the importance of modeling for struggling writers. By actually showing students how to use a particular strategy, the teacher helps the student create a mental picture of how it works. Of course, the modeling also demonstrates for the student that all writers, even the teacher, need to use strategies to guide their writing.

Finding a Topic

> "The best books come from someplace deep inside."
> —Judy Blume

While discussing with the classroom teacher a recent writing workshop lesson that Russ had observed, the focus moved to two students who seemed to have trouble settling down to the writing task. The conversation went something like this:

Teacher: Sometimes during writer's workshop, those two are right on task. They have produced some good writing. Other times, like today, I have trouble keeping them focused.
Russ: What have you noticed about the times when they were on task?
Teacher: They were writing about something they really cared about.
Russ: So, you have your answer.
Teacher: But I give them lots of choice in their writing now.
Russ: Yes, you do. Perhaps what these students need is instruction in how to make good choices of things to write about.

No teacher who has ever attempted to get a young struggling writer to put pencil to paper can fail to recognize the plaintive cry: "I don't know what to write about." Students, and especially struggling writers, tend to think of writing topics either as something mundane, like My Trip to Disney World, or something grand, rooted in television or the movies: The Aliens Who Came to Earth. Teachers need to help children discover what it is they have to write about. This discovery process takes time. Students need to learn to look inside themselves to find where the stories reside. They need to learn, and to believe, that they have something to say and that that something is not a reworked version of a cartoon show they saw on television. Writing is first and foremost about communication. Once students view writing as an opportunity to communicate their unique experience to others, stories will pour out of them the way they often pour out of our parents and grandparents around a dinner table.

A good place for students to begin their search for writing topics is their writer's notebook, or as some teachers call it, their idea journal. This type of journal is a repository for brief writings and musings called *quick-writes*, where the young author can gather ideas in the same way professional authors gather ideas. Authors such as Calkins (1991), Bomer (1995), and Fletcher (1996) have been advocates for the use of some type of writer's journal. Regardless of what it is called, the idea journal or writer's notebook is uniquely useful in helping struggling writers develop fluency through short, focused writing experiences. After numerous journal entries have been recorded, it becomes a place where teacher and student can look together to find writing topics.

Here's how to introduce this sort of journal to students:

1. Make a list on the board of things that you know a great deal about, explaining to students that writers need to write about things they know well.

2. Ask the students to make a similar list in their journals.
3. Tell the students that this is not a list of topics, but simply a list from which a topic could grow. For example, "baseball" might be on Russ's list because he knows a lot about baseball, but the topic he wants to write about might be the time he played baseball in the snow.
4. Ask the students to choose one thing from their list and use it to decide on a topic.
5. Do a ten-minute quickwrite on the topic in the journal—teacher as well as students.
6. Allow for a brief sharing period so students can see what others are writing about; this may cause them to add items to their own Things I Can Write About list.

Some students have difficulty moving from the list of Things I Can Write About to a topic. The teacher must guide these students toward a topic focused enough for a quickwrite. Russ shows us one way this can be done:

David: I don't know what to write.
Russ: Well, David, let's have a look at your list. I see several things on here. What is jumping out at you right now?
David: Losing Teeth.
Russ: OK, let's focus on losing teeth. How many teeth have you lost?
David: I don't know. About six. I always get five dollars for a loose tooth.
Russ: Wow! I used to get a dime.
David: Yeah, but one time I got ten dollars.
Russ: Ten dollars. Why was that time so special?
David: Well, I lost two teeth at one time.
Russ: David, I think we have found a topic. Why don't you try a quick-write on the time you lost two teeth at the same time?

This was enough to give David a jump start. He went on for several minutes to write the comical story of losing two teeth at once in a wrestling match with his dad.

After the journal has been introduced and students are familiar with quickwrites, virtually everything that happens in the classroom can become the focus for a quickwrite. Sometimes students may write in response to literature. For example, after reading *Knots on a Counting Rope* by Bill Martin, Jr,. and John Archambault, a book that features a story told over and over again by grandfather to grandson, teachers might sit in a circle with their students and tell family stories, stories that are known because they have been told over and over. After the oral storytelling, everyone might do a quickwrite. Another time Cynthia Rylant's *Every Living Thing* might serve as the impetus for a quickwrite on how an animal has touched the students' lives.

Students can do quickwrites about incidents in the cafeteria or on the playground. They can do a quickwrite in response to a special assembly program. They can interview grandparents, neighbors, and friends. They can look at pictures and tell what they see or make up a story to fit the picture. In short, teachers can awaken students to all the possibilities for communication and encourage students to record observations and thoughts about them in an idea journal. Throughout these activities, teachers must help developing writers realize that they do indeed have something to write about and that what they have to write about comes from inside.

Once students have made a number of entries in their idea journals, they are ready to craft a piece of writing. In Lucy Calkins's (1991) words, this is the time to "nudge" the students toward a writing project. Start by asking the students to reread their journals. Have them try to identify an entry that they like best, one that has particular meaning. Next, help them to find connections between this important entry and other entries. The search is for something that really matters to the student: a theme that resonates throughout the journal, a writing topic that is so engaging that the student will be able to experience the kind of flow described in Chapter 2. This is where the nudge comes in. We must help students identify this personal "understory" and nudge them toward developing a project around it.

Teachers can begin this nudge by opening up their own idea journals and sharing entries with the students. Russ recently went through his journal and then discussed his insights with a group of students as a means of helping them discover the underlying story in their own journal entries. As he describes it,

> I noticed that many of my entries dealt with waiting for my father for one thing or another when I was a child. The entries included a time when, waiting for my dad to come home to dinner, I sat looking out the big picture window in our dining room, watching car headlights and trying to predict which ones might be from my father's car. Another entry had me standing on the basketball court during a lineup for a free throw and scanning the stands to see if my father had arrived yet. I shared these vignettes with my students and said that I had discovered a topic for my writing project. I thought I would try a poem called, "Waiting for Daddy." This poem would explore my feelings about my own dad, who often worked long hours and missed many dinners.

We can see from this example that the teacher must guide student choice by helping students find those topics that truly matter. When children are helped to focus on what really matters to them, deeply and personally, and when they come to realize that these deep personal feelings are the best place to search for topics, they can be freed from the concern over what to write about.

Determining the Form, and Shaping the Writing: The Mentor Text

Once children have discovered *what* they want to write about, they need to decide *how* they are going to write about it. Many options are open to them. A topic may lend itself to a short story, a memoir, a poem, a persuasive essay, a letter, a report, or other possibilities. For example, a student who has found a recurring theme in his journal entries related to his pet Labrador retriever might choose to have the dog be a character in a story, write a memoir of an experience with the dog, write a dog poem, write a letter to the editor of the local newspaper arguing for responsible dog ownership, or do a report on the proper care and feeding of Labrador retrievers. Another student who has discovered a number of entries related to playing soccer might decide to write a picture book about a soccer game, relate a funny incident that happened at soccer practice, or write an explanation of the rules of soccer for a soccer novice. A third student who discovers lots of journal entries relating to battles with an older sibling might want to write a story about two sisters struggling to get along in a family, a poem that voices her feelings about the problem, or a report on the causes of sibling rivalry.

Whatever the choice, the student will need some guidelines to help shape the writing. For struggling writers, especially, these guidelines need to be clear and concrete. One way to accomplish this is to direct the students to *mentor texts*. A mentor text is simply an example of writing in the mode the student has chosen. Students opting to write factual reports might be directed to feature articles clipped from newspapers or magazines. Students interested in writing poetry should be directed to a variety of poems and poetic forms, especially nonrhyming types of poetry. A student who wishes to write a picture book must investigate a variety of picture books. Other writers might want to look at editorials, letters to the editor, plays, diaries, and other resources.

The teacher's role during this part of writing instruction continues to be that of facilitator. The teacher provides mini-lessons that demonstrate the various genres available to the writer. Well-chosen picture books, poems, and feature articles presented through book talks and read-alouds can help children see the many shapes their writing can take. A special section of the classroom library can be set aside for exemplars of the various types of writing, labeled for easy access. In conference, the teacher helps students explore the various options for their topics, suggests some possible forms for the writing, and steers the students to relevant mentor texts. The mentor text provides the struggling writer with a map of the possibilities for the writing. This map forms a foundation for building a topic into an extended piece of writing. Wendy Katz uses mentor texts regularly in her sixth-grade classroom. Following is an account of her experiences:

Mentoring is an essential part of teaching. We look to the more experienced teachers to guide us in our work. Students also need to look to mentors to help them be successful. In the writing workshop in my classroom, students look to published authors and students who can help them to create pieces of writing. With every writing unit that we do, my students are introduced to writers who are published in that particular genre.

This year my students took on the writing challenge of creating picture books. Before we even thought about writing, students sat and read picture books and identified what they saw the authors or illustrators doing with their words or pictures. We talked about the craft of the writing and the possible authors' intentions behind the writing.

After reading for roughly three days and categorizing the types of picture books, we discussed how we could model our own writing after some of the amazing picture books we had read. As a part of the writing process, students chose a "seed," or topic they wanted to focus on and nurtured their idea in a writer's notebook. From that nurturing, they determined what type of picture book they were interested in writing and for their mentors, turned to the picture books we had read.

Mentors were chosen on the basis of a variety of criteria. Some students chose books because they liked the craft that the author used, such as repetition or simile; others chose books because they were writing about a similar topic. After a mentor was chosen, students reread the picture book and made a list of "noticings," crafting techniques that the author had used in the writing. Using this list, the students continued to nurture their seeds by trying to write like their mentor.

Although some people believe that all writing has to be unique, I believe that all writing builds upon what we know to be good writing. Therefore, when we write, we model our own style after writers we have read. The use of mentors allows students to write about their own thoughts or ideas by building on the shoulders of accomplished writers: their style, structure, or crafting techniques.

While writing feature articles, we created the following list of things to think about when choosing a mentor:

How Do I Choose a Mentor Piece?

1. Read the piece, and make sure you understand it.
2. Reread the piece, and think through the following questions:
   - Am I writing in this genre?
   - Do I like this piece of writing?
   - Do I notice the author doing any crafting techniques? (If so, be sure to write them down in the form of a list.)
   - Do I like the author's use of crafting techniques?
   - Do I like the structure of the piece?
   - Can I model my writing after this piece?

Developing Topics into Stories, Poems, and Reports

Framing Stories

Most teachers know numerous prewriting strategies. Activities such as brainstorming, outlining, and creating webs are used to help students gather and organize their thoughts before drafting a story. For struggling writers such strategies may not be enough. These students may require another level of structure to plan and develop their written drafts—they may need to consider the specific elements of their story.

Many teachers introduce students to the concept of story elements—setting, characters, problem/goal, plot, resolution—in the context of reading instruction (see Chapter 8). Read-alouds, guided reading, and literature circles afford excellent opportunities for students to learn about story elements. Once students have a good working knowledge of story elements in their reading, teachers can help them apply this knowledge to their writing. A planning sheet like the one shown in Figure 9.3 serves much the same purpose in writing as it does in reading: it encourages students to carefully consider and think through their stories. The plan makes it easier for struggling writers to keep their story draft focused and helps them develop the story beyond simple initiating and ending events. Students should be encouraged, through peer and teacher conferences, to fill out the planning sheet as completely as possible. Asking students to "talk through" the story using the planning sheet as a guide can alert them to missing information. This oral rehearsal may also help students get words down on paper as they begin drafting.

Composing Poems

Because it is usually a short form of writing, and because it does not make as many demands on knowledge of sentence structure and mechanics, poetry is a good choice of expression for struggling writers. However, two problems exist in the teaching of poetry writing. The first problem is with rhyming. Most children, and many adults, equate poetry with rhyme.

Figure 9.3 Story Planning Guide

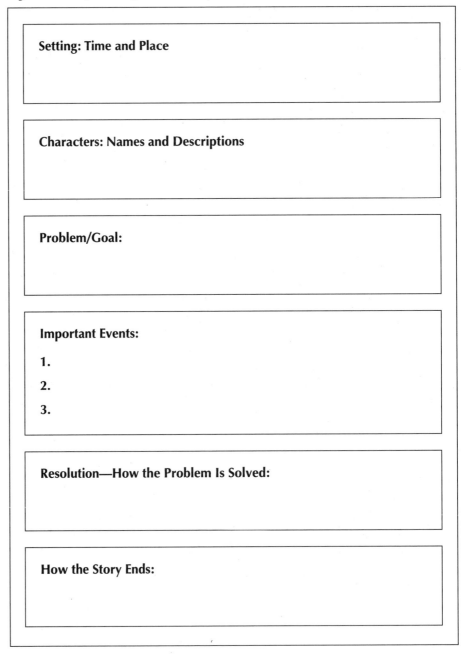

Setting: Time and Place

Characters: Names and Descriptions

Problem/Goal:

Important Events:

1.

2.

3.

Resolution—How the Problem Is Solved:

How the Story Ends:

Unfortunately, writing rhyming poetry that maintains meter—the rhythmical pattern in verse—and meaning is a task that even the most skilled young writers find daunting. For this reason, we recommend avoiding rhyming poetry for writing instruction. The second problem is form. Many teachers limit their poetry instruction to cinquains, diamantes, haiku, and the like. Although there is certainly nothing wrong with form in poetry, and these forms have a certain utility, the formula the students are to follow often takes precedence over the message the author would like to communicate. Therefore, we recommend teaching children to write free verse.

Begin by reading and showing students numerous free-verse poems; a good book to start with is Deborah Chandra's *Balloons*. Read these poems to the students and display them on chart paper or the overhead. Discuss what makes free verse true poetry: the use of similes, metaphors, imagery, and alliteration. Show students that poetry is condensed language, in which small words are sometimes left out. Point out how free verse moves down the page and not across the page like a story. Discuss how the poem is arranged on the page. (Why did the poet place the line break there?) Gather a file of free-verse poetry that students can use as mentor texts. (For an in-depth look at mentor poems, see Flynn and McPhillips 2000.)

Once students have been exposed to free-verse poetry they are ready to try it. A free-verse poem can start from a quickwrite or other journal entry, or any short piece of prose. Often we tell students to close their eyes and picture a movie running in their mind's eye. We ask them to stop the movie, focus on the image they see, and then open their eyes and write a two- or three-sentence description of it. This brief prose piece becomes the raw material to be crafted into a poem.

Once the prose piece is on paper the student can go to work to craft a poem. The steps that follow will help students create a free-verse poem:

1. Rearrange the sentences so that they move down the page.
2. Guide the reader to read the poem the way you want it to be read by deciding where the line breaks should be.
3. Take out any extra or unneeded words or replace weak words with more powerful words. Remember: Poetry is condensed language.
4. Add images to your poem. Try to use metaphors, similes, and powerful verbs and adjectives to create a picture in your reader's mind.
5. Take your rough draft to a partner. What suggestions does your partner have? Look at some sample free-verse poems. What would you like to change in your poem?
6. Revise your poem.

Free verse can free struggling writers to create successful communication.

Writing Reports: The I-Search Paper

Of all the scary writing assignments that confront the struggling writer, perhaps the scariest is the research report. Oftentimes, the struggling writer is also a struggling reader, so the idea of gathering information from a variety of print sources and then somehow weaving that information into a coherent report that is written "in your own words" is truly intimidating.

Students, struggling and otherwise, often resort to copying something out of the encyclopedia. The entire exercise ends up as unsatisfactory, for both student and teacher.

Macrorie (1980) suggests a remedy, the I-Search paper. As the name implies, the I-Search paper encourages young writers to search their own interests and knowledge, and to use a variety of sources—print and non-print—to create a successful piece of research.

The outline that follows describes an instructional plan for helping struggling young learners write an I-Search report. As we discussed earlier in the chapter, start by modeling all the processes using an example of personal interest.

1. *Topic Selection.* Good I-Search projects evolve from the genuine interests and needs of authors. Planning family vacations, investigating hobbies, learning about careers, and studying the needs of pets all make good topics for I-Search papers. When Russ models his topic choice for students, he thinks aloud, talking about his childhood interest in collecting baseball cards, about his mother throwing out all his baseball cards, and about his interest in how baseball cards have changed over the years since he was a boy. To help students, talk to them and help them find topics they are passionate about and are interested in researching. The idea journal may contain the seeds of a good I-Search topic.

2. *What I Already Know.* Direct students' attention to the I-Search Planning Sheet (see Figure 9.4). After demonstrating the process, have students brainstorm a list of everything they know about their topic.

3. *What I Want to Find Out.* This is a key column for the I-Search plan. Students must be able to identify their personal need for doing this I-Search. Again, modeling is important. Russ, for example, points out to students that his first column shows that he knows a great deal about baseball cards from many years ago, but not much about modern-day baseball cards. So, he wants to know about that. Have students identify what they would like to find out and fill in the column.

4. *How I Will Find It Out.* As students move to this column, they should be encouraged to think of a wide variety of sources. For example, on his planning sheet Russ identifies student collectors, card collector magazines, card dealers, Web sites, and even his mother as possible sources.

5. *What I Learned.* Finally, students conduct their research and complete the final column on the planning sheet. Keeping the report to a fairly short length (two to three pages) makes the task more manageable for students and reduces the temptation to copy.

Once students have completed their research and the four columns of the planning sheet are filled in, it is time to write the research report.

Figure 9.4 I-Search Planning Sheet

What I Know	What I Want to Find Out	How I Will Find Out	What I Learned

Adapted from K. Macrorie. 1980. *The I-Search Paper.* Portsmouth, NH: Heinemann; and D. Ogle. 1986. "K-W-L: A Teaching Model That Develops Action Reading of Expository Text." *The Reading Teacher* 40: 564–570.

Macrorie (1980) suggests that students write the report in a language and style that is comfortable and natural, not stiff and formal. The I-Search Planning Sheet provides the scaffold for the writing, and the report follows this general outline:

1. What I Knew
2. Why I'm Writing This Report
3. The Search (the story of how I got the information)
4. What I Learned

Students should also be required to make a list of the sources they used to get their information: interview, informal conversation, Web site, book, or other. Asking them to follow a simple works cited format for this purpose works well.

Revising

Of all the aspects of the writing process, students probably have the most difficulty with revision. This is doubly true for struggling writers. Getting a first draft down on paper is hard enough; it is not surprising that they are reluctant to revisit the writing to make it better. Struggling students often do not see the need to revise, or are hesitant to acknowledge it, knowing well the difficulties that revising may cause them. Even when they do recognize the need, they may feel powerless to do anything about it.

Teachers can help students become aware of the need to revise by guiding them to reflect on their writing and assess its effect on the reader: "Will the reader understand this? Will this make sense to the reader? What do I need to add to help the reader make sense?" As students learn to step back and put themselves in the role of audience they learn to spot "holes" that may trip up the reader, resulting from confusing or missing information. The monitoring for meaning that students engage in during guided silent reading and literature circles is good preparation (see Chapter 5). Also, teachers can model the process through think-alouds with their own writing, or by sharing their writing with the class and asking students if they have any questions. Suggesting that students read their pieces aloud to themselves often makes it easier for them to assume the role of listener and detect problem areas.

Once struggling writers are aware that their writing can profit from revision, they need the necessary support to make it happen. Two key points must be kept in mind. First, teachers should not expect students to correct everything that needs work on a particular piece of writing but should be satisfied with one or two targeted revisions. We must remember that the goal is to help the writer write better, not make the writing perfect. Second, teachers must give students specific strategies that will help them revise and make the revision task seem less overwhelming.

One reason students struggle with revision is that it is difficult to know exactly what to do. Directions that tell them to read over their story to see what they left out or to see how they could add detail are too vague. Specific, easy-to-apply strategies such as those below help struggling writers feel like revision is something they can do.

Drop a Bomb

Once students have begun to develop a reflective stance, the question becomes, "Do I have to recopy my whole story to add this part in?" Struggling writers are loath to recopy work that has, after all, demanded so much effort in the first place. The Drop a Bomb strategy is popular with students for just this reason—recopying is not necessary. The extra material is added to the text by simply "dropping a bomb" on an open area of the paper, such as a margin or space at the end of the story, and then drawing a line to the text location where it should be inserted (see Figure 9.5).

When students realize that revision does not mean rewriting, they are much more willing to consider changes to the text. Indeed, after a recent introduction to this strategy, students in one third-grade class were dropping bombs all over their stories.

Figure 9.5 Teacher Modeling of the Drop a Bomb Strategy

> Over the Christmas holidays, I had an exciting adventure. My brother and I drove a moving van all the way to Florida. The trip down would take three days. I had not spent that much time with my brother since I was sixteen. My brother and I had never been really close, so I was wondering how this would all turn out.
>
> > We were moving my parents to their new retirement home in Clearwater.

Box and Explode

Barry Lane (1993) suggests this strategy in his excellent book on revision, *After the End*. The strategy is a good one to use when students write stories in which every incident is given equal weight. This is a problem for many novice writers. Stories lack focus and tend to read like a laundry list of linked sentences starting, "And then . . ." Here is a brief example of such a story.

The Scary Ride

My family and I went to Great Adventure. We drove a long time to get there. After we got there my little sister was hungry so we had to stop and have lunch before we even went on any rides. After lunch, we went on lots of rides. My dad and I like the roller coasters the best. We went on Rolling Thunder, Runaway Railroad and Scream Machine. The best roller coaster of all was the Batman. The line was real long. Finally, we got on. It was real scary.

I wanted to go on Batman again, but my mom said my little sister was too tired, so we had to go home.

This story is an excellent candidate for the Box and Explode strategy. Lane suggests telling students that Box and Explode is like using the slow-motion button on a video camera. The object is to slow down the motion at the most important point of the story, to draw the reader in. In the story above, riding the Batman roller coaster is clearly the high point of the story, yet the author has given it roughly the same weight as stopping for lunch. A conference to help the student expand this part of the story might go like this:

Teacher: What do you want the reader to know after reading this story?
Student: About my trip to Great Adventure.
Teacher: I notice that you called the story "The Scary Ride."
Student: Yeah, the Batman ride was the best!
Teacher: So the Batman ride is important to your story.
Student: That was the best part.
Teacher: Put a box around the part about the Batman ride. What do you notice?
Student: I didn't say much about it.
Teacher: What else could you say?
Student: Well, I guess I could talk about what makes it so scary.
Teacher: Sounds like a good idea. Try to explode this part of the story.

Box and Explode usually takes more room than the Drop a Bomb strategy. Still, it is important to make students feel that they don't need to do a lot of recopying. Simply have them tape the exploded segment onto the rough draft, where it can be added later.

Powerful Verbs

Joan Warner, a third-grade teacher, noticed that her students overused the verb *went* in their stories. She devised this mini-lesson to help students use more powerful verbs in their writing.

First, Joan put the following paragraph on chart paper and called the students over to the meeting area:

Last week my family and I went to Grandma's house. We went in our new car. While we were there we went into Grandma's attic. My brother and I went up a ladder. It was scary in the attic. There were lots of cobwebs and the light went on and off. We found an old trunk. A piece of rope went all around the trunk. We wondered what was inside.

Joan said to the students, "I reread this piece and realized that I had used *went* too much. Can you help me brainstorm a list of words that have a similar meaning as *went*, but might make my story more powerful?"

Joan then recorded the students' words on the chart. Next, she used their words and a few she added herself to revise the paragraph as

Last week my family and I traveled to Grandma's house. We drove in our new car. While we were there we sneaked into Grandma's attic.

My brother and I climbed up a ladder. It was scary in the attic. There were lots of cobwebs and the light flickered on and off. We found an old trunk. A piece of rope wound all around the trunk. We wondered what was inside.

After rereading the story aloud, Joan discussed with the students how these verbs improved the story. She helped them to see that well-chosen verbs can vivify writing. As a follow-up Joan told the students to return to their seats, find a place in one of their stories where they used *went*, and try to replace it with a more powerful verb. In case students couldn't find an example in their own writing, Joan had on hand a few sentences with *went* for them to use. Later, during their share time, students talked about the revisions they had made using the strategy.

Editing

Struggling writers are often identified by the difficulties they have with spelling, mechanics, and grammar. It is vital that teachers devise strategies that help struggling writers improve the technical correctness of their writing. This can be a difficult proposition. The teacher emphasizes technical correctness at the risk of having struggling writers "shut down" with frustration at their lack of ability to control spelling and mechanics. Yet, a failure to emphasize these aspects of writing is also a disservice to the child who, after all, needs to have spelling and mechanical aspects of writing under control to become a fluid and fluent writer. Also, the teacher may find that there is pressure from parents, colleagues, and administrators to "teach these kids correct spelling and punctuation."

The key concept for productive editing with struggling writers is focus. Focus on a few misspellings; focus on a narrow range of mechanical and grammatical concerns. Focus on those aspects of correctness that the student *can* bring under control. The instructional design for this focused editing instruction will include small-group mini-lessons, targeted editing checklists, peer editing, and teacher editing.

Small-Group Mini-Lessons

In any fourth-grade classroom there will be a group of students who have full command and control of capitalization, another group who has pretty good control of capitalization, and a group who struggles with capitalization. These students don't all need a mini-lesson on capitalization, but clearly the third group does. Teachers need to take time, during writer's workshop, while most of the class is working on their writing, to present brief, targeted lessons for those who struggle with aspects of grammar and mechanics. Providing immediate feedback on the targeted skill will enhance the effect of these lessons. For example, the teacher who has just presented a small-group mini-lesson on capitalization might say to the students, "Now I want you to return to your seats, take out a draft you are working on, and read it over to check for correct capitalization. I will be coming around to see how you are doing." Note that this follow-up is rooted in the student's own writing and not on a capitalization worksheet.

Targeted Editing Checklists

For students who have the basics of spelling, grammar, and mechanics fairly well under control, an editing checklist of six or eight items may be reasonable. For the struggling writer, lengthy editing checklists are overwhelming and dispiriting. Checklists for struggling writers should focus on no more than three or four items (see Figure 9.6). The choice of what goes on the checklist should be guided by what is possible for the students and what has been the subject of recent mini-lessons. For example, after a mini-lesson on capitalization, a teacher would want the list to include checking for correct capitalization. Directions on checklists should be narrow, clear, and most of all, something that the struggling writer can handle. Rather than having a checklist that says "Check for capitalization," the list might read, "Did I capitalize the first word of each

Figure 9.6 Editing Checklist

Read over your story and make sure that you can answer these questions with a *yes*. Then take your work to a friend and have that person check your story using the same questions. Your partner must put checks in the blank spaces and sign your editing checklist. Staple this sheet to your rough draft.

	Me Yes	Partner Yes
1. Do all sentences start with a capital?	_____	_____
2. Do all sentences end with a period, question mark, or exclamation point?	_____	_____
3. Are misspelled words circled?	_____	_____
4. Are apostrophes used correctly in contractions (can't) and possessives (Roy's toy)?	_____	_____

My Initials _____

Partner's Initials _____

new sentence?" Checklists should also change as student abilities and teacher targets change.

Peer Editing

Students in grades 3 through 6 are often quite good at helping each other edit, particularly if the editing is narrowly focused. Peer editing should take place only after the individual author has done an initial edit guided by a checklist. As Figure 9.6 illustrates, the same checklist is used for the peer-editing conference. Including a space for the peer editor to sign encourages editors to take the task seriously.

Early in the year, teachers need to provide mini-lessons on proper peer-editing etiquette and procedures. It is also a good idea to occasionally have two students role play an exemplary peer-editing conference while the rest of the class observes and takes notes. A debriefing session with the class after the role play will help students focus on how successful peer-editing conferences are held. Occasionally, teachers must also sit down with a pair of peer editors and help them negotiate the process.

The Teacher Edit

We each present workshops for teachers on writing instruction, and a consistent and persistent question is, "Is it okay to display student work that has misspellings and mechanical errors?" Generally when teachers ask this question they are concerned with the response of parents and administrators to "final drafts" that are still littered with errors. However, another player in this public display needs to be considered—the student. Every student, from the budding Hemingway to the most struggling writer in the room, deserves to have published work displayed. The major motivation for taking a story through the writing process to publication is the opportunity to share it with others and to be celebrated for one's efforts. For the struggling writer, however, this celebration is fraught with peril. Despite the best of efforts, a struggling writer's published piece is sure to expose deficiencies to the world. Students do not deserve to have their lack of knowledge on display for all to see.

Clearly, this creates a dilemma for the teacher: how to provide for the celebration that every writer deserves and yet protect the struggling writers as they continue to develop command of the written language? The problem can be resolved through the teacher edit.

The teacher edit takes place after the writer has finished a personal edit and a peer edit. The teacher edit prepares the paper for publication. It is conducted side by side with the student, but it is not a time for lengthy teaching of skills. During the teacher edit, the teacher corrects mechanical and spelling errors while explaining to the student why the changes are necessary. The tone of the teacher edit is cheerful and upbeat. The writer should get the message that they have done a good job preparing the manuscript and that this final edit will clean up the piece for publication. It is important to remember all the good teaching and learning that has taken place before this. The teacher edit simply fills in gaps in the student's knowledge so that the published piece can be displayed.

The Special Case of Spelling

Students who struggle with spelling need the kind of developmentally appropriate instruction described in Chapter 6 so that they can increase their knowledge of how words work and expend less energy on this aspect of their writing. However, word knowledge develops over time, and struggling writers need to be able to cope with the problems associated with being poor spellers on a daily basis. They must bring two things to the editing process to improve the spelling of a piece: (1) a spelling conscience, and (2) a knowledge of tools that can help with spelling.

A *spelling conscience* is the awareness that spelling does indeed matter and that correct spelling enhances the communicative effect of the writing. Teachers help students develop a spelling conscience by sending consistent messages that spelling matters and by holding students accountable for correct spelling of *all the words they know how to spell*. A student who can spell the word *they* out of context must be held responsible for correctly spelling *they* in a composition. Although struggling writers may correctly spell many of the words that occur frequently in their reading and writing, they may need to have others, such as *because, where,* and even *done* reinforced. Students should be taught these words a few at a time and be held accountable for them. When lists of high-frequency words that students have trouble spelling are displayed in the room and/or in a student's personal dictionary, students with a spelling conscience can use them to check their spelling while they are writing and when they are editing.

Holding students accountable for high-frequency words does not preclude allowing them to construct temporary spellings for less frequently used words. It is important that students use constructed spellings so they can continue the flow of writing without stopping every few lines to look up a word. The writer with a spelling conscience, however, checks the spelling of these words during editing.

Many tools beyond the dictionary are available for the struggling speller. We discussed some of these earlier in the chapter: index cards or bookmarks with high-frequency words, a personal dictionary, and handheld spell-checkers. In addition, if a student is composing on a word processor, of course, the spell-check feature is readily available. Spell-check is actually an excellent teaching tool, because it typically gives the student an array of choices for correcting a spelling. A word of caution here: the spell-check does not check meaning, so mistakes such as misused homophones—words that are pronounced alike but have different spellings and different meanings (*there, they're, their*)—pass unnoticed. The classroom is another good resource for spelling when words are displayed on word walls and when story maps and charts relevant to what is being studied are readily available. Moreover, classmates and the teacher are at hand to offer assistance.

The dictionary, too, is a valuable though sometimes difficult-to-use tool for the struggling writer. When a student needs to look up a word, teachers should view it as a teachable moment. Teachers must not abandon the struggling writer with a curt suggestion to "Look it up." Many struggling writers have trouble navigating the dictionary. A better response is to say, "Let's look that up." In this way teacher and student can explore the skills needed for finding a word quickly and efficiently in a dictionary. Making sure that the classroom reference area includes several types of dictionaries—some easier, some more comprehensive—is also beneficial.

Assessment Strategies

The best assessment for struggling writers is one that supports their efforts to improve at writing without penalizing them for what they have not yet learned to do. Assessment should acknowledge what novice writers are doing well while helping them make informed decisions about what they need to work on. In this section, we will suggest that the best way to accomplish an assessment that improves a struggling writer's performance is through classroom criteria charts and student self-assessment.

Criteria Charts

Criteria charts, or rubrics, are relatively easy to make and extraordinarily useful as assessment tools for students. The best way to construct a criteria chart is in collaboration with the entire class. After several weeks of writing instruction, the teacher might ask the students in the classroom two questions: (1) What do good writers do? and (2) What makes writing good? As students raise their hands to contribute, the teacher records their ideas on chart paper, clarifies the students' comments, and contributes his or her own responses to the question. The results of one such brainstorming session follow:

What Do Good Writers Do? What Makes Writing Good?
beginning, middle, end
choose a good topic
write about what they know
start sentences in different ways
use powerful verbs

use revision strategies
confer with the teacher
confer with other students
make several drafts
check spelling
check for capitals at the beginning of sentences
use lots of details
write neatly
keep a journal
make sense
share what they write

Student responses will fall into three categories: writing process; the qualities of good writing; and grammar, spelling, and mechanics. The teacher ends the brainstorming session by asking the students which of the items on the list deal with the writing process (WP); which deal with the qualities of good writing (Q); and which deal with grammar, mechanics, and spelling (GMS). Each of the items on the criteria chart is then labeled appropriately. The teacher recopies the criteria chart, organizing it into the categories cited above, for display in the classroom. Following is an example of a completed criteria chart:

**Classroom Writing Criteria Chart
(What Do Good Writers Do?)**

Writing Process
- Choose a good topic
- Keep a journal
- Confer with the teacher
- Confer with other students
- Use revision strategies
- Make several drafts
- Share what they write

Qualities of Good Writing
- Include beginning, middle, end
- Start sentences in different ways
- Use powerful verbs
- Use lots of details
- Make sure it makes sense

Grammar, Mechanics, Spelling
- Check spelling
- Check for capitals at beginning of sentences
- Write neatly

Figure 9.7 Student Self-Evaluation T-Chart

Things I Am Doing Well in Writing	One Thing I Need to Work On

Student Self-Assessment

Once the criteria chart has been incorporated into the classroom environment, it is relatively easy to start students on productive self-assessment. The teacher gives each student a self-assessment T-chart (see Figure 9.7). On the left-hand side the students write things that they do well in writing—at least one thing for each of the three criteria chart categories. On the right-hand side the students write one thing, and only one, in each of the categories that needs work. If given a choice, many students who are struggling with literacy would focus only on spelling and mechanics, so the T-chart forces everyone to set a goal in the three areas of process, content, and mechanics. This T-chart is placed in the student's writing folder and referred to over the next several weeks as the teacher helps the student focus on the areas that were identified as needing greater attention.

Teachers who create classroom writing environments that support risk-taking and who model and guide students' learning of effective strategies, encourage and enable all students to become better writers. As reluctant writers increase their competence and confidence during writing workshop, they are likely to become more engaged and less intimidated by the many other literacy tasks they face each day that have a writing component; such involvement is critical to their progress.

PART TWO

STRATEGY BANK

Instruction

A. Interest Surveys for Reading and Writing
B. Paired Script Writing
C. Double-Entry Journals
D. Planning in Departmental/Pullout Programs

Assessment

E. Anecdotal Records
F. Assessing Response Groups
G. Assessing Small Groups with Teacher-Made Tests
H. Assessing Decoding
I. Assessing Fluency

Test Taking

J. Multiple Choice Items
K. Open-Ended Questions
L. Attending to Writing Prompts
M. Making Rubrics Friendly

Home/School Connections

N. Home/School Literature Connections
O. Reading Buddies
P. Home Newsletters
Q. Shared Goals: Parents, Students, Teachers

Professional Development

R. Professional Development Guidelines for Using This Text
S. Preservice Guidelines
T. Peer Coaching
U. Study Groups

What It Does

Interest surveys provide an opportunity for students to identify and teachers to discover information about students' reading and writing interests. They also help students identify possible reading and writing topics, and assist teachers in providing resources and instruction that appeal to students' interests. Knowing that their teachers care about their interests can be highly motivating for some students.

How to Do It

1. Determine the questions that will help you identify your students' interests and preferences for reading and writing activities. Think about the resources available to support student choice and the information you need from students to use those resources most effectively. Your questions should be designed to help you assist your students in making choices they find motivating.
2. Conduct an initial survey early in the school year, so that you can use the information they provide as early as possible. Consult the surveys periodically, particularly when you need information to help a particular student make choices for reading and writing.
3. Allow students to complete the surveys again later in the year to determine whether their preferences and attitudes have changed.
4. Interest surveys may be used to form clubs in which students share and discuss books around a given topic or genre, such as a Mystery Book Club, or a Nature Science Book Club.

What to Look For

1. Are students who struggle less aware of their own interests than other students in the class? Do they report fewer interests?
2. Do students who struggle indicate less positive attitudes about reading and writing than do other students in the class?
3. Are there ways that you can adjust your teaching, your materials, or your assignments to better match the interests of your less motivated students?

For More Information

Worthy, J., M. Moorman, and M. Turner. 1999. "What Johnny Likes to Read Is Hard to Find in School." *Reading Research Quarterly* 34 (1): 12–27.

Routman, R. 1991. *Invitations*. Portsmouth, NH: Heinemann.

Here are some sample surveys.

Reading Survey

1. What are your favorite types of books?
2. Who are your favorite authors?
3. What do you like to read other than books (for example, magazines, comics, newspapers, encyclopedias)?
4. What are you working on to improve in your reading?
5. What do you like least about reading?
6. What are your favorite hobbies, activities, and or sports?
7. What do you know a lot about?
8. Where do you usually get your reading materials?
9. How do you decide which books or materials to read?
10. When and where do you like to read?

Writing Survey

1. What sort of writing do you do at home (for example, e-mail, letters, lists, diary)?
2. What is your favorite kind of writing assignment in school?
3. What are your strengths as a writer?
4. What are you working on to improve in your writing?
5. What do you like least about writing?
6. What topics for writing do you like best?
7. What are your favorite hobbies, activities, and or sports?
8. What topics do you know a lot about?
9. What are your favorite types of books?
10. Who are your favorite authors?

Supporting Struggling Readers and Writers: Strategies for Classroom Intervention 3–6 by Dorothy S. Strickland, Kathy Ganske, and Joanne K. Monroe. Copyright © 2002. Stenhouse Publishers

What It Does

Paired script writing is a highly motivational writing technique that involves creativity, writing, reading, and collaboration. Through a series of script exchanges, students write one character's lines and a partner writes the other. This back-and-forth trading of scripts makes this strategy particularly engaging; students never know what their partner has written until they get the script back. Even struggling writers rarely have trouble thinking of what to write next. In fact, teachers often have to caution students that they have only a few more minutes to end the episode. When complete, students can practice reading their scripts and share them with the class as a readers' theater (see Chapter 7).

How to Do It

1. Explain to students that scripts are dialogues between characters and that they often involve a conflict. Have students brainstorm a list of characters who might have a dilemma. Examples might be a brother and sister, soccer coach and player, dentist and patient, dog and cat, King George of England and a colonist, a pencil and a piece of paper.

2. Choose one of the examples to demonstrate the process of writing a dialogue in script form. Make students aware that after a character's first speech or line, the character's name is abbreviated and just an initial is used, as below:

    Brother:

    Sister:

    B:

    S:

3. Model how to write the dialogue by recording a series of speeches between two characters while describing the process through a think-aloud. As an alternative, you may want to determine the dialogue for just one of the characters and let the students dictate the other character's responses.

4. After several speeches have been recorded for each character, write a speech that will begin to resolve the conflict. Discuss with the class how this can be accomplished, since this is a task they will face with their own scripts. Some form

of closure can usually be brought to the dilemma in two or three exchanges.

5. Ask the students to take out a sheet of paper and write the names of two characters who might have a conflict at the top. Have them circle the one whose lines they will write, and give them time to write that character's first speech, usually two to four lines of text.

6. After students have finished the first speech they should exchange papers with a partner. This works best if it is someone within "handing distance" so students do not have to move around. Although it is not essential for students to give their paper to the same person who gave them one, it is important for individuals to keep the characters they start out with.

7. Continue the exchanges until dilemmas have been resolved, or if necessary, until time runs out.

8. Give the students time to practice reading the scripts with their partner. Although most students do fine with just one copy, they enjoy being able to retain one for themselves.

9. Encourage the students to share their scripts as a readers' theater.

What to Look For

1. Do students begin writing promptly and stay engaged throughout several exchanges?
2. Are they able to resolve the conflicts?
3. What mini-lessons might be beneficial to help students with their script writing?

For More Information

To learn more about readers' theater refer to Chapter 7 and the Resources section of this book.

What It Does

Double-entry journals are journals in which the pages are divided into two columns. In one column students write a quote from their reading; in the other they write their reaction. The use of double-entry journals encourages students to respond to events, characters, or new information in their reading by relating the information to their own lives or the world around them. Although in its truest form an entire journal is devoted to double entries, many teachers combine the use of double-entry responses with other types of written response.

How to Do It

1. Have students divide a page in their reading log into two columns. Have them label the left column "Quote" and the right "Reactions" or "Reflections."
2. As students read, have them select a quote that is of particular interest. Their selection will just as likely be based on *how* the author said something as on *what* the author said. Have them write down the quotation under the Quote column and record the page number where they found it. If they prefer, they may mark the location with a sticky note and record the quote after they complete their reading.
3. Ask students to record their reactions. They might recall a similar experience and tell about it, relate a character's description to one in another book they have read, explain why they chose a particular phrase (simile, metaphor, idiom) and what they think it means, compare a time or location in their reading to another with which they are familiar, and so on.

What to Look For

1. Does the personal response show elaboration, or is the reaction very brief?
2. Over time, is there a pattern to the type of quotes that are selected (for example, focused on characters or phrases, or located at the beginning or end of the assigned reading)?
3. Do your responses to the writing encourage the reluctant student to share more personal reactions?

Variations

This type of journal entry can easily be adapted for content-area use as well as reading, by altering the headings to fit a new purpose. For example, column labels such as the following might be used:

1. "I Predict" and "What Happened"
2. "I Want to Find Out" and "What I Learned"
3. "Math Problem" and "What I Did to Solve It"
4. "What I Thought About the Ending" and "What [peer's name] Thought"
5. "What I Did in the Experiment" and "What I Discovered"
6. "What I Know Already" and "What I Learned"
7. "How the Character Looks" and "What the Characters' Actions Are"

Supporting Struggling Readers and Writers: Strategies for Classroom Intervention 3–6 by Dorothy S. Strickland, Kathy Ganske, and Joanne K. Monroe. Copyright © 2002. Stenhouse Publishers

What It Does

This strategy provides a structure for planning that extends beyond the daily, highly fragmented instruction found in many departmental programs characterized by forty- to fifty-minute periods. By projecting plans for the year, marking period, and week, teachers provide a more comprehensive and cohesive program.

How to Do It

1. *Consider the reading and writing goals for the entire year.* Goals should be based on the literacy standards for your district. In reading, you might want to do an author study, a genre study, an intensive study of a content-area theme related to students' work in science or social studies, and so on. In writing, you might want to study several writing forms: essays, memoirs, and a particular form of poetry. Select one reading and one writing focus for each marking period. Most schools have four marking periods each year. Add some time for work on test-taking strategies such as those outlined in the Assessment section of the Strategy Bank.

2. *Divide an eight-week marking period as follows:*
   Three-Week Unit: Reading Focus (example: biography genre study)
   One Week Unit: Test-Taking Strategy (example: open-ended questions)
   Three-Week Unit: Writing Focus (example: memoir writing)
   One Week Unit: Test-Taking Strategy (example: responding to writing prompts)

3. *Plan for each week.* (A sample outline follows, based on the above examples.)
   I. Weeks 1 through 3: Reading Focus
      A. Select an area of emphasis for the unit.
         Example: Genre study, biographies
      B. Select the materials you will use.
         Example: Choose biographies about people you think the students will be interested in and read portions aloud. You will also need sets of biographies (six to eight books in each set) at various reading levels for small-group instruction and literature circles.

   C. Decide on certain strategies you want to teach through this unit.
      Examples: How the writers of biography reveal character traits of their subjects, how biographers gather information, plus a range of more general comprehension strategies.
   D. Plan assignments.
      Examples: Students write character sketches of someone they know; students interview an older person in their family or in the community and write a brief biography; students read as a whole group or in small groups from biographies they choose from sets of texts the teacher has selected; their reading is guided through prompts given by the teacher; they respond to these in logs and share in group discussions; throughout the unit, specific reading comprehension strategies are taught and applied to texts used in the unit; one mini-reading assignment, such as reading the character sketches, is due at the end of the week and is given each week; and one longer-term culminating activity with some type of response (written, oral, or graphic), is due at the end of the three-week unit. This activity may be a group project.
   II. Week 4: Test-Taking Strategies. Select one of the test-taking strategies offered in the Strategy Bank or some other strategy and work on it over the period of a week.
   III. Weeks 5 through 7: Writing Focus
      A. Select an area of emphasis for the unit.
         Example: Memoir writing
      B. Select the materials you will use.
         Example: Select memoirs and portions of memoirs to read aloud and discuss with the class so that the students will have a clear understanding of what a memoir is.
      C. Decide on specific strategies you want to teach.
         Examples: how to use descriptive language in writing; how to brainstorm memories about an event and use the brainstorming to plan the writing; how to

use a writer's checklist for self-assessment; how to apply specific writing strategies to their memoir writing. Use the unit to focus on any aspect of the writing process or specific writing strategies that you feel your students need to strengthen.

D. Decide on short- and long-term assignments.

Example: three mini-writing assignments due at the end of each week (write about your favorite birthday celebration); one longer-term writing assignment due at the end of the three-week unit. You might wish to connect this assignment with a social studies theme. Students would create a hypothetical character living in a particular period of time or location under study, then write a memoir describing events and scenes from the period and/or place.

IV. Week 8: Test-Taking Strategies. Select one of the test-taking strategies offered in the Strategy Bank or some other strategy and work on it over the period of a week.

4. *Plan for one week within each three-week unit of study*. Note: Each week of the three weeks should be integrated with the others to form a coherent sequence. The point here is to plan in larger chunks than each daily fifty-minute period.

Monday—Introduce texts, writing forms, or strategy under study.

Teacher works with whole group.

Tuesday, Wednesday, Thursday—Follow up to Monday.

Students begin some independent work.

Teacher works with small groups and individuals.

Friday—Review, continue with previous day's work, wrap up, and share.

5. *Grading*. Many teachers assign points to student assignments and grade accordingly. For example, in reading, the following would be assigned points: quality of response logs, participation in literature circles, quality of other types of response such as projects and longer writing

assignments. Students should be aware of the grading system and the fact that they are held accountable. They should be encouraged to seek help when they need it. Small-group and individual instruction offered within the instructional period helps assure students and parents that teachers are attending to individual needs.

What to Look For

1. Is there a sense of continuity and internal integrity to the curriculum?
2. Is there sufficient looping back to previously taught skills and strategies so that students constantly build on what they have learned?
3. Is the overall vision of the curriculum clear to me and to my students?

Supporting Struggling Readers and Writers: Strategies for Classroom Intervention 3–6 by Dorothy S. Strickland, Kathy Ganske, and Joanne K. Monroe. Copyright © 2002. Stenhouse Publishers

Supporting Struggling Readers and Writers: Strategies for Classroom Intervention 3–6 by Dorothy S. Strickland, Kathy Ganske, and Joanne K. Monroe. Copyright © 2002. Stenhouse Publishers

What It Does

Anecdotal records are a means for teachers to keep dated notes of their observations of students working in small groups or independently. These recorded observations are enormously helpful in planning instruction and assessing student growth.

How to Do It

To maintain good anecdotal records teachers need to be able to make notes easily and quickly and store them for ready access. Here are two suggestions to help you organize and stay organized.

1. A clipboard makes it easy to take notes "on the run," which is usually the circumstance in which teachers find themselves when taking notes for anecdotal records.
2. Recording sheets already marked with students' names make it easy to document the observations. We recommend the use of sheets like the one below that allow you to place a small stack of 3 x 5 sticky notes in the box next to each student's name. The notes are large enough for you to jot down the date and brief observations. A glance to see which sticky notes are blank on the record sheets will quickly let you see whom you still need to observe. At the end of the day or session, the filled notes are lifted from the sheet and placed in each student's file. Depleted piles of sticky notes are replenished as necessary in preparation for the next day's observations. These recording sheets, clipped onto a clipboard, make a portable, manageable system for maintaining anecdotal records.

Variation

Teachers have used many variations to this system. Any approach that allows you to make quick notes that can be filed by individual student names will be effective. Some teachers like to use a small three-ring notebook with a tabbed divider for each student. They insert several sheets of paper after each divider. To make their notes, they simply turn to the student's page and record the date and observation.

What to Look For

1. Are you making regular notations of your observations?
2. Is your record-keeping system portable enough that you have it with you when you need it?
3. Is it easy for you to access your notes about each of your students?

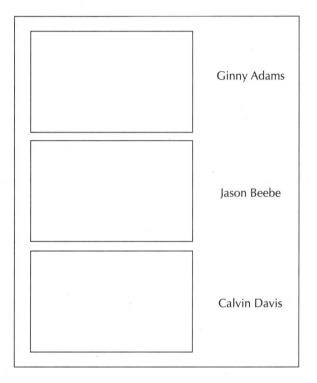

Ginny Adams

Jason Beebe

Calvin Davis

4. Are you able to determine growth (or lack of growth) over time in reviewing your anecdotal records for individual students?
5. Are you using the information you gather to inform your instruction?

For More Information

See Assessing Response Groups in the Strategy Bank.

What It Does

Many teachers express concern about assessing the quality of response and discussion during literature circles. They are more comfortable with paper and pencil assessments. Yet, literature circles provide an opportunity to use oral response as a window into how children are thinking about and reacting to texts.

How to Do It

1. Prepare an assessment form such as the one on page 209.
2. Discuss the contents of the form with students so that they have a clear idea of the expectations. Explain the following:

   Focus. Refers to the prompt that students respond to or other topics of discussion.

   Preparation. Students are expected to come to the response group prepared with all materials and a completed assignment (book, response log with completed entry, pencil if needed, etc.).

   Participation. Students are expected to understand and adhere to established guidelines for discussion. Individual student progress in oral language should be monitored throughout the year.

   Comments. Students are expected to demonstrate understandings about text structures and literary devices under study as they apply what they know to the material under discussion. For example, students may discuss literary concepts such as character development, setting, problem, problem resolution, and poetic devices. The student's ability to apply comprehension processes such as making inferences, recalling details, and making predictions is also noted.

3. Use the form to enter comments about students in the three categories.

What to Look For

1. Do students understand their responsibilities for making reader response groups interesting and productive?
2. Are students making progress in the categories under assessment?
3. Are the assessment results used to inform instructional decisions for individuals and for the entire group?

For More Information

Peterson, R., and S. Eeds. 1990. *Grand Conversations: Literature Groups in Action.* New York: Scholastic.

Strickland, D. S., R. M. Dillon, L. Funkhouser, M. Glick, and C. Rogers. 1989. "Research Currents: Classroom Dialogue During Literature Response Groups." *Language Arts* 66: 193–200.

Supporting Struggling Readers and Writers: Strategies for Classroom Intervention 3–6 by Dorothy S. Strickland, Kathy Ganske, and Joanne K. Monroe. Copyright © 2002. Stenhouse Publishers

Response Group Assessment Form

Date _____   Book _____

Knowledge/Skills

	• Ready with materials • On task • On time	• Listens and responds appropriately • Has a sense of audience • Uses language with confidence	• Literary concepts • Comprehension
Name	**Preparation**	**Participation**	**Application**
Emilio			
Dawn			
Terry			
Shirika			
James			
Comments:			

What It Does

This strategy encourages teachers to (1) test only their stated objectives and (2) vary the formats they use for end-of-book tests. It helps students demonstrate their understanding and/or recall of what they read or their ability to apply learned comprehension strategies.

How to Do It

1. Recognize that you should test only what you taught. In assessing guided silent reading, for example, the purposes you set for your students on their bookmarks will help to determine what questions you should ask. In the case of literature circles, the assigned roles and your prompts will guide the question making. Consistency between what was taught and what is tested assures alignment of objectives, instruction, and assessment. For example, if students used a bookmark like the one shown as Figure 5.4 in their guided silent reading, they should be assessed on their ability to
   a. make connections ("When I read . . ., I thought about . . ."),
   b. generate questions and answers ("Questions I would ask if I were the teacher . . ."),
   c. monitor for meaning ("I was confused when . . ."),
   d. use context to learn new words ("Words that are new to me . . .").

2. Consider the type of format that will be most effective for the assessment. A traditional closed-book format is appropriate if you want to determine what students remember from their reading and discussion. Students who were taught to identify and discuss new words in context might be tested in this format. The traditional method of matching words to their definitions will reveal whether the students learned enough about the words through their use of context and discussion to know them in isolation. We recommend that you use only a sampling of the words discussed and limit your choices to important words that you know students will see and use again.

   An open-book format is recommended if you want to see how well students can use their recall and the text itself to answer questions, just as they will often need to do when answering open-ended questions on a state test. If you

taught students to generate questions, you might test in this format using some of their questions. Asking students to support their answers with information from the text is a way to help them use all available resources to answer effectively.

If you want to determine how well students can apply the strategies they learned, just as they will in standardized and state tests, it is effective to have them use a short, unfamiliar piece for part of the test. (In fact, the sample passages that are frequently provided for test practice work well, as do short pieces from *Reader's Digest* and *Parade* magazines or from children's magazines.) If you asked students to monitor for meaning by identifying confusing parts of the text, this format is especially useful. Your question might be phrased in this way: "We have been working on learning to monitor for meaning by noticing parts that are confusing in our reading. Find one or more parts of the test story that confused you or might confuse another reader. Tell why those parts are confusing, and what you did (or recommend) to better understand them."

You may decide to use a combination of the closed-book and open-book format in a single test, or you may choose to use an alternative format such as the one below:

Variation

You might write an open-bookmark test rather than an open-book test. Telling your students at the start of their reading that they will be able to use their bookmarks during the test at the end of the unit will encourage note taking and allow you to ask open-ended questions, even if the students do not have access to their book.

What to Look For

1. Do you have evidence that students are able to use and articulate their use of the strategies you have taught them?
2. Are your students able to demonstrate their learning in a variety of types of test?

For More Information

See Assessing Response Groups, Open-Ended Questions, and Multiple Choice Items, all in the Strategy Bank.

Supporting Struggling Readers and Writers: Strategies for Classroom Intervention 3–6 by Dorothy S. Strickland, Kathy Ganske, and Joanne K. Monroe. Copyright © 2002. Stenhouse Publishers

Supporting Struggling Readers and Writers: Strategies for Classroom Intervention 3–6 by Dorothy S. Strickland, Kathy Ganske, and Joanne K. Monroe. Copyright © 2002. Stenhouse Publishers

What It Does

Patricia Cunningham (1990) has developed the Names Test as a measure for assessing children's decoding skills. As its title suggests, the source of words for the Names Test is people's names. Because most children have heard many more first and last names than they have seen in print, names provide "an ideal source of words for use in assessing decoding skills" (p. 125). The process consists of the three steps outlined below. The assessment can provide teachers with information about their students' general decoding ability.

How to Do It

Procedures for administering and scoring the Names Test

Preparing the Instrument

1. Type or print legibly twenty-five names on a sheet of paper or card stock. Make sure the print size is appropriate for the age or grade level of the students being tested.
2. For students who might perceive reading an entire list of names as too formidable, type or print the names on index cards, so they can be read individually.
3. Prepare a protocol (scoring) sheet. Do this by typing the list of names in a column and following each name with a blank line to be used for recording a student's responses.

Administering the Names Test

1. Administer the Names Test individually. Select a quiet, distraction-free location.
2. Explain to the student that she or he is to pretend to be a teacher who must read a list of names of students in the class. Direct the student to read the names as if taking attendance.
3. Have the student read the entire list. Inform the student that you will not be able to help with difficult names, and encourage him or her to "make a guess if you are not sure." This way you will have sufficient responses for analysis.
4. Write a check on the protocol sheet for each name read correctly. Write phonetic spellings for names that are mispronounced.

Scoring and Interpreting the Names Test

1. Count a word correct if all syllables are pronounced correctly regardless of where the student places the accent. For example, either Yo´/lan/da or Yo/lan´/da would be acceptable.
2. For words in which the vowel pronunciation depends on which syllable the consonant is placed with, count them correct for either pronunciation. For example, either Ho/mer or Hom/er would be acceptable.
3. Count the number of names read correctly, and analyze those mispronounced, looking for patterns indicative of decoding strengths and weaknesses.

The Names Test

Jay Conway	Wendy Swain
Tim Cornell	Glen Spencer
Chuck Hoke	Fred Sherwood
Yolanda Clark	Flo Thornton
Kimberly Blake	Dee Skidmore
Roberta Slade	Grace Brewster
Homer Preston	Ned Westmoreland
Gus Quincy	Ron Smitherman
Cindy Sampson	Troy Whitlock
Chester Wright	Vance Middleton
Ginger Yale	Zane Anderson
Patrick Tweed	Bernard Pendergraph
Stanley Shaw	

What to Look For

1. What differences do you notice in the student's ability to read one-, two- and three-syllable words?
2. How willing is the student to attempt longer words?
3. Do you notice any general trends in terms of how the student tries to decode words? For example, is the student successful with most initial consonants but not blends or digraphs, or perhaps with short vowels but not long vowels?

For More Information

Cunningham, P. 1990. "The Names Test: A Quick Assessment of Decoding Ability." *The Reading Teacher* 44: 124–129. (Reprinted with permission.)

What It Does

Martinez, Roser, and Strecker (1999) have developed a tool for assessing fluency in the classroom. The process involves the five components of fluency outlined below and provides teachers and students with concrete information with which to work.

How to Do It

To monitor student progress, assess them periodically with material that is on their independent level or only mildly challenging. Children may be assessed on materials that have been used instructionally or with which they have otherwise become familiar. Below are the assessment components and scoring rubrics.

Diagnostic Fluency Assessment
1. Rate: words per minute
2. Accuracy: percentage of words correctly recognized.
3. Fluidity (smoothness/flow of the reading):
   a. Hesitates in every line of print with many false starts; frequent prompting; no rhythm or cadence
   b. Several extended pauses; hesitations, and/or repetitions that are disruptive to the reading; occasional prompting; impression of choppiness
   c. Occasional inappropriate pauses; only occasional hesitation or repetition; rare prompting; only occasional choppiness
   d. Smooth reading overall with few pauses, hesitations, or repetitions; word or structural difficulties are quickly self-corrected; no choppiness
   e. Smooth, connected reading with no inappropriate pauses or hesitations; rare false start is immediately self-corrected; appropriate varied rhythm and cadence
4. Phrasing
   a. Reads in a word-by-word manner; ignores phrase boundaries and punctuation or creates inappropriate boundaries
   b. Overuses inappropriate phrasing; breaks phrasing within meaningful units; may break between subject and verb; some attention to punctuation boundaries

   c. Some inappropriate phrasing; attends to punctuation boundaries
   d. Usually chunks text into syntactically meaningful units; attends to punctuation boundaries
   e. Consistently chunks text into syntactically meaningful units; attends to punctuation boundaries
5. Expressiveness
   a. Reads with equal stress to each word; reads in a monotone with no expression; fails to mark end of sentences or dialogue with rise/fall of voice
   b. Uses minimal expression; reads with inappropriate stress; uses intonation that fails to mark end of sentences and clauses
   c. Uses some appropriate expression; reads with reasonable stress; uses intonation that marks end of sentences and clauses
   d. Generally uses appropriate stress and intonation with adequate attention to expression, including voice change at quotations and appropriate rise and fall of voice
   e. Consistently attends to appropriate stress, intonation, and expression, including consistent voice changes for quotations; demonstrates sensitivity to mood and tone; alters rate as needed for dramatic effect

For More Information

Martinez, M., N. L. Roser, and S. K. Strecker. 1999. "'I Never Thought I Could Be a Star': A Readers Theater Ticket to Fluency." *The Reading Teacher* 52: 326–334. (Used with permission.)

Strecker, S. K. 2001. "Questions Teachers Are Asking About Reading Fluency." *The California Reader* 34: 23–26.

Supporting Struggling Readers and Writers: Strategies for Classroom Intervention 3–6 by Dorothy S. Strickland, Kathy Ganske, and Joanne K. Monroe. Copyright © 2002. Stenhouse Publishers

What It Does

This strategy provides a technique for students to approach multiple choice items in a way that stresses reading for meaning. It helps them to understand how these items work so that they can discriminate among the possible answers with confidence.

How to Do It

1. Choose a multiple choice item from an old test booklet. Each item will consist of a passage and several questions with possible answers listed under them. Make sure the item is at the reading level of the students.

2. You may either enlarge the passage part of the item and put it on a transparency so that everyone can read it, or make sufficient copies for everyone. In either case, separate the passage part of the item from the questions and have students read it first silently.

3. After students have read the passage, discuss its meaning with them. Let them know that it is important to "think" about the passage as they read it before going on to work with the questions.

4. Have students read the first question and decide what the answer might be. Have them justify their answer based on information in the passage.

   a. Continue with two or three additional questions.

   b. Note that the point of this exercise is not to practice multiple choice items, but to understand how best to address them.

What to Look For

1. Are students really thinking about what the passage means as they read it?

2. Can they justify their answers based on information in the text. Or are they simply guessing?

3. Are students getting a sense of how these items are constructed?

4. Are students learning how to most efficiently use their time when addressing multiple choice items?

What It Does

As with any literacy strategy, students need to be shown how to approach the tasks related to test taking. This is particularly true of students experiencing difficulty, since they tend to be easily confused by new situations or literacy demands. For these students it is critical to use a scaffolding process that starts with observation and discussion of the task and gradually allows them to participate until they gain enough confidence to act independently. Most important, this kind of help benefits students beyond test taking, as they can use it to work with texts in other situations.

How to Do It

1. Obtain sample items from test booklets or from testing guidelines from your state department of education. Start by actually sharing with students some test passages, open-ended questions, and satisfactory answers to those questions. Discuss why a particular answer was a good one. Refer back to the question and note that the responder really paid attention to what was asked. This is particularly important in the case of questions that ask the reader to "support your answer with information from the selection"; many students neglect this. If your state or district provides a scoring rubric for open-ended questions, guide students in analyzing open-ended responses with the rubric. For example, answers may be judged in terms of (1) understanding of the task, (2) completion of the requirements, (3) quality of explanations or opinions, and (4) use of references to the text.

2. Over several days, introduce other test passages and involve students in group activities. First, actually demonstrate a good response by reading a passage and writing on the chalkboard or a chart as you think aloud about why you are responding as you do. This helps students get a sense of how a good reader thinks. Next, lead the students in a whole-group open-ended response to another test selection. This can be followed by small groups or pairs of students working in this way. Answers can be shared, compared, and discussed in terms of the rubric.

This helps give students a better idea of just what is expected of them.

3. Finally, allow students to practice one or two on their own. It is important to remember that this kind of practice comes after a variety of experiences with the task. Too often, teachers go directly to item practice, giving students little opportunity to truly understand the nature of the task. Mindless item practice simply reinforces what struggling readers and writers already suspect: "This is much too hard for me and I have no idea what to do."

What to Look For

1. Are students able to examine and identify specific aspects of a well-written open-ended response?

2. Do they demonstrate understanding of the task, completion of requirements, high-quality explanations or opinions, and the use of references to the text in their own attempts at open-ended responses?

Supporting Struggling Readers and Writers: Strategies for Classroom Intervention 3–6 by Dorothy S. Strickland, Kathy Ganske, and Joanne K. Monroe. Copyright © 2002. Stenhouse Publishers

What It Does

How well students understand and pay attention to the prompts used in writing assessments directly affects the efficiency with which they respond and, of course, how well they score. Teachers can help by discussing the nature of this type of writing task as opposed to the writing activities in which they normally engage. Deconstructing the task as well as modeling and guiding students through a few sample writing activities will also go a long way toward making them feel more confident about their ability to perform.

How to Do It

Assessments differ from one state to another. However, certain general features are usually present and can be discussed in advance. For example,

1. Students should be told to read the directions carefully. Let them know that the prompts act as the guide for how their answer will be scored. Unfortunately, interesting and well-written information may not be counted if it does not link directly to the prompts. Prompts usually consist of two or three parts. Response to all parts must be included in what they write. This can be demonstrated by modeling for students and by examining writing samples in relation to a scoring rubric.

2. Test instructions generally encourage students to engage in some type of prewriting activity, though students are told these will not count in their grade. For this reason, some students skip outlining or webbing and go directly to writing. Others spend too much time on prewriting activities, leaving less time for the actual writing. Students should be encouraged to plan their writing based on the prompt. Prewriting helps to generate and organize ideas. But it should be done quickly and they should move on to the writing as soon as possible.

3. Students should know that writing in a test situation is different from "real" writing for their own purposes. Making that distinction should help them focus on what is a very deliberate and prescribed task. Time spent showing students

how tests work and helping them to understand the task goes hand in hand with opportunities to improve the actual writing they will do.

What to Look For

1. Are the students able to determine the ways in which a writing sample responds or does not respond to all parts of a given prompt?
2. Do the students effectively allocate time for prewriting activities?
3. Do students respond to all parts of the prompt in their writing?

What It Does

Rubrics or scoring guides are useful tools for helping students get a sense of what they should strive for in their writing. It is important that students actually see good examples of writing that conform to the rubrics being used. Photocopies of writing samples may be made into transparencies and shown on an overhead projector. In this way, groups of children can read and discuss the writing in terms of the rubrics. For struggling readers and writers, it may be useful to reword state or district rubrics so that they are understandable to the learner.

How to Do It

Below is an example of how a state department rubric was rewritten in child-friendly language so that all fourth and fifth graders could read and understand it.

Writer's Checklist

(New Jersey State Department of Education Test Specification Booklet, Trenton, NJ, 1998, p. 55)

Did you remember to
- keep the central idea or topic in mind?
- keep your audience in mind?
- support your ideas with details, explanations, and examples?
- state your ideas in a clear sequence?
- include an opening and a closing?
- use a variety of words and vary your sentence structure?
- state your opinion or conclusion clearly?
- capitalize, spell, and use punctuation correctly?
- write neatly?

Writer's Checklist

(simplified version)

Did you remember to
- stick to the topic?
- think about your audience?
- give details and examples?
- put things in order?
- include an opening and a closing?
- use a variety of words and sentences?

- make your opinion clear?
- use capitals and punctuation correctly?
- write neatly?

What to Look For

1. Are students able to refer to the rubric with understanding as they talk about their writing and the writing of others?
2. Do students use the rubric to revise what they have written?

Supporting Struggling Readers and Writers: Strategies for Classroom Intervention 3–6 by Dorothy S. Strickland, Kathy Ganske, and Joanne K. Monroe. Copyright © 2002. Stenhouse Publishers

What It Does

Literature studies and book discussions can be used to help students deepen their understanding of their own cultural backgrounds and connect to the backgrounds of others. Students and their families learn that people like themselves can be found in print. Making sense of print takes on a new dimension for all involved.

How to Do It

1. Learn about students' backgrounds and cultural contexts through class discussions, talking with parents, and students' school journals.
2. Choose tasks and literature that are relevant to the students' lives. Multicultural literature not only lets students connect text to their own backgrounds, but can also serve as a stimulus for discussion about race, social class, and gender issues. Journal response questions can be included that deal with the students' own lives, especially regarding issues that have emerged in their reading.
3. Connect experiences to literature by sharing your own personal stories and encouraging students to share theirs. Use knowledge about the children (such as a trip they took or an interest they have) to bring them into a discussion and enable them to contribute their experiences. A class news board could be a helpful medium to share events from home. When possible, interrelate books, students' experiences, your own experiences, and the news board throughout classroom discussions.
4. Communicate with parents. Newsletters can be written to let parents know about what is going on in the classroom, including the topics being read and discussed. Parents might feel more comfortable talking to the teacher when the need arises if you give them a phone call at the beginning of the year to tell them about some of their children's strengths.

What to Look For

1. Has a safe classroom climate been developed so that the students feel comfortable sharing their thoughts and experiences?
2. Are the students increasingly able to make their own connections to the texts they are reading?
3. Do parents feel comfortable talking to the teacher as the need arises?

For More Information

McCarthey, S. 1999. "Identifying Teacher Practices That Connect Home and School." *Education and Urban Society* 32 (1): 83–107.

Supporting Struggling Readers and Writers: Strategies for Classroom Intervention 3–6 by Dorothy S. Strickland, Kathy Ganske, and Joanne K. Monroe. Copyright © 2002. Stenhouse Publishers

What It Does

Connecting home and school is important for all students. Parents of students who are experiencing difficulty are generally eager to do something to assist their child's reading. Probably the best help is to have parent and child read together in material that is slightly below the child's instructional level. The procedure below helps to establish a routine for sharing books at home and providing feedback.

How to Do It

Create a memo similar to the one below and send it home with each child.

To: At-Home Reading Buddy

From: (teacher's name)

Please make sure that your child reads each evening for at least twenty minutes. After the reading you may wish to do the following:

- Have your child retell what was read.
- Discuss what was read with your child.
- Have your child read selected parts aloud to you.
- Encourage your child to use sticky notes to indicate words or sections of the material that were difficult and need further explanation.

Keep a reading log, including the title of the book and the number of pages read each day.

At the end of each month, please sign the log and have your child bring it to school.

A log might look like this:

Reading Buddy Log

Name of child: _____

Date   Book Title; Pages Read

_____

_____

_____

What to Look For

1. Does the student establish an independent reading routine with a partner at home?
2. What kind of reading materials does the student choose to read independently?
3. Is the student becoming more confident as a reader?

Supporting Struggling Readers and Writers: Strategies for Classroom Intervention 3–6 by Dorothy S. Strickland, Kathy Ganske, and Joanne K. Monroe. Copyright © 2002. Stenhouse Publishers

Supporting Struggling Readers and Writers: Strategies for Classroom Intervention 3–6 by Dorothy S. Strickland, Kathy Ganske, and Joanne K. Monroe. Copyright © 2002. Stenhouse Publishers

What It Does

High-stakes testing and increasing calls for accountability have caused the public to be more questioning of the schools. At the elementary level, most questions are directed toward the reading program. Parents want to know what methods and materials are used and how students are assessed. The parents of children who are not performing up to local or state standards want to know what programs are available for extra help. Schools can offset misunderstandings and public criticism by answering some of these questions before they are asked. A school or classroom newsletter can be an effective way to do this.

How to Do It

1. School newsletters can be published monthly. Although contributions from all grades may be included, the teachers at different grades can share responsibility each month.
2. Information about the school's reading and writing instruction program should be included each month. This should be written in language that is accessible to people other than educators with examples given whenever possible. For example, *Research shows that small-group instruction promotes children's learning. At Lincoln School we involve students in varied kinds of groupings as well as some whole-class and individualized instruction. At least two or three times a week, your child participates in small-group guided reading. This kind of grouping ensures that your child practices skills and strategies on materials that are challenging but not frustrating. He or she also works in literature circles, where books are read, responded to, and discussed. Research groups in social studies and science involve students in reading and writing as well. The groups vary according to our purposes.*
3. One or two suggestions for informal activities that parents can do with their children are helpful.
4. A parent's question box with frequently asked questions can be included. For example,
   - Is there a homework policy at Lincoln School?
   - Are those workbooks in the department store useful?
   - How much television should I allow my child to watch?

     Very specific answers may not be suitable in all cases. However, parents welcome guidelines. Also, you might want to query some parents and have them offer their solutions to some questions.
5. Other suggestions for inclusion are children's work, a calendar of activities, and suggestions for community resources.

What to Look For

1. Did you note and respond to the comments of parents and students about the newsletter?
2. What seems to be particularly helpful?
3. Discuss with faculty how to improve the newsletter and how to make the process both effective and efficient in terms of faculty time and resources.

What It Does

Children's difficulties with schoolwork often cause considerable anxiety in the family. Parents often feel defensive and may want to blame the child or the school. Speaking frankly with parents about school expectations and their child's progress in relationship to them is important. Equally important is the development of a plan of action that involves everyone in a constructive way. Collaborative goal setting by child, parent, and teacher is a good way to start.

How to Do It

1. In a joint conference with parents and child, discuss the child's strengths as well as those areas needing work. Agree on some key areas to work on over a given time—perhaps a marking period.
2. Let the parents know some of the things you will be doing at school. This is important, since parents need to know that you are attempting to address the problems.
3. Give some specific suggestions for parents to do at home. These need not be suggestions for direct instruction. They can be suggestions about establishing routines for homework, supervising it to see that it is completed, and making sure that their child reads for a certain number of minutes each night. Parents want and need to share responsibility for the child's progress.
4. Specific goals may be written down in the child's portfolio so that they can be returned to at the end of the semester.

What to Look For

Use periodic meetings, perhaps one each marking period, with parents and student to review the child's progress. All can share what they have done and how things seem to be progressing. Note disparities in expectations between home and school and discuss those that might need clarification on both sides. This type of collaboration helps avoid the suspicion and blame that often occurs when parents think the school is not doing enough. More important, parents have a better sense of what is expected and feel involved in efforts to see that their child succeeds.

Supporting Struggling Readers and Writers: Strategies for Classroom Intervention 3–6 by Dorothy S. Strickland, Kathy Ganske, and Joanne K. Monroe. Copyright © 2002. Stenhouse Publishers

Supporting Struggling Readers and Writers: Strategies for Classroom Intervention 3–6 by Dorothy S. Strickland, Kathy Ganske, and Joanne K. Monroe. Copyright © 2002. Stenhouse Publishers

What It Does

Following are some suggestions for administrators and supervisors who are planning on-site, long-term professional development. They point to ways that a school or district faculty can create a staff development program to address their specific needs.

How to Do It

1. Collect and analyze data of student performance. Standardized test scores often precipitate staff development efforts. Be sure to collect other types of information as well, such as the mobility of students and their linguistic backgrounds, as well as work samples and performance-based assessments.

2. Identify any gaps or discrepancies that exist between desired and actual performance. If the problems appear too numerous and overwhelming, it might be best to preselect a few key areas on which to focus. These may be brought to the attention of the staff so they can decide where they want to begin. This will expedite the planning.

3. Identify possible causes for the discrepancies. Participants might wish to select several chapters in this book as a common basis for discussion. Staff should work together to create clear problem statements based on the discrepancies discovered. These problem statements may be linked to areas such as curriculum, instructional materials, classroom management, assessment, or teachers' knowledge of the content area or teaching methodology.

4. Use the content of selected chapters to brainstorm possible sources of staff development material that would address the causes that have been named. Select the material based on its potential for addressing the causes and bringing about student learning.

5. Determine the kinds of evidence that would demonstrate that the desired outcomes have been achieved. Do not limit the evidence to standardized test scores alone. Initiate a plan of classroom assessment and documentation of learning that can be brought to subsequent meetings and shared.

6. Discuss the level of support that should and can be maintained through the implementation phases. This may include release time, support staff, supplies, and financial resources and may involve adjustments in administrative structures.

What to Look For

1. Is the staff development process and content relevant to the needs of the particular school site?

2. Is the content compatible with other practices that are in use? If not, what adjustments need to be made?

3. What evidence is there that instruction is improving? that learning is improving?

For More Information

National Staff Development Council and National Association of Elementary School Principals. 1995. *Standards for Staff Development: Elementary School Edition.* Oxford, OH: National Staff Development Council.

What It Does

Preservice students are often unprepared for the range of abilities and backgrounds of the students they will teach. At the intermediate grades, in particular, new teachers often assume that all students will possess a certain level of capability. Following are some suggestions for using this book to build the knowledge base and skills required for prospective teachers to cope successfully with the realities they will face. This book may be used as a co-textbook in a basic reading course or as a basic text in a course designed for content-area reading. Although it addresses issues of academic diversity found in any school district, it is especially relevant for students preparing to work in areas where large numbers of students are not performing well.

What Preservice Students Need to Know and Be Able to Do About Classroom Intervention

1. Knowledge of risk factors for difficulties in reading;
2. Capacity to assess children appropriately for screening;
3. Capacity to assess children in order to design appropriate instruction;
4. Ability to tailor instruction to children with specific needs;
5. Knowledge and ability to apply the features of effective intervention programs;
6. Ability to make appropriate referrals and coordinate instruction within and outside the classroom.

How to Do It

What preservice teachers need to know and be able to do about classroom intervention can be acquired through

1. assigned readings with follow-up discussion;
2. instructor and peer demonstrations in the college classroom;
3. direct experience administering instruments for assessment and analyzing the results;
4. opportunities to plan instruction to meet student-specific needs;
5. field observations in classrooms;
6. interviews with teachers and other school personnel.

If *Supporting Struggling Readers and Writers* is used as a co-text, students may be assigned readings that supplement the sister text, but go into greater depth on issues related to students who present learning dilemmas.

Activities such as the following can heighten students' awareness of the diversity they will face:

- Discussion of the causes of reading problems with a special focus on the cultural and linguistic issues surrounding the teaching and learning of literacy.
- Classroom observations of how teachers in the intermediate grades organize instruction to accommodate the needs of diverse learners, followed by sharing and class discussion.
- Observations and interviews of teachers on how they document progress and tailor instruction to individual needs, followed by sharing and class discussion.
- Observations and interviews with a reading specialist to determine how the supplementary programs function in a school and the relationship between those programs and that of intervention in the regular classroom.
- Demonstrations and in-class simulations of various strategies discussed in the text, particularly those related to word study, fluency, writing, and reading comprehension.

Reinforce the reality of the diversity in literacy achievement found in any given classroom by collecting (or having students collect) and sharing writing samples from several children in the same class. Guide students in using a rubric or scoring guide to analyze the writing for both strengths and potential teaching points. Point out differences in how the children are developing though they are at the same grade level, and stress that this is typical in any school. Have teacher candidates suggest how they might differentiate instruction among them.

Supporting Struggling Readers and Writers: Strategies for Classroom Intervention 3–6 by Dorothy S. Strickland, Kathy Ganske, and Joanne K. Monroe. Copyright © 2002. Stenhouse Publishers

What It Does

Peer coaching is an effective means of providing ongoing professional development. Because it involves teachers in a long-term, collaborative effort, it has the potential to dramatically affect instruction. Coaching teams might be formed to address specific goals. Each team might wish to read and discuss several chapters in this book and decide on two or three areas to work on, such as integrating new writing or comprehension strategies in the classroom. One or two teachers on each team who are more familiar with the strategies might take the lead. Teachers would commit to trying at least one or two strategies, reporting on the results, and soliciting feedback on what worked and did not work.

How to Do It

The first steps of the coaching process involve acquiring skills through practice, observation, and feedback. Later, as skills develop, coaching sessions are used to examine how to best apply the skills to the classroom context.

1. Study the theory behind a targeted skill or strategy. The theoretical framework can be ascertained through discussions, readings, presentations, or other means.
2. Find a way to observe a demonstration of the strategy. Demonstration can take place by means of a videotape or a live presentation.
3. Practice new skills. Practicing with other teachers helps participants to clarify mistakes, develop peer-coaching skills, and learn from others' ideas and skills. The more similar the simulated conditions of the practice are to the workplace, the better.
4. Provide feedback. Teachers can observe and provide feedback for each other, or they can critique themselves through the use of cassette and video recordings. Feedback should take place as soon as possible after the training event and should be specific and nonevaluative.
5. Continue follow-up in the coaching process. The teachers continue to meet together to do collaborative problem-solving, joint planning of lessons, and analysis of curriculum materials for the appropriate use of strategies. As needed, the teachers continue to serve as coaches for each other in the classroom.

Variations

Instead of having the teacher who observes be the coach, switch roles so that the observer becomes the learner and the teacher who is teaching becomes the coach. This approach can be less threatening and can foster collegiality.

What to Look For

1. Is the feedback given supportive and helpful?
2. Are teachers developing greater confidence and mastery over the strategies implemented?
3. In addition to learning skills, is the coaching team engaged in solving problems and generating new ideas?

For More Information

Joyce, G., and B. Showers. 1995. *Student Achievement Through Staff Development* pp. 68–69, 84–87. New York: Longman.

Showers, B., and B. Joyce. 1996. "The Evolution of Peer Coaching." *Educational Leadership* 53: 17–20.

What It Does

Study groups may involve the whole faculty or they may involve faculty at specific grade levels or with similar goals. At times, all new faculty might be involved in a study group during their first year of teaching. Faculty study groups may be used to (a) support curricular and instructional innovations, (b) integrate the school's instructional programs, (c) target a schoolwide instructional need, and (d) monitor the effect of changes on students.

How to Do It

1. Groups of six members or fewer seem to work best. The topic determines who participates in a given group. Weekly hour-long meetings often work well.
2. Establish norms at the first meeting. Discuss issues such as expected participation, punctuality, respect for others' opinions, and openness to change. A pattern for leadership should also be established. Leaders confirm the time and location of the meeting, complete the log after the meeting, and report back to faculty/staff who are not part of the group. Rotating leaders will help all members maintain an equal status.
3. Create a study group action plan. The plan should include
   - the specific needs that the group will investigate;
   - how student change that results from the work of the study group will be ascertained;
   - the resources the group will use;
   - training events that include presentation of the theory that supports a given skill and opportunities to observe and practice with each other in the classroom.
4. Report what happened after each study group meeting. Recording helps group members confirm why they took a certain action and see the progress of group relationships and their thinking. A report could consist of
   - date, time, place;
   - attendance at the meeting;
   - how participants applied what was learned in the classroom;
   - a summary of the group's discussions and activities;

- plans for the next meeting;
- concerns and recommendations.

5. Periodically evaluate the effectiveness of the study group. Use the action plan as a reference for formulating evaluation questions. Evaluate the way the study group is functioning as well as how the study group is affecting students and the school culture.
6. Establish communication networks. This can be done in various ways:
   - Every four to six weeks have representatives from each group meet to share and discuss their logs. These meetings, in turn, can be discussed in the study groups.
   - Post the study group logs so that everyone has access to them.
   - Create newsletters, brochures, and videos describing findings and activities.
   - Hold exhibits. Groups can advertise a time when others can find out what the study group is doing.
   - Create a bulletin board for notes from the study groups.
   - Hold a whole-faculty study group meeting every four to six weeks. Invite district leaders.
   - Plan special celebrations.
   - Assign a liaison to other study groups.
   - Tell students what is happening in the study groups.

What to Look For

1. Are the topics of the study groups substantive and practical so that the focus is on the content rather than on the individuals in the group?
2. Do the members freely participate in the discussions and show appreciation for each other's ideas?
3. Are the study group members effective in implementing their action plan?
4. Are any changes seen in the students as a result of the study groups?

For More Information

Murphy, C. U., and D. W. Lick. 1998. *Whole-Faculty Study Groups: A Powerful Way to Change Schools and Enhance Learning* pp. 51–60, 98–99. Thousand Oaks, CA: Corwin Press.

Supporting Struggling Readers and Writers: Strategies for Classroom Intervention 3–6 by Dorothy S. Strickland, Kathy Ganske, and Joanne K. Monroe. Copyright © 2002. Stenhouse Publishers

RESOURCES

A Selected List of High-Interest, Low-Vocabulary Books and Books with Predictable Text

Picture Books for Read-Aloud/Think-Aloud Instruction

More Resources

Good Sources for Leveled Fiction and Nonfiction Text for Guided
    Silent Reading
Resources for Choral Reading
Selected Resources for Readers' Theater

A Selected List of High-Interest, Low-Vocabulary Books and Books with Predictable Text

Chapter Books

(see also Series That Feature the Same Characters)

Ackerman, K. 1994. *The Night Crossing*. New York: Random House.

Blume, J. 1971. *Freckle Juice*. New York: Dell Yearling.

Bulla, C. R. 1990. *White Bird*. New York: Random House.

Cameron, A. 1988. *The Most Beautiful Place in the World*. New York: Knopf.

Clements, A. 2001. *Jake Drake: Bully Buster*. New York: Aladdin.

Cohen, B. 1983. *Molly's Pilgrim*. New York: Bantam.

Christopher, M. 1997. *Stranger in Right Field*. Boston: Little, Brown. (A great author for books that deal with sports)

Dahl, R. 1966. *The Magic Finger*. New York: Puffin.

———. 1970. *Fantastic Mr. Fox*. New York: Puffin.

———. 1978. *The Enormous Crocodile*. New York: Knopf.

———. 1991. *George's Marvelous Medicine*. New York: Puffin.

Dalgliesh, A. 1954. *The Courage of Sarah Noble*. New York: Scribner.

Fleischman, P. 1980. *The Half-a-Moon Inn*. New York: HarperCollins.

Fleischman, S. 1986. *The Whipping Boy*. New York: William Morrow.

Gardner, J. R. 1980. *Stone Fox*. New York: Harper & Row.

Graeber, C. 1983. *Mustard*. New York: Bantam Skylark.

Hesse, K. 1994. *Sable*. New York: Henry Holt.

Kinsey-Warnock, N. 1989. *The Canada Geese Quilt*. New York: Dell Yearling.

MacLachlan, P. 1985. *Sarah, Plain and Tall*. New York: HarperCollins.

McSwigan, M. 1942. *Snow Treasure*. New York: Dutton.

Mowat, F. 1981. *Owls in the Family*. New York: Dell Yearling.

Naylor, P. 1991. *Shiloh*. New York: Simon & Schuster.

Park, B. 1982. *Skinnybones*. New York: Knopf.

Rockwell, T. 1973. *How to Eat Fried Worms*. New York: Dell Yearling.

Schwartz, A. 1981. *Scary Stories to Tell in the Dark*. New York: Lippincott.

———. 1984. *In a Dark, Dark Room and Other Scary Stories*. New York: Harper & Row.

Smith, R. K. 1989. *Chocolate Fever*. New York: Penguin Putnam.

Taylor, M. 1990. *Mississippi Bridge*. New York: Bantam Skylark.

Series That Feature the Same Characters (sample title listed)

Adler, D. A. 1980. *Cam Jansen and the Mystery of the U.F.O.* New York: Scholastic.

Allard, H. 1985. *Miss Nelson Is Missing*. Boston: Houghton Mifflin.

Cameron, A. 1981. *The Stories Julian Tells*. New York: Knopf.

Etra, J., and S. Spinner. 1988. *Aliens for Breakfast*. New York: Random House.

Hurwitz, J. 1989. *Rip-Roaring Russell*. New York: Puffin.

Kline, S. 1990. *Horrible Harry's Secret*. New York: Puffin.

Marshall, J. 1984. *George and Martha Back in Town*. Boston: Houghton Mifflin.

Namioka, L. 1995. *Yang the Third and Her Impossible Family.* Boston: Little, Brown.

Osborne, M. P. 1995. *Afternoon on the Amazon.* New York: Random House (Magic Tree House).

Osborne, W., and M. P. Osborne. 2001. *Mummies and Pyramids.* New York: Random House. (Magic Tree House Research Guide).

Peterson, J. 1979. *The Littles and the Big Storm.* New York: Scholastic.

Rylant, C. 1992. *Henry and Mudge and the Long Weekend.* New York: Aladdin.

———. 1997. *Mr. Putter and Tabby Row the Boat.* San Diego: Harcourt Brace.

Sachar, L. 1993. *Marvin Redpost: Why Pick on Me?* New York: Random House.

Scieszka, J. 1991. *Knights of the Kitchen Table.* New York: Penguin. (Time Warp Trio Series).

Sharmat, M. W. 1974. *Nate the Great Goes Undercover.* New York: Dell.

Sobol, D. J. 1971. *Encyclopedia Brown Tracks Them Down.* New York: Crowell.

Text Series

Esiason, B., NFL Quarterback. 1995. *A Boy Named Boomer.* New York: Scholastic. (Hello Reader).

Hänel, W. 1999. *Rescue at Sea.* New York: North-South Books. (Easy-to-Read).

Hayes, G. 1985. *The Mystery of the Pirate Ghost.* New York: Random House. (STEP into Reading).

Kunhardt, E. 1987. *Pompeii: Buried Alive.* New York: Random House. (STEP into Reading).

Levinson, N. S. 1992. *Snowshoe Thompson.* New York: HarperCollins. (An I Can Read Book).

Lowry, L. 1999. *Aunt Clara Brown: Official Pioneer.* Minneapolis: Carolrhoda Books. (On My Own: Biography).

Nirgiotis, N. 1996. *Volcanoes: Mountains That Blow Their Tops.* New York: Grosset & Dunlap. (All Aboard Reading).

O'Connor, J. 1986. *The Teeny Tiny Woman.* New York: Random House. (STEP into Reading).

Standiford, N. 1989. *The Bravest Dog Ever: The True Story of Balto.* New York: Random House. (STEP into Reading).

Picture Books

Clement, R. 1997. *Grandpa's Teeth.* New York: HarperCollins.

Fleischman, P. 1999. *Westlandia.* New York: Scholastic.

Polacco, P. 1994. *Pink and Say.* New York: Scholastic.

Ringgold, F. 1992. *Aunt Harriet's Underground Railroad.* New York: Scholastic.

Fractured Fairy Tales and Fairy Tale/Fable Variations (all are picture books)

Jackson, E. 1994. *Cinder Edna.* New York: Mulberry Press.

Lobel, A. 1980. *Fables.* New York: Scholastic.

Minters, F. 1997. *Cinder-Elly*. New York: Viking.

Palatini, M. 1995. *Piggie Pie*. New York: Clarion.

San Souci, R. D. 1989. *The Talking Eggs*. New York: Scholastic.

Sciezska, J. 1989. *The True Story of the Three Little Pigs*. New York: Scholastic.

———. 1991. *The Frog Prince Continued*. New York: The Trumpet Club.

Trivas, E. 1993. *The Three Little Wolves and the Big Bad Pig*. New York: Aladdin.

Predictable Books

Gelman, R. G. 1977. *More Spaghetti, I Say!* New York: Scholastic. (Hello Reader Series).

Grossman, B. 1996. *My Little Sister Ate One Hair*. New York: Crown.

McPhail, D. 1993. *Pigs Aplenty, Pigs Galore!* New York: Penguin Putnam.

Slier, D. 1997. *The Enormous Turnip*. New York: Star Bright Books.

Wood, D., and A. Wood. 1984. *The Napping House*. Orlando, FL: Harcourt Brace.

Picture Books for Read-Aloud/Think-Aloud Instruction

The following lists of picture books were recommended by a small sampling of teachers of grades 3 through 6 who were asked to identify titles that are highly effective for read-aloud/think-aloud instruction. Most of the books were recommended by more than one teacher and by teachers of all four grade levels. All of the books were recommended for more than one purpose. Because teachers named *creating visual images* and *monitoring for meaning* as strategies for many of these titles, they are not listed as categorizing criteria. The categories that are listed may be helpful for making book choices.

We suggest that you read selected books with an aware mind, noticing the comprehension strategies that the texts and pictures stimulate during reading. The strategies you notice yourself using as you read are the right ones to demonstrate in your think-aloud. We recommend that you limit your strategy demonstration to one per read-aloud. For example, think aloud only about the predictions that occur to you while reading *The Wednesday Surprise* (Bunting 1991), despite the other thinking and connecting that may occur to you as you read. This will make the selected strategy more evident and clear to your students.

To provide background knowledge; to support making text-to-world connections; to identify important information; to make inferences:

Agra Deedy, C. 2000. *The Yellow Star: The Legend of King Christian X of Denmark.* Atlanta: Peachtree.

Bunting, E. 1990. *The Wall.* Boston: Houghton Mifflin.

———. 1994. *Terrible Things.* Philadelphia: Jewish Publication Society.

———. 1996. *Smoky Night.* New York: Harcourt.

Cannon, J. 1996. *Verdi.* New York: Harcourt.

Golenbock, P. 1992. *Teammates.* New York: Harcourt.

Heide, F. P., and J. H. Gilliland. 1990. *The Day of Ahmed's Secret.* New York: Scholastic.

Lawrence, J. 1992. *The Great Migration.* New York: HarperCollins.

Martin, B., Jr., and J. Archambault. 1987. *Knots on a Counting Rope.* New York: Henry Holt.

Maruki, T. 1982. *Hiroshima No Pika: The Flash of Hiroshima.* New York: HarperCollins.

Miles, M. 1976. *Annie and the Old One.* Boston: Little, Brown.

Mochizuki, K. 1993. *Baseball Saved Us.* New York: Lee & Low Books.

Polacco, P. 1994. *Pink and Say.* New York: Putnam.

Ryan, P. 1996. *The Flag We Love.* Boston: Charlesbridge Publishing.

San Souci, R. 1989. *The Talking Eggs.* New York: Scholastic.

Say, A. 1993. *Grandfather's Journey.* Boston: Houghton Mifflin.

Siebert, D. 1995. *Mojave*. New York: HarperCollins.

Steptoe, J. 1987. *Mufaro's Beautiful Daughters*. New York: HarperCollins.

Tsuchiya, Y. 1997. *Faithful Elephants: A True Story of Animals, People and War*. Boston: Houghton Mifflin.

To highlight interesting language devices; to support recognizing multiple meanings and generating questions:

Barrett, J. 1978. *Cloudy with a Chance of Meatballs*. New York: Simon & Schuster.

Base, G. 1987. *Animalia*. New York: Harry N. Abrams.

Baylor, B. 1986. *The Way to Start a Day*. New York: Simon & Schuster.

Levitt, P., E. Guralick, and D. Burger. 1989. *The Weighty Word Book*. Longmont, CO: Bookmakers Guild.

To promote theme-related connections; to provide models for student writing; to highlight mood, tone, humor, or parody; to support making text-to-self connections and predictions:

Brown, M. 1951. *The Important Book*. New York: HarperCollins.

Bunting, E. 1991. *The Wednesday Surprise*. Boston: Houghton Mifflin.

———. 1993. *Fly Away Home*. Boston: Houghton Mifflin.

Calmenson, S. 1991. *The Principal's New Clothes*. New York: Scholastic.

Cole, B. 1997. *Princess Smartypants*. New York: Putnam.

Cronin, D. 2000. *Click Clack Moo: Cows That Type*. New York: Simon & Schuster.

Henkes, K. 1991. *Chrysanthemum*. New York: HarperCollins.

Hoffman, C. 1991. *Amazing Grace*. New York: Dial Books.

Houston, G. 1991. *My Great-Aunt Arizona*. New York: HarperCollins.

Howard, E. 1995. *Aunt Flossie's Hats*. Boston: Houghton Mifflin.

McNulty, F. 1994. *A Snake in the House*. New York: Scholastic.

Meddaugh, S. 1995. *Martha Speaks*. Boston: Houghton Mifflin.

Munsch, R. 1986. *The Paper Bag Princess*. Willowdale, Ontario: Firefly Books.

———. 1988. *Thomas' Snowsuit*. Willowdale, Ontario: Firefly Books.

Numeroff, L. 1985. *If You Give a Mouse a Cookie*. New York: HarperCollins.

Pfister, M. 1997. *Milo and the Magic Stones*. New York: North-South Books.

Rylant, C. 1981. *When I Was Young in the Mountains*. New York: Viking Penguin.

———. 1986. *The Relatives Came*. New York: Random House.

———. 1996. *The Whales*. New York: Scholastic.

———. 1998. *Scarecrow*. New York: Harcourt.

Schubert, D. 1987. *Where's My Monkey?* New York: Penguin.

Scieszka, J. 1989. *The True Story of the Three Little Pigs*. New York: Viking.

———. 1992. *The Stinky Cheese Man and Other Fairly Stupid Tales*. New York: Viking.

———. 1995. *Math Curse*. New York: Viking.

Steig, W. 1973. *Sylvester and the Magic Pebble*. New York: Simon & Schuster.

———. 1993. *Shrek!* New York: Farrar, Straus & Giroux.

Van Allsberg, C. 1983. *The Wreck of the Zephyr*. Boston: Houghton Mifflin.

———. 1984. *The Mystery of Harris Burdick*. Boston: Houghton Mifflin.

———. 1986. *The Stranger*. Boston: Houghton Mifflin.

———. 1988. *Two Bad Ants*. Boston: Houghton Mifflin.

———. 1990. *Just a Dream*. Boston: Houghton Mifflin.

———. 1992. *The Widow's Broom*. Boston: Houghton Mifflin.

Viorst, J. 1972. *I'll Fix Anthony*. New York: HarperCollins.

———. 1976. *Alexander and the Terrible, Horrible, No Good, Very Bad Day*. New York: Simon & Schuster.

Wells, R. 1992. *Shy Charles*. New York: Penguin.

Wiesner, D. 1991. *Tuesday*. Boston: Houghton Mifflin.

Wood, A. 1995. *King Bidgood's in the Bathtub*. New York: Harcourt Brace.

Yolen, J. 1987. *Owl Moon*. New York: Putnam.

———. 1997. *Miz Berlin Walks*. New York: Putnam.

See also:

Benedict, S., and L. Carlisle, eds. 1992. *Beyond Words*. Portsmouth, NH: Heinemann.

Hall, S. 1990. *Using Picture Storybooks to Teach Literary Devices*. Phoenix: Oryx Press.

Keene, E., and S. Zimmerman. 1997. *Mosaic of Thought: Teaching Comprehension in a Reader's Workshop*. Portsmouth, NH: Heinemann.

More Resources

Good Sources for Leveled Fiction and Nonfiction Text for Guided Silent Reading

Celebration Press. Pearson Learning, 299 Jefferson Road, Parsippany, NJ 07054; 800-321-3106

Newbridge Educational Publishing, 333 East 38th Street, New York, NY 10016; 800-867-0307

Pacific Learning, 15342 Graham Street, Huntington Beach, CA 92649-0723; 800-279-0737

Perma-Bound, 617 Vidalia Road, Jacksonville, IL 62650; 800-637-6581

Rigby Education, P.O. Box 797, Crystal Lake, IL 60039-0797; 800-822-8661

Shortland Publications, 50 S. Steele Street, Suite 755, Denver, CO 80209; 800-775-9995

Resources for Choral Reading

Angelou, M. 1978. *Life Doesn't Frighten Me*. New York: Stewart, Tabori, & Chang.

Cullinan, B. E., ed. 1996. *A Jar of Tiny Stars: Poems by NCTE Award–Winning Poets*. Honesdale, PA: Wordsong.

Hughes, L. 1994. *The Dream Keeper and Other Poems*. New York: Scholastic.

Lansky, B. 1991. *Kids Pick the Funniest Poems: Poems That Make Kids Laugh*. New York: Meadowbrook Press.

O'Neill, M. 1961. *Hailstones and Halibut Bones*. New York: Delacorte Press.

Silverstein, S. 1996. *Falling Up*. New York: HarperCollins.

Sword, E. H., ed. 1995. *A Child's Anthology of Poetry*. Hopewell, NJ: The Ecco Press.

Viorst, J. 1981. *If I Were in Charge of the World and Other Worries: Poems for Children and Their Parents*. New York: Aladdin.

Selected Resources for Readers' Theater

Bauer, C. F. 1987. *Presenting Reader's Theater: Plays and Poems to Read Aloud*. New York: H. W. Wilson.

Braun, W., and C. Braun. 1996. *A Readers Theater Treasury of Stories*. Calgary, Alberta: Braun & Braun Associates.

Fredericks, A. 1993. *Frantic Frogs and Other Frankly Fractured Folktales for Readers Theater*. Englewood, CO: Teacher Ideas Press.

Gander Academy: Readers Theater. (June 14, 2001). [Internet]. Available: www.stemnet.nf.ca/CITE/langrt.htm.

Laughlin, M. 1990. *Reader's Theater for Children: Scripts and Script Development*. Englewood, CO: Teacher Ideas Press.

Pugliano, C. 1997. *Easy to Read Folk and Fairy Tale Plays*. New York: Scholastic.

Reader's Theater Online Canada. (June 14, 2001). [Internet]. Available: www.loiswalker.com.

Shepard, A. 1993. *Stories on Stage: Scripts for Reader's Theater.* New York: H. W. Wilson.

Shephard, A. (June 14, 2001). [Internet]. Available: www.aaronshep.com (Once there, search for *scripts*.)

Sierra, J. 1996. *Multicultural Folktales for Feltboard and Reader's Theater.* Westport, CT: Greenwood Publishing Group.

REFERENCES

Children's Books

Bagert, B. 1995. *Elephant Games and Other Playful Poems to Perform*. Honesdale, PA: Boyds Mills Press.

Baylor, B. 1995. *I'm in Charge of Celebrations*. New York: Aladdin.

Blume, J. 1971. *Freckle Juice*. New York: Dell Yearling.

Bunting, E. 1991. *The Wednesday Surprise*. Boston: Houghton Mifflin.

Chandra, D. 1993. *Balloons: And Other Poems*. New York: Sunburst.

Ciardi, J. 1983. "Read This with Gestures." In J. Prelutsky, ed., *The Random House Book of Poetry for Children*. New York: Random House.

———. 1996. "Mummy Slept Late and Daddy Fixed Breakfast." In B. E. Cullinan, ed., *A Jar of Tiny Stars: Poems by NCTE Award–Winning Poets*, p. 40. Honesdale, PA: Wordsong.

Cleary, B. 1981. *Ramona Quimby, Age 8*. New York: Dell.

Clements, A. 1996. *Frindle*. New York: Aladdin.

———. 2001. *Jake Drake: Bully Buster*. New York: Aladdin.

Dahl, R. 1982. *The BFG*. New York: Viking Penguin.

Facklam, M. 1994. *The Big Bug Book*. Boston: Little, Brown.

Fleischman, P. 1980. *The Half-a-Moon Inn*. New York: HarperCollins.

———. 1985. *I Am the Phoenix: Poems for Two Voices*. New York: Harper & Row.

———. 1988. *Joyful Noise: Poems for Two Voices*. New York: Harper & Row.

———. 1999. *Westlandia*. New York: Scholastic.

Gardner, J. R. 1980. *Stone Fox*. New York: Harper & Row.

Gunning, M. 1993. *Not a Copper Penny in Me House*. Honesdale, PA: Wordsong/Boyds Mills Press.

Hillock, G. T. 1986. "Woodpecker in Disguise." In J. Prelutsky, ed., *Read Aloud Rhymes for the Very Young*. New York: Knopf.

Jackson, E. 1994. *Cinder Edna*. New York: Mulberry Press.

Kline, S. 1990. *Horrible Harry's Secret*. New York: Penguin.

Lester, J. 1998. *From Slave Ship . . . To Freedom Road*. New York: Puffin.

Lobel, A. 1980. *Fables*. New York: Harper & Row.

Lowry, L. 1990. *Number the Stars*. Boston: Houghton Mifflin.

———. 1993. *The Giver*. Boston: Houghton Mifflin.

————. 2000. *Gathering Blue*. Boston: Houghton Mifflin.

MacLachlan, P. 1985. *Sarah, Plain and Tall*. New York: HarperCollins.

Martin, B., Jr., and J. Archambault. 1987. *Knots on a Counting Rope*. New York: Henry Holt.

Namioka, L. 2000. *Yang the Eldest and His Odd Jobs*. Boston: Little, Brown.

Naylor, P. 1991. *Shiloh*. New York: Simon & Schuster.

Patalini, M. 1995. *Piggie Pie*. New York: Clarion.

Perez, E. 1993. *A Look Around Rain Forests*. St. Petersburg, FL: Willowisp Press.

Rowling, J. K. 1997. *Harry Potter and the Sorcerer's Stone*. New York: Scholastic.

Rylant, C. 1985. *Every Living Thing*. New York: Aladdin.

Sachar, L. 1998. *Holes*. New York: Farrar, Straus, & Giroux.

Savran, S. 1997. *Penguins*. New York: Scholastic.

Stott, C. 1991. *Observing the Sky*. New York: Troll.

Thayer, E. L. 1995. "Casey at the Bat." In E. H. Sword, ed., *A Child's Anthology of Poetry*. Hopewell, NJ: The Ecco Press.

Yep, L. 1997. *The Imp That Ate My Homework*. New York: HarperCollins.

Professional Books

Adams, M. J. 1990. *Beginning to Read: Thinking and Learning About Print*. Cambridge, MA: MIT Press.

Allen, J. 1999. *Words, Words, Words: Teaching Vocabulary in Grades 4–12*. Portland, ME: Stenhouse.

Allington, R. L. 1983a. "Fluency: The Neglected Reading Goal." *The Reading Teacher* 36 (6): 556–561.

————. 1983b. "The Reading Instruction Provided Readers of Differing Reading Abilities." *Elementary School Journal* 83: 548–559.

Anderson, R. C., P. T. Wilson, and L. G. Fielding. 1988. "Growth in Reading and How Children Spend Their Time Outside of School." *Reading Research Quarterly* 23: 285–303.

Aronson, E., C. Stephan, J. Sikes, N. Blaney, and M. Snapp. 1978. *The Jigsaw Classroom*. Beverly Hills, CA: Sage.

Atwell, N. 1987. *In the Middle: Writing, Reading, and Learning with Adolescents*. Portmouth, NH: Heinemann Boynton/Cook.

Au, K., J. Carroll, and J. Scheu. 1997. *Balanced Literacy Instruction: A Teacher's Resource Book*. Norwood, MA: Christopher-Gordon.

August, D. A., and K. Hakuta, eds. 1997. *Improving Schooling for Language-Minority Children: A Research Agenda*. Washington, DC: National Academy Press.

Avery, C. 1999. Making Children the Heart of Our Practice. Speech presented at the Rutgers Literacy Curriculum Network. New Brunswick, NJ: Rutgers University.

Baker, L., and A. Wigfield. 1999. "Dimensions of Children's Motivation for Reading and Their Relationships to Reading Activity and Reading Achievement." *Reading Research Quarterly* 34 (4): 452–477.

Baker, T. K., S. A. Bisson, I. H. Blum, T. S. Creamer, P. S. Koskinen, and S. M. Phillips. 1999. "Shared Reading Books, and Audiotapes: Supporting Diverse Students in School and at Home." *The Reading Teacher* 52: 430–444.

Bauer, C. F. 1987. *Presenting Reader's Theater: Plays and Poems to Read Aloud*. New York: H. W. Wilson.

Baumann, J. F., and A. M. Duffy. 1997. *Engaged Reading for Pleasure and Learning: A Report from the National Reading Research Center*. Athens, GA: National Reading Research Center (NRRC).

Baumann, J., H. Hooten, and P. White. 1999. "Teaching Comprehension Through Literature: A Teacher-Researcher Project to Develop Fifth Graders' Reading Strategies and Motivation." *The Reading Teacher* 53 (1): 38–51.

Bear, D., M. Invernizzi, S. Templeton, and F. Johnston. 2000. *Words Their Way: Word Study for Phonics, Vocabulary, and Spelling Instruction*. 2d ed. Upper Saddle River, NJ: Merrill.

Beattie, J. 1994. "Characteristics of Students with Disabilities and How Teachers Can Help." In K. Wood and B. Algozzine, eds., *Teaching Reading to High-Risk Learners: A Unified Perspective*. Boston: Allyn and Bacon.

Bomer, R. 1995. *Time for Meaning*. Portsmouth, NH: Heinemann.

Braun, W., and C. Braun. 1996. *A Readers Theater Treasury of Stories*. Calgary, Alberta: Braun & Braun Associates.

Calfee, R. C., and E. H. Hiebert. 1991. "Classroom Assessment of Reading." In R. Barr, M. Kamil, P. Mosenthal, and P. D. Pearson, eds., *Handbook of Research on Reading*. 2d ed. New York: Longman.

Calkins, L. 1991. *Living Between the Lines*. Portsmouth, NH: Heinemann.

———. 1994. *The Art of Teaching Writing*. Portsmouth, NH: Heinemann.

Cazden, C. 1988. *Classroom Discourse: The Language of Teaching and Learning*. New York: Teachers College Press.

Clay, M. 1985. *The Early Detection of Reading Difficulties*. Portsmouth, NH: Heinemann.

Collins, J. 1999. *Strategies for Struggling Writers*. New York: The Guilford Press.

Committee on the Prevention of Reading Difficulties in Young Children. 1998. *Preventing Reading Difficulties in Young Children*. Washington, DC: National Academy Press.

Conrad, R. 1979. *The Deaf School Child*. London: Harper & Row.

Csikszentmihalyi, M. 1990. "Literacy and Intrinsic Motivation." *Daedalus* 119: 115–140.

Cullinan, B. 1974. *Black Dialects and Reading*. Urbana, IL: National Council of Teachers of English.

Cummins, J. 1984. *Bilingualism and Special Education: Issues in Assessment and Pedagogy*. San Diego: College-Hill Press.

Cunningham, A., and K. Stanovich. 1998. "What Reading Does for the Mind." *American Educator* 22: 8–15.

Cunningham, P. 1990. "The Names Test: A Quick Assessment of Decoding Ability." *The Reading Teacher* 44 (2): 124–129.

Cunningham, P. M. 2000. *Phonics They Use: Words for Reading and Writing*. 3d ed. New York: HarperCollins College Publishers.

Cunningham, P. M., and J. W. Cunningham. 1992. "Making Words: Enhancing the Invented Spelling-Decoding Connection." *The Reading Teacher* 46: 106–115.

Daniels, H. 1994. *Literature Circles: Voice and Choice in the Student-Centered Classroom.* Portland, ME: Stenhouse.

Darling-Hammond, L. 1994. "Performance-Based Assessment and Educational Equity." *Harvard Educational Review* 64: 5–30.

Deci, E. I., and R. M. Ryan. 1985. *Intrinsic Motivation and Self-Determination in Human Behavior.* New York: Plenum.

Dole, J. A., S. W. Valencia, E. A. Greer, and J. L. Wardrop. 1991. "Effects of Two Types of Prereading Instruction on the Comprehension of Narrative and Expository Text." *Reading Research Quarterly* 26: 142–158.

Duffy, G. G. 1990. *Reading in the Middle School.* 2d ed. Newark, DE: International Reading Association.

Durkin, D. 1978–1979. "What Classroom Observations Reveal About Reading Comprehension Instruction." *Reading Research Quarterly* 14: 481–533.

———. 1993. *Teaching Them to Read.* 6th ed. Boston: Allyn & Bacon.

Ehri, L. C. 1998. "Grapheme-Phoneme Knowledge Is Essential for Learning to Read Words in English." In J. L. Metsala and L. C. Ehri, eds., *Word Recognition in Beginning Literacy.* Mahwah, NJ: Lawrence Erlbaum.

Fletcher, R. 1996. *Breathing In, Breathing Out: Keeping a Writer's Notebook.* Portsmouth, NH: Heinemann.

Flynn, N., and S. McPhillips. 2000. *A Note Slipped Under the Door: Teaching from Poems We Love.* Portland, ME: Stenhouse.

Fountas, I. C., and G. S. Pinnell. 1996. *Guided Reading: Good First Teaching for All Students.* Portsmouth, NH: Heinemann.

———. 1999. *Matching Books to Readers: Using Leveled Books in Guided Reading, Grades K–3.* Portsmouth, NH: Heinemann.

———. 2001. *Guiding Readers and Writers Grades 3–6: Teaching Comprehension, Genre, and Content Literacy.* Portsmouth, NH: Heinemann.

Fredericks, A. 1993. *Frantic Frogs and Other Frankly Fractured Folktales for Readers Theater.* Englewood, CO: Teacher Ideas Press.

Gambrell, L. 1996. "Creating Classroom Cultures That Foster Reading Motivation." *The Reading Teacher* 50 (1): 14–25.

Ganske, K. 2000. *Word Journeys: Assessment-Guided Phonics, Spelling, and Vocabulary Instruction.* New York: The Guilford Press.

Garcia, G. E. 2000. "Bilingual Children's Reading." In M. Kamil, P. Rosenthal, P. D. Pearson, and R. Barr, eds., *Handbook on Reading Research*, Vol. 3. Mahwah, NJ: Lawrence Erlbaum.

Gasparro, M., and B. Falletta. 1994. *Creating Drama with Poetry: Teaching English as a Second Language Through Dramatization and Improvisation.* ERIC Digest. www.cal.org/ericcll/digest.gaspar01.html.

Gentry, J. R. 1980. "Three Steps to Teaching Beginning Readers to Spell." In E.H. Henderson and J. W. Beers, eds., *Developmental and Cognitive Aspects of Learning to Spell: A Reflection of Word Knowledge.* Newark, DE: International Reading Association.

Gersten, R. 1999. "The Changing Face of Bilingual Education." *Educational Leadership* 56: 41–45.

Gilger, J. W., B. F. Pennington, and J. C. DeFries. 1991. "Risk for Reading Disability as a Function of Family History in Three Family Studies." *Reading and Writing: An Interdisciplinary Journal* 3: 205–217.

Gillet, J. W., and L. Beverly. 2001. *Directing the Writing Workshop: An Elementary Teacher's Handbook.* New York: The Guilford Press.

Goodman, Y., and A. Marek. 1996. *Retrospective Miscue Analysis.* Katonah, NY: Richard C. Owen.

Gopaul-McNicol, S., S. Reid, and G. Wisdom. 1998. "The Psychoeducational Assessment of Ebonics Speakers: Issues and Challenges." *Journal of Negro Education* 67: 16–24.

Graves, D. 1983. *Writing: Teachers and Children at Work.* Portsmouth, NH: Heinemann.

———. 1994. *A Fresh Look at Writing.* Portsmouth, NH: Heinemann.

Greaney, V. 1980. "Factors Related to Amount and Type of Leisure-Time Reading." *Reading Research Quarterly* 15: 337–357.

Guthrie, J. T., and E. Anderson. 1999. "Engagement in Reading: Processes of Motivated, Strategic, Knowledgeable, Social Readers." In J. T. Guthrie and D. E. Alvermann, eds., *Engaged Reading: Processes, Practices, and Policy Implications.* New York: Teachers College Press.

Harris, T. L., and R. E. Hodges. 1995. *The Literacy Dictionary: The Vocabulary of Reading and Writing.* Newark, DE: International Reading Association.

Henderson, E. 1990. *Teaching Spelling,* rev. ed. Boston: Houghton Mifflin.

Hidi, S., and V. Anderson. 1986. "Producing Written Summaries: Task Demands, Cognitive Operations, and Implications for Instruction." *Review of Educational Research* 56: 473–494.

Hidi, S., and J. Harackiewicz. 2000. "Motivating the Academically Unmotivated: A Critical Issue for the 21st Century." *Review of Educational Research* 70 (2): 151–179.

Hiebert, E. H. 1983. "An Examination of Ability Grouping for Reading Instruction." *Reading Research Quarterly* 18: 231–255.

Holdaway, D. 1979. *The Foundation of Literacy.* New York: Ashton Scholastic.

Invernizzi, M. A., M. P. Abouzeid, and J. T. Gill. 1994. "Using Students' Invented Spellings as a Guide for Spelling Instruction That Emphasizes Word Study." *Elementary School Journal* 95: 155–167.

Ivey, G. 1999. "A Multicase Study in the Middle School: Complexities Among Young Adolescent Readers." *Reading Research Quarterly* 34 (2): 172–192.

Johnston, P. 1999. Learning Disabled Students and Their Literacy Instruction. Presentation handout, Rutgers Literacy Curriculum Network, New Brunswick, NJ.

———. 2000. *Running Records: A Self-Tutoring Guide.* Portland, ME: Stenhouse.

Juel, C. 1988. Learning to Read and Write: A Longitudinal Study of Fifty-Four Children from First Through Fourth Grade. Paper presented at the annual meeting of the American Educational Research Association, New Orleans, LA.

Just, M., and P. Carpenter. 1987. *The Psychology of Reading and Language Comprehension*. Boston: Allyn and Bacon.

Kagan, S. 1994. *Cooperative Learning*. San Juan Capistrano, CA: Kagan Cooperative Learning.

Keegan, S., and K. Shrake. 1991. "Literature Study Groups: An Alternative to Ability Grouping." *The Reading Teacher* 44 (8): 542–547.

Keene, E. O., and S. Zimmerman. 1997. *Mosaic of Thought: Teaching Comprehension in a Reader's Workshop*. Portsmouth, NH: Heinemann.

Kibby, M. W. 1993. "What Reading Teachers Should Know About Reading Proficiency in the U.S." *Journal of Reading* 37: 28–39.

Klinger, J. K., and S. Vaughn. 1999. "Promoting Reading Comprehension, Content Learning, and English Acquisition Through Collaborative Strategic Reading (CSR)." *The Reading Teacher* 52: 738–747.

Koskinen, P. S., and I. H. Blum. 1986. "Paired Repeated Reading: A Classroom Strategy for Developing Fluent Reading." *The Reading Teacher* 39 (2): 70–75.

Labov, W. 1995. "Can Reading Failure Be Reversed? A Linguistic Approach to the Question." In V. L. Gadsden and D. A. Wagner, eds., *Literacy Among African-American Youth*. Cresskill, NJ: Hampton Press.

Laminack, L., and K. Wood. 1996. *Spelling in Use: Looking Closely at Spelling in Whole Language Classrooms*. Urbana, IL: National Council of Teachers of English.

Lane, B. 1993. *After the End: Teaching and Learning Creative Revision*. Portsmouth, NH: Heinemann.

Laughlin, M. 1990. *Reader's Theater for Children: Scripts and Script Development*. Englewood, CO: Teacher Ideas Press.

Macrorie, K. 1980. *The I-Search Paper*. Portsmouth, NH: Heinemann.

Martinez, M., N. L. Roser, and S. K. Strecker. 1999. "'I Never Thought I Could Be a Star': A Readers Theater Ticket to Fluency." *The Reading Teacher* 52: 326–334.

McKeown, M. G. 1985. "The Acquisition of Word Meaning from Context by Children of High and Low Ability." *Reading Research Quarterly* 20: 482–496.

McMahon, S. 1996. "Guiding Student-Led Discussion Groups." In L. B. Gambrell and J. F. Almasi, eds., *Lively Discussions! Fostering Engaged Reading*. Newark, DE: International Reading Association.

Monroe, J. 1998. Guided Reading: Meeting the Needs of Elementary Children (Grades 3–6). Speech presented at the Rutgers' 30th Annual Conference on Reading and Writing. New Brunswick, NJ: Rutgers University.

Morris, D. 1992. *Case Studies in Teaching Beginning Readers: Howard Street Tutoring Manual*. Boone, NC: Fieldstream Publications.

Murray, D. 1986. *A Writer Teaches Writing*. New York: Harcourt Brace.

National Center for Education Statistics. 1999. *Teacher Quality: A Report on the Preparation and Qualifications of Public School Teachers*. Washington, DC: U.S. Department of Education, Office of Educational Research and Improvement.

National Center for Fair and Open Testing. 1998. www.fairtest.org.

National Reading Panel. 2000. *Teaching Children to Read*. Washington, DC: National Institute of Child Health and Human Development.

National Research Council. 1997. *Educating One and All: Students with Disabilities and Standards-Based Reform*. Washington, DC: National Academy Press.

Ogle, D. 1986. "K-W-L: A Teaching Model That Develops Action Reading and Expository Text." *The Reading Teacher* 40: 564–570.

Palincsar, A., and A. Brown. 1984. "Reciprocal Teaching of Comprehension-Fostering and Comprehension-Monitoring Activities." *Cognition and Instruction* 1 (2): 117–175.

Pallas, A. M., D. R. Entwisle, K. L. Alexander, and M. F. Stluka. 1994. "Ability-Group Effects: Instructional, Social, or Institutional?" *Sociology of Education* 67: 27–46.

Peterson, R., and S. Eeds. 1990. *Grand Conversations: Literature Groups in Action*. New York: Scholastic.

Pikulski, J. 1994. "Preventing Reading Failure: A Review of Five Effective Programs." *The Reading Teacher* 48: 30–39.

Pinnell, G. S., J. J. Pikulski, K. K. Wixson, J. R. Campbell, P. B. Gough, and A. S. Beatty. 1995. *Listening to Children Aloud*. Washington, DC: Office of Educational Research and Improvement, U.S. Department of Education.

Raphael, T. E. 1986. "Teaching Question-Answer Relationships, Revisited." *The Reading Teacher* 39 (6): 516–523.

Raphael, T., and S. McMahon. 1994. "Book Club: An Alternative Framework for Reading Instruction." *The Reading Teacher* 48: 102–116.

Ray, K. W. 1999. *Wondrous Words*. Urbana, IL: National Council of Teachers of English.

Read, C. 1971. "Pre-School Children's Knowledge of English Phonology." *Harvard Educational Review* 41 (1): 150–179.

Reader's Theater Online Canada. www.loiswalker.com.

Reader's Theater Script Service. www.readers-theater.com.

Reinking, D., and J. Watkins. 2000. "A Formative Experiment Investigating the Use of Multimedia Book Reviews to Increase Elementary Students' Independent Reading." *Reading Research Quarterly* 35 (3): 384–419.

Roller, C. M. 1996. *Variability Not Disability*. Newark, DE: International Reading Association.

Roser, N., and M. Martinez, eds. 1995. *Book Talk and Beyond: Children and Teachers Respond to Literature*. Newark, DE: International Reading Association.

Rueda, R. 1991. "Characteristics of Literacy Programs for Language-Minority Students." In E. H. Hiebert, ed., *Literacy for a Diverse Society: Perspectives, Practices, and Policies*. New York: Teachers College Press.

Samuels, S. J. 1979. "The Method of Repeated Reading." *The Reading Teacher* 32 (4): 403–408.

Scarborough, H. H. 1998. "Early Identification of Children at Risk for Reading Disabilities: Phonological Awareness and Some Other Promising Predictors." In K. Shapiro, P. J. Accardo, and A. J. Capute, eds., *Specific Reading Disability: A View of the Spectrum*. Timonium, MD: York Press.

Schlagal, R. 1989. "Constancy and Change in Spelling Development." *Reading Psychology* 10 (30): 207–232.

———. 1992. "Patterns of Orthographic Development in the Intermediate

Grades." In S. Templeton and D. Bear, eds., *Development of Orthographic Knowledge and the Foundations of Literacy: A Memorial Festschrift for Edmund H. Henderson.* Hillsdale, NJ: Lawrence Erlbaum.

Shaywitz, B. A., J. M. Fletcher, and S. E. Shaywitz. 1995. "Defining and Classifying Learning Disabilities and Attention-Deficit/Hyperactivity Disorder." *Journal of Child Neurology* 10 (Suppl. 1): S50–S57.

Shepard, A. 1993. *Stories on Stage: Scripts for Reader's Theater.* New York: H. W. Wilson.

Short, K. 1995. "Foreword." In B. C. Hill, N. J. Johnson, and K. L. S. Noe, eds., *Literature Circles and Response.* Norwood, MA: Christopher-Gordon.

Sierra, J. 1996. *Multicultural Folktales for Feltboard and Reader's Theater.* Westport, CT: Greenwood Publishing Group.

Smitherman, G. 1977. *"Talkin' and Testifyin'": The Language of Black America.* Boston: Houghton Mifflin.

Snow, C. E., W. S. Barnes, J. Chandler, I. F. Goodman, and L. Hemphill. 1991. *Unfulfilled Expectations: Home and School Influences on Literacy.* Cambridge, MA: Harvard University Press.

Snow, C., M. S. Burns, and P. Griffin. 1998. *Preventing Reading Difficulties in Young Children.* Washington, DC: National Academy Press.

Spear-Swerling, L., and R. J. Sternberg. 1996. *Off Track: When Poor Readers Become Learning Disabled.* Boulder, CO: Westview Press.

Stahl, S. 1986. "Three Principles of Effective Vocabulary Instruction." *Journal of Reading* 29 (7): 662–668.

Stanovich, K. E. 2000. *Progress in Understanding Reading: Scientific Foundations and New Frontiers.* New York: The Guilford Press.

Strickland, D. S. 1998. "What's Basic in Reading Instruction: Finding Common Ground." *Educational Leadership* 55: 7–10.

Strickland, D. S., R. M. Dillon, L. Funkhouser, M. Glick, and C. Rogers. 1989. "Research Currents: Classroom Dialogue During Literature Response Groups." *Language Arts* 66: 193–200.

Teachers of English to Speakers of Other Languages, Inc. 1997. *ESL Standards for Pre-K–12 Students.* Alexandria, VA: Author.

Teddlie, C., P. Kirby, and S. Stringfield. 1989. "Effective vs. Ineffective Schools: Observable Differences in the Classroom." *American Journal of Education* 97: 221–236.

Templeton, S., and D. Bear, eds. 1992. *Development of Orthographic Knowledge and the Foundations of Literacy: A Memorial Festschrift for Edmund H. Henderson.* Hillsale, NJ: Lawrence Erlbaum.

Templeton, S., and D. Morris. 1999. "Questions Teachers Ask About Spelling." *Reading Research Quarterly* 34 (1): 102–112.

Tierney, R. J., J. E. Readence, and E. K. Dishner. 1995. *Reading Strategies and Practices: A Compendium.* 3d ed. Boston: Allyn and Bacon.

Volger, G. P., J. C. DeFries, and S. N. Decker. 1985. "Family History as an Indicator of Risk for Reading Disability." *Journal of Learning Disabilities* 18: 419–421.

Vygotsky, L. 1978. *Mind in Society.* Cambridge, MA: MIT Press.

Whitehead, D. 1994. "Teaching Literacy and Learning Strategies Through a Modified Guided Silent Reading Procedure." *Journal of Reading* 38 (1): 24–30.

Worthy, J., and J. V. Hoffman. 1996. "Critical Questions." *The Reading Teacher* 49: 656–657.

Worthy, J., M. Moorman, and M. Turner. 1999. "What Johnny Likes to Read Is Hard to Find in School." *Reading Research Quarterly* 34 (1): 12–27.

Zutell, J., and T. Rasinski. 1991. "Training Teachers to Attend to Their Students' Oral Reading Fluency." *Theory into Practice* 30 (3): 212–217.

INDEX

instructional strategies to promote, 94–102

role of, 91–92

P

paired repeated reading, 130–132

paired script writing, 203

parents

  communicating with, 217

  goals setting with, 220

  newsletters for, 55, 219

  as reading buddies, 218

  with reading disabilities, 8

  support programs involving, 54–55

peer coaching, 223

peer editing, 195

Penguins (Savran), 150

Perez, Ed, 149

phrasing, 134–135

picture books

  for guided silent reading, 67

  list of, 227

  for read-aloud/think/aloud instruction, 229–231

picture sorts, 102

picture walk, 147–148

pictures, 147–149

Piggie Pie (Patlini), 123

Plays, 126

poetry

  for choral reading, 124

  English-language learners and, 33–34

  writing, 185–187

powerful verbs, 192–193

predictable books, 228

prereading

  guiding silent reading and, 74–75

  literature circles and, 86–87

preservice guidelines, 222

prewriting strategies, 185

prior knowledge, 145–150

professional development strategies

  for administrators and supervisors, 221

  peer coaching, 223

preservice guidelines, 222

  study groups, 224

prompts, writing, 215

publishing activities, 28

punctuation marks, 135

Q

Question-Answer-Relationships (QARs)

  explanation of, 156–158

  introducing students to, 158–162

questions

  guidelines for quality, 155–156

  helping readers to answer, 154–155

  helping struggling readers generate, 162–163

  open-ended, 214

R

Ramona Quimby, Age 8 (Cleary), 123

rank ordering, 63–65

read-alouds

  benefits of, 125

  to foster reading fluency, 123–124

"Read This with Gestures" (Ciardi), 33

reader response groups, 52–53

reader response journals, 53

readers

  characteristics of successful, 6–7

  expectations for elementary-level, 3–4

  self-monitoring by, 154

readers' theater, 126–128

reading

  creating situations that inspire, 26

  management of independent, 53–54

  repeated, 36

reading buddies, at-home, 218

reading comprehension

  background and issues related to, 142–145

  guided silent reading and, 70–72

  helping readers monitor their own, 154